The Independent Director in Society

Gerry Brown • Andrew
Kakabadse • Filipe Morais

The Independent
Director in Society

Our current crisis of governance
and what to do about it

palgrave
macmillan

Gerry Brown
GBrown Associates Ltd
READING, UK

Andrew Kakabadse
Henley Business School
Henley on Thames, UK

Filipe Morais
Henley Business School
University of Reading
Reading, Berkshire, UK

ISBN 978-3-030-51302-3   ISBN 978-3-030-51303-0   (eBook)
https://doi.org/10.1007/978-3-030-51303-0

This Palgrave Macmillan imprint is published by the registered company Springer Nature Switzerland AG.
The registered company address is: Gewerbestrasse 11, 6330 Cham, Switzerland

To my wife Clemencia, sons, daughters and family for their unfailing interest and support for this very demanding and absorbing adventure.
Gerry

Preface

Just as this book went to press, the coronavirus pandemic erupted in China and spread rapidly throughout the world. Millions are infected, and tens of thousands have already died of Covid-19, the illness caused by the virus. In their initial response, most nations have gone into lockdown to stop the spread of the virus. The world economy has ground to a halt. Few, if any, institutions have been unaffected by the crisis, which has become the greatest challenge to governance in living memory.

The pandemic, and our responses to it, throw into sharp relief the failings and weaknesses of leadership and governance, in every sector and at every level, in the UK and around the world. Richard Horton, editor of *The Lancet*, has called the crisis 'the greatest global science policy failure in a generation', and the philanthropist and former Microsoft chairman Bill Gates tweeted that 'few governments will get an A-grade' for their response to the challenge.

These failures of leadership and governance have played out on many levels. One of these was the failure to prepare adequately for the coming crisis. It has been argued that this crisis is a 'black swan' event, unforeseeable and unimaginable, but this simply is not so. Nassim Nicholas Taleb, the person who first popularised the phrase 'black swan', is one of many who have pointed out that the prospect of a major global pandemic has been predicted, and its health and economic impacts modelled, many times in the past.

Another failure was the hesitant and often ineffective responses to the crisis once it began, with particularly dire consequences for health care workers on the front line. Britain is not the only country suffering shortages of testing kits and personal protective equipment (PPE). President Macron of France has been forced to apologise for shortages and delays in his own country. Without the necessary protection, health care workers are falling ill and dying in ever-increasing numbers.

These failures of preparation and response also highlight the failings of boards. Our original research, conducted before the crisis began, had already raised many important issues, and Covid-19 has thrown these into sharper relief. Are boards able to respond adequately and quickly to crisis? Are they able to make informed decisions and respond promptly? Does the size and composition of boards—particularly their lack of diversity—hinder their decision-making ability? Are independent directors sufficiently engaged, and do they take their responsibilities seriously? Judging by the apparent powerlessness of many institutions in the face of the exploding medical, social and financial crisis, the answer is often 'no'.

But the real challenge for governance is only just beginning. At some point the virus will be brought under control, enabling the rebuilding of our damaged societies and shattered economies to begin. But are our institutions robust enough to achieve this? Are they fit for purpose? As our book points out, the answers depend to a very large extent on how well those institutions are organised and governed, and in particular, how well boards are engaged with their organisations and with their stakeholders.

The purpose of the board is 'engaged stewardship', ensuring the organisation is run to the maximal benefit of all stakeholders. The key word here is 'engaged'. This requires a deep understanding of the needs of stakeholders and the service the institution provides for them. As our research shows, boards add value when they are truly engaged. Most board members are well aligned with each other and their management—that is, they share common values, aims and beliefs and are committed to making positive change—but they are not sufficiently engaged with other internal stakeholders nor have enough understanding of the circumstances and environment within which their organisations operate. When this happens, boards are unable to make the best possible decisions and the value they add to organisations is diminished. The current crisis has shone a bleak light on this problem and forces us to confront weaknesses in governance across a wide swathe of society.

The health care sector, as already highlighted, is on the front line, and this includes not just hospitals and the National Health Service (NHS) but also Public Health England (which has revealed the awkward split in responsibilities between them). It includes also hospices and care homes, where both private and public sectors had already been under strain for some time, in part due to poor supervision and governance. While magnificent efforts have been made to find enough beds, the shortages of equipment such as PPE, ICU beds and ventilators—plus the risk to their own health—have put NHS and care home workers under terrible and sometimes lethal stress. What long-term damage will have been done to the health care sector once the crisis is over? What damage will have been done to the nation's health more generally by the cancellation of non-urgent operations along with GP and hospital appointments in the meantime? And further, what changes will have to be made to health policy? Over the past fifteen years, government-led initiatives in health care, combined with the impacts of austerity, have moved away from an emphasis on curative care and hospitals towards preventative care in the community. The assumption has been that epidemics are things of the past and that the greatest challenge now is lifestyle-related health problems. Clearly that assumption is false, and, as the editor of *The Lancet* suggests, a dramatic rethink of health policy is needed. Boards of NHS Trusts, Public Health England and other health care institutions collectively have a mountain to climb.

But the same is true everywhere. Governments and central banks have torn up the rules on borrowing in order to prop up the economy, but how exactly will the massive debts they are incurring be paid for? Decisions about long-term borrowing and increased taxation will need to be made, and these decisions will have far-reaching consequences for us all. Businesses too face a crisis even more drastic than the global financial crashes of 2008 and 1987. Stock markets have plunged, drastically reducing the market value of many companies with a corresponding impact on pension funds. Oil prices have fallen through the floor. Some sectors have prospered: technology firms, especially online retailers, are doing well. But automobile manufacturing has ground to a halt, high streets are deserted with all but essential shops closed, and airlines and the travel industry are staring into an abyss with seemingly little sign of a bridge to the other side. Unemployment is already at record levels not seen in many countries since the 1930s, and is forecast to rise still further. How well businesses and industries recover from the crisis will often depend on the leadership their boards give them. But are boards fit for purpose and ready for these tasks?

Universities are struggling too. The switch from classroom to online teaching has been a major challenge, which some have begun to master and others have not. What will the long-term impact be on pedagogy and the delivery of higher education, when the lived student experience remains a vital part (and selling point) of the educational equation? Another looming problem is a severe reduction in the numbers of overseas students, particularly those from East Asia coming to Europe and America, so long as travel restrictions remain in place. As a result, universities will take a significant financial hit. As we point out in this book, university boards were already struggling to meet the challenges they faced. The crisis could force them to cut staff and departments, and even push some of them over the edge in to bankruptcy, unless their boards are brave and resilient enough, and their balance sheets are robust enough, to navigate through the dangerous times ahead.

Sport, both professional and amateur, has virtually ceased. The 2020 Olympics have, after much dithering, finally been postponed. When some professional sports do resume, they will have to do so behind closed doors. For many sports and institutions, the loss of revenue from audiences and sponsorship represents an existential crisis. Semi-professional and amateur sports clubs along with other local facilities like leisure centres will be dependent on whatever financial lifeline governments can throw them through local councils or organisations like Sport England.

Also caught in the middle are charities. Many, like food banks, domestic abuse charities, hospices and providers of care for the elderly and homeless people—and, it is beginning to emerge, animal rescue charities—are seeing a huge upsurge in demand for their services. At the same time their funding is being squeezed; fundraising and volunteer work is hampered by social distancing, high street charity shops are forced to close, and donors are pledging money instead to a relatively narrow range of charities associated with institutions like the NHS. Most charities also rely on volunteers, who are often retired people and therefore more at risk to the virus. When the crisis is over, many charities will need to look hard at their governance, operations and funding models and think about how to make themselves more crisis-resilient and future-proof. That will not be easy. Our research for this book already asks some searching questions about whether charity boards are up to the task.

This crisis is testing us all, not just our institutions, but as our way of life as nations and societies—as people—in ways that most of us have never been tested before. One of the many questions that needs to be asked now is 'do we have the courage, the skill and the will to respond and rebuild when the crisis has passed?' And even, ideally, to make it a better place than it was before?

The answer, we think, is yes. We have already seen magnificent and also humbling efforts. A million people in the UK alone have volunteered contribute to and support the front-line services in whatever capacity is needed. But having willing volunteers on the ground is not enough. In the long run, we need this same spirit of selflessness, that same energy and dedication, to enter the boardrooms of our institutions. We need to rethink and recast board culture, so that board members are truly independent in thought and action so they can play a full part in governance. Independent directors are the stewards of the organisation. They owe a duty not just to the institution itself but also to all its stakeholders, including customers, clients and service users, employees, shareholders and communities, and ultimately society itself.

The time for reform is now. We call on everyone who has the motivation, experience and ability, from all ages and from all backgrounds, to come forward and volunteer for service as independent directors. Your commitment, skills, talent and vision are needed now as never before. Being an independent director sometimes requires sacrifice; we have to put the needs of others ahead of our own concerns but—as the crisis is showing—personal sacrifice can often result in a much greater good and, we would argue, personal reward and satisfaction in the long run as well. How our institutions are governed affects us all, and everyone has a part to play. The time to begin rebuilding is now.

What happens after will be the real challenge.

Reading, UK   Gerry Brown
Henley on Thames, UK   Andrew Kakabadse
                                                        Filipe Morais
                                                         April 2020

Acknowledgements

My thanks go to many people.

To my fellow authors Professor Andrew Kakabadse and Dr Filipe Morais. It has been a pleasure to share the journey with you.

To Andrew Myers for bringing a quantification and statistical perspective to our deliberations.

To Morgen Witzel for helping another dream to become reality.

To Jeff Scott for his persistence in bringing the perspective of the reader and preparing the marketing and publicity plan.

To Marilyn Livingstone for creating the index.

To son Mario for preparing the Infographics and granddaughter Aurora for designing the book cover.

To daughter Cayetana for preparing the book launch.

To daughter Francisca for the digital marketing plan.

To son-in-law Chris for the 4global case study.

To Edmee for her help with the virtual book launch.

To Professor Nada Kakabadse for her advice and preparing case studies.

To Professor Sir Steve Smith and Professor Sir William Wakeham for their continuing support, interest and critical review of this project from start to finish.

To the organisations who supported the carrying out of the research for the book including Chris Hopson NHS Providers, Niall Dickson The NHS Confederation, Chris Sayers Committee of University Chairs. Mike Shore NYE Association of Heads of University Administration, Rosalind Oakley The Association of Chairs of Charities, Karl Wilding National Council of Voluntary Organisations, Phil Smith Sport England.

To all of the key opinion leaders who agreed to be interviewed and who are listed in Appendix 6.

To all those who contributed case studies and who are listed in Appendix 8.

To those who have endorsed the book, including Barry Bateman, Lord Crisp, Sir Dennis Gillings, David Gregson, Dr Ann Limb.

To The Chartered Governance Institute for their financial donation.

To G Brown Associates Ltd for funding the research carried out by Henley Business School.

To numerous others for their interest and support including my brother Ben, friends Peter Weston, Michael Bundy, David Parfett, Dr Robin Headlam-Wells and the staff of the Financial Times NED programme, Lesley Stephenson, Sarah Boulton, Murray Steele and Patrick Dunne.

—Gerry Brown

Contents

List of Figures

List of Tables

Part I

The Challenge

1

Introduction

Society faces a crisis of governance. In the UK and around the world, we depend on institutions to deliver us the goods and services we need in order to be healthy and happy. How well those institutions carry out their mission and meet the needs of the people depends in large part on how well they are governed. But far too often, those who are responsible for governance are failing in their responsibilities and duties.

This is equally true whether we are discussing corporations, government institutions and public sector bodies like the National Health Service (NHS), or third sector institutions such as charities. Governance is equally important in all, and yet in every sector the signs of crisis can be seen. The impact on society, as we shall demonstrate, is colossal. At best, many of our institutions are underperforming and failing to deliver, meaning other people suffer the consequences: loss of jobs and income, poor quality education or shortages of urgently needed medicines or medical care, to name just a few examples. At worst, the consequences are corruption and scandal, mismanagement, value destruction, the failure of entire institutions, and sometimes—too often— injury or death.

This book is about the crisis of governance, and what can be done about it. We argue that much of the problem is due to widespread ignorance about what governance actually is, and specifically about the role played by boards of directors. The general public, the media, governments, even boards of directors themselves do not fully understand the concept of governance or what is involved. This ignorance means that all too often people don't realise what good governance looks like or, much more dangerously, do they recognise bad governance when they see it.

© The Author(s) 2020
G. Brown et al., *The Independent Director in Society*,
https://doi.org/10.1007/978-3-030-51303-0_1

We will focus particularly on the role of the *independent directors* who serve on boards, explaining their responsibilities and defining the tasks they face. Independent directors are the lynchpin of governance. If they do their job well, then we can be reasonably certain that the institution is well governed and able to carry out its mission. If they fail, then the institution is, at the very least, at risk. It is vitally important that we have independent directors who fully understand their task and are prepared to engage with the institutions they serve.

In writing this book, we want to help independent directors—and prospective independent directors—learn more about their role and purpose and better equip themselves for the challenges we face. But the core messages of this book will be important to anyone who cares about good governance: executives, regulators, political leaders or anyone who is affected by governance issues and wants to see positive change. In short, practically everyone.

Governance and Management

There is a sharp distinction between governance and management, and the role of the former is not always fully appreciated. The day-to-day running of these institutions is the task of the *executive* team and the managers who report to them. They prepare budgets, execute strategy, deliver products and services to clients and customers, and do all the myriad things any organisation must do in order to carry out its mission.

Governance, on the other hand, is about oversight. Managers and executives come and go, but governance structures are permanent. It is the independent directors—sometimes also known as non-executive directors, governors or trustees, depending on the type of institution—who are the real custodians of the organisation. Their task is to ensure that the organisation stays focused on its mission, balances the interests of its stakeholders and works to the benefit of all. Theirs is the ultimate responsibility. If the organisation has a failure or breaks down in some way—a human or financial scandal, perhaps, or a case of corruption, or a breach of regulations or procedures that puts people's lives in danger—it is up to the independent directors to put things right. It is also part of their role to ensure that these failures do not happen in the first place.

Businesses, large and small, provide employment and generate wealth. Government regulates society and provides vital services such as infrastructure, policing and defence. The National Health Service tends to the ill and the hurt and tries to keep the rest of us healthy. Schools and universities provide the education we need if we are to thrive. Sporting bodies provide us with entertainment and recreation that helps keep us fit. Charities are active everywhere providing vitally needed services ranging from medical research and health care to libraries and the arts. And so on, and on.

Each of these sectors has their own particular and unique challenges. In particular, some distinctions must be drawn between governance in business, on the one hand, and in the private and third sectors on the other. The onus to provide good governance in business is on the owners of the business (or at least, the owners of the share capital of the business). In current business theory, ownership and control of business should be kept separate, with owners staying out of the day-to-day running of the business, but this does not mean they are excused from all responsibility; shareholders have a duty of stewardship and should continue to exercise oversight over the company's management. How well they do so varies wildly from case to case; some shareholders take their responsibilities seriously, others appear to have little concern for the companies they apparently own. But, in theory at least, owners are able to exercise governance over private sector companies. In practice there can be a clear benefit to listed companies' governance from shareholder involvement. The recent action by Blackrock in regard to the requirement for companies to pay more attention to sustainability issues is a good example. Notwithstanding the above points some of the largest and most successful companies today (e.g. Amazon, Facebook, Google, Microsoft) are companies where those managing and controlling the business are also major shareholders, often founders. These companies pose particular challenges for governance and independent directors.

Charities and public sector bodies are different in that they usually have no owners (though within the third sector some organisations are organised along mutual lines, meaning that independent directors are also nominally the owners, even though the organisation has no actual share capital). Unlike in business, where independent directors have a responsibility to shareholders, in these organisations the independent directors are the last line of responsibility; the buck stops with them. This creates different expectations of governance, and different challenges for directors.

But what all these organisations have in common is that they are under pressure like never before. Economic and political uncertainties and the challenges of the digital age mean the future is becoming harder and harder to predict. What will the market look like? What strategies will be needed for survival and growth? Even these basic questions are fraught with uncertainty. At the same time, austerity and budget cuts, the vagaries of government policy, the increasing costs of skilled labour, medicines and technology—to name but a few of the many issues we face—mean that all of our institutions are under mounting pressure to do more with less, to deliver more value to society while coping with diminishing resources. And all this was before the coronavirus epidemic of 2020 caused the worst health emergency and economic crisis in living memory. The pressure before the epidemic was nothing compared to what we face now.

The challenge facing independent directors and boards is, how to overcome these formidable obstacles and have real positive impact on society? That is the endgame; that is the purpose for which independent directors exist. Their function is to provide governance, support and oversight, ensuring that the executives meet the goals that have been set for them and that the needs of stakeholders are served. With good governance, organisations can expect to overcome most of their challenges, if not all, and go on to fulfil their purpose and mission. Without it, they have little hope of doing so.

We must be careful not to overstate the problem. Many boards are dealing with these challenges; some are overcoming them and forging ahead. There are many high-performing boards, many excellent independent directors and many hard-working and dedicated chairs who give tirelessly of themselves and work hard in the service of society. But sadly, there is also a long tale of underperformance; and sometimes that underperformance leads to disaster.

Fatal Consequences

Good governance is often lacking, and when it is, the consequences for society can be severe. When failures happen, responsibility can nearly always be traced back to the board. In the words of one recent report by Alvarez & Marsal and Henley Business School, 'many boards are arguably not currently equipped to deal with major or extraordinary disruptions and discontinuities and are often found to be unaligned with their management team and not effective in addressing the most pressing issues.'[1]

Kevin Carey, chairman of the charity Royal National Institute for the Blind (RNIB), was much more blunt. 'Most charities don't fail because they lack a governance code, a risk register and a charity handbook', he said in a recent essay for the charity think-tank New Philanthropy Capital (NPC). 'They do so because of trustee cowardice... Assemble all the 360 degree appraisals, skills audits and Nolan Principles you like; they are redundant if no one has the guts to say the CEO is useless, the deficit is structural or, more widely, that the emperor has no clothes.'[2]

Some might think that 'cowardice' is too harsh a word. But when we look at the litany of collapses and failures in recent years, we are certainly entitled to ask what might have happened if the independent directors had stood up and properly held the executive team to account, as they are supposed to do.

Business has had a steady stream of disasters, so many, that at times one can hardly open the newspaper or turn on the television news without seeing yet another one. Sometimes businesses collapse through mismanagement: we can think of Lehman Brothers, Swissair, Royal Ahold, Ratner's, Royal Bank of Scotland, Nortel, Carillion and many others. Sometimes they are hit by unethical behaviour such as fraud, often sanctioned at the highest level: examples include Enron, Parmalat, Global Grossing, Tyco, Takata, Rolls Royce, Satyam, and of course the endless stream of scandals that unfolded in the banking industry especially in the years following the 2008 collapse, resulting in fines of over $300 billion. In nearly every case the board's ignorance or inability to curtail reckless or unethical behaviour played a part in the disaster.[3]

There are many other types of business scandals, ranging from the accusations of false accounting at Tesco, the culture of corruption and machismo that plagued Uber, the failure to address data security issues that still continues to haunt Facebook in the aftermath of the Cambridge Analytica affair, Volkswagen's now infamous 'defeat device' that allowed its cars to falsely pass emissions standards tests, accusations of tax evasion that have hit Facebook and Amazon, or quarrels over executive compensation that have broken out at British Petroleum (BP). All of these have caused reputational damage, loss of customer confidence which in turn led to loss of revenue, fines imposed by regulators, and significant reputational damage and loss of brand value. And finally, how far did bad management or mismanagement contribute to the structural weakness of so many companies that were brought to their knees by the coronavirus pandemic? It may sound harsh to judge their performance given that the pandemic caught them by surprise; but given how long its arrival had been forecast, *why* were they surprised and why were they not better prepared?

Scandals and financial disasters in sports have also been a feature of our times, from the Chicago 'Black Sox' scandal of 1919 when the Chicago White Sox baseball team conspired with a gambling syndicate to throw the World Series, right up to the collapse of Bury football club, expelled from the English Football League after it became apparent that the club could no longer pay its creditors in August 2019. Another club, Bolton Wanderers, only just escaped a similar fate after a last-minute rescue deal. Other examples include drug-taking in athletics, weight-lifting and cycling; the ball-tampering scandal that hit the Australian national cricket team in 2018; accusations of bullying and harassment in the British national cycling team; bribery in the run-up to the awarding of the Olympic games and the persistent accusations of corruption that plague FIFA, the international football governing body.

When scandals at sports teams and sporting organisations are exposed, the consequences can be long-lasting. They include damage to reputation and image, which means even die-hard fans can sometimes become disillusioned and turn against the team or lose interest in the sport altogether. A declining fan base means loss of revenue, and this can turn into a downward spiral where the organisation contracts towards the point of non-existence. When sports organisations suffer significant reputational harm, the consequences can range from job losses and poor performance to failure to carry out their mission to bring health and fitness benefits to society. And the weaker these organisations become, the fewer people support them.

Scandals have hit charities too. The collapse of Kids Company, the sexual abuse scandal at Oxfam, the revelations of sexual harassment and worse at fundraising dinners held by the Presidents Club, Age UK's recommending to pensioners a deal through a tie-up with an energy company that was not actually to the advantage of pensioners and the severe problems of governance at the RSPCA that forced the regulator, the Charities Commission, to intervene are just some examples that made headlines. Scandals in charities result in loss of reputation, which in turn means loss of revenue through funding and donations, loss of stakeholder confidence and difficulties in recruiting good people. All this makes it difficult for charities to carry out their mission.

Here in the UK, the NHS has sadly had many problems. High-profile scandals have broken out at many hospitals and trusts: the Alder Hay organ scandal, Mid Staffordshire Trust, Cumbria Furness General Hospital, Gosport War Memorial Trust, Shrewsbury and Telford Trust, South East Coast Ambulances Trust, University of Wales Hospital and Morecombe Bay Maternity Hospital, to name just some of the most recent. The consequences of these scandals are harm to patients—the people, the hospital or trust is supposed to protect—including suffering pain and death. Beyond this, there are severe consequences for the organisations themselves. Reputational damage can lead to difficulties in hiring key staff; no one wants to work for a tainted organisation. Morale among existing staff declines, which in turn can affect the quality of care. Again, the cycle of failure begins to perpetuate itself. Structural and morale problems were already plaguing the NHS even before coronavirus arrived, and though front-line staff responded heroically, it remains to be seen what long-term damage the NHS as an institution has suffered.

UK universities have also had their problems. Racist and sexist behaviour by staff and students has contributed to scandals such as the one that engulfed the Oxford Union in November 2019, when a visually impaired student was dragged out of a meeting, allegedly by his ankles, by security guards. The president of the Oxford Union was eventually compelled to resign, but the incident was symptomatic of the prejudice that still remains engrained in many university campuses.[4] Around the same time, staff at many universities launched a series of strikes over pay, pensions and working conditions. The reputation of UK universities, once considered among the best in the world, is being tarnished, with the consequent risk that the best and brightest students may start looking elsewhere for higher education.

Challenging Times

It is easy, of course, to point the finger of blame. We need also to recognise the excellent and often selfless service put in by independent directors at other institutions which quietly get on with their business, serving people efficiently without making headlines. In the corporate sector, independent directors are usually paid, but in many charities, sports bodies and universities they are volunteers who give up their own time and serve without pay, sometimes without even taking expenses. We salute these people who do so much work that is essential to society, and feel that more effort should be made to praise and recognise them. They do a very hard job.

Governing modern institutions in an age of uncertainty and constraint is an onerous task, to say the least. The duties of independent directors and the burdens placed upon them are heavy in the extreme. Commenting on the duties of the independent director a few years ago, the *Financial Times* described it as 'a job for which no one is qualified':

> The list of attributes required of the non-executive director is so long, precise and contradictory that there cannot be a single board member in the world that fully fits the bill. They need to be supportive, intelligent, interesting, well-rounded and funny, entrepreneurial, objective yet passionate, independent, curious, challenging and fit. They also need to have a financial background and real business experience, a strong moral compass, and be first-class all-rounders with specific industry skills.[5]

Nor is this a uniquely British problem. Global research published annually by the recruitment consultancy Harvey Nash and London Business School (LBS) shows that the problems of governance are equally severe in other parts of the world.[6] Historically, the UK has had very high standards of corporate governance, and other countries have followed our lead when introducing codes and standards. But there is a danger that those standards are beginning to erode. Not only are people inside the system struggling to cope with the burdens placed on them, but the system itself is increasingly coming under attack. An editorial in *The Times* in 2019, commenting on the leaked diplomatic cables that forced the resignation of the British ambassador in Washington, Sir Kim Darroch, highlighted both the importance of institutions and the danger they are in:

> Robust institutions are an essential safeguard against the arbitrary exercise of power. Parliament, the judiciary, a free press, an independent civil service and independent regulators and agencies all play a vital role in ensuring that decisions are taken transparently on the basis of expertise and evidence. That is essential to maintain public trust in the political system… these attacks on the civil service fit into a wider pattern of attacks…on other independent institutions, including the judiciary, the free press and even parliament itself. Halting these attacks and restoring faith in the machinery of British liberal democracy is one of the most urgent challenges facing Britain's next prime minister.[7]

What is true of politics is also true of all our institutions, everywhere. No matter how difficult or complex the job of governance is, it must be done. The question is, how can we best support our independent directors in order to maintain and enhance standards of good governance, to the benefit of society as a whole?

Research at Henley Business School

To understand the problem more fully and to hopefully arrive at some solutions, in 2017 we set up the Independent Director in Society Research Programme at Henley Business School. The project, which lasted for two years, focused on governance in the UK in four important sectors: health care, higher education, charities and sports. It had support from a number of major institutions within those sectors, including the Committee of University Chairs and the Association of Heads of University Administrators (higher education); NHS Providers, the NHS Confederation and NHS Improvement (the NHS); the National Council for Voluntary Organisations, the Fundraising Authority and the Association of Chairs (charities); and Sport England (sport).

We interviewed forty-three key opinion leaders (e.g. chairs, vice-chancellors, CEOs, independent directors) across the NHS, charity, sports and university sectors. The interviews explored board governance across these sectors and focused on independence and the independent director role. Interviewees were asked one key question: how can independence be gained, sustained and lost? The ensuing report identified a number of themes and insights that subsequently formed the base for the survey design. The survey was tested with directors both face to face and online to eliminate ambiguities, duplications and clarify questions.

After this process the length of the survey was substantially reduced. The final version of the survey was also discussed with key stakeholders in each sector who have made some final suggestions. With the support of these organisations, the survey was sent to directors in each of these sectors. The survey returned 623 completed responses from across the 4 sectors including: NHS (n = 203), university (n = 135), sports (n = 129) and charities (n = 156). In addition, the research team has undertaken a desk review of latest literature on each of the sectors, as well as conducting case studies in each of the four sectors under scrutiny (each of these cases is included later in the book). The result is a robust and detailed picture of the state of boards and independent directors in all four sectors (Fig. 1.1–1.4).

The appendices provide more detailed descriptive statistics for all four sectors. Appendices 1–5 cover board and director demographics, board operation and director time, director recruitment, selection, induction, remuneration and evaluation, board challenges, and board and director behaviour. These issues will also be covered in more detail in the text of the book as we go forward. Further appendices give details of the individuals surveyed and case studies included in the book.

To these findings we added previous research into governance in business and politics, including the Kakabadse Report on civil service effectiveness, presented to the House of Commons Public Administration and Constitutional Affairs Committee in 2018, and a series of reports on board effectiveness in the corporate world over the last five years. In this book we have also incorporated additional research from external organisations including Harvey Nash and management consultants McKinsey & Company, and from Gerry Brown's book *The Independent Director*, his own personal observations on the role and function of the independent or non-executive director in the private sector.[8]

Some of the research results make for grim reading. In the charities sector, for example, our research found that 33% of independent directors received no training for their role at all, not even induction into their organisations. Further, 43% had no other not-for-profit board experience currently to inform them about their new roles. In other words, they were simply parachuted in and expected to know from day one what was expected of them. Given the complex world of charities regulation—and given that many

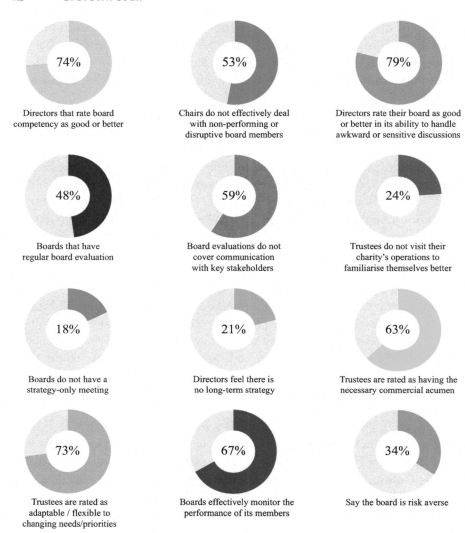

Fig. 1.1 Key findings from the charities sector

charities work with children and vulnerable people—these statistics are almost terrifying.

A survey of media articles about charities reveal that most journalists do not seem to understand the role of the trustee or chairman. We realised that one of the main challenges of governance today must be to create a better understanding of what the role of independent director entails and what the

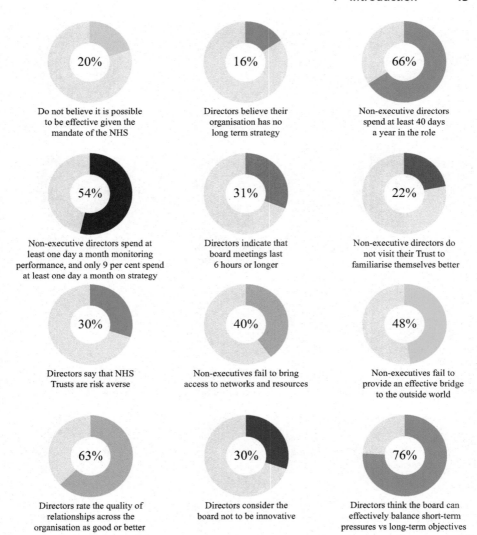

Fig. 1.2 Key findings from the NHS

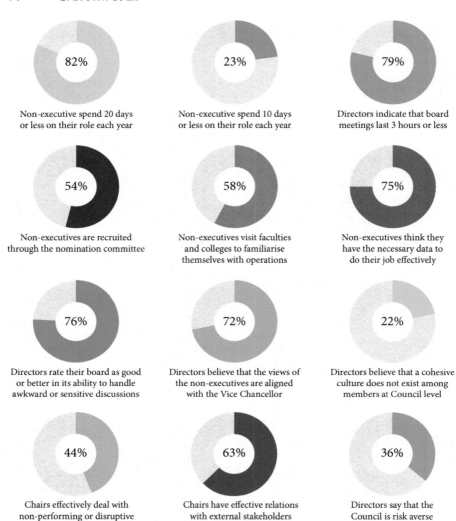

Fig. 1.3 Key findings from higher education

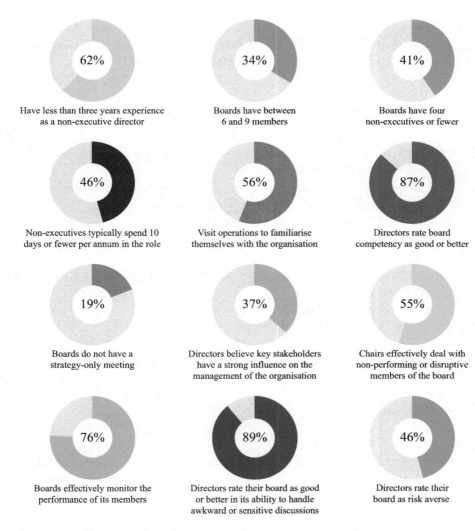

Fig. 1.4 Key findings from sports organisations

director's responsibilities are. The fact that we have independent directors in vital posts where they do know not what they should do or what is expected of them is not a situation that can be allowed to continue.

> **Key Findings from the Charities Sector**
>
> only 74% of directors rate board competency as good or better
> over 50% of chairs do not effectively deal with non-performing or disruptive board members
> only 79% of directors rate their board as good or better in its ability to handle awkward or sensitive discussions
> only 48% of boards have a regular board evaluation
> only 41% cover communication with key stakeholders where a board evaluation exists
> 24% of trustees do not visit their charity's operations to familiarise themselves better
> 18% of boards do not have a strategy-only meeting
> over 20% of directors feel there is no long-term strategy
> only 63% of trustees are rated as having the necessary commercial acumen
> only 73% of trustees are rated as adaptable/flexible to changing needs/ priorities
> only 67% of boards effectively monitor the performance of its members
> 34% say the board is too risk averse.

Knowledge of digital economy issues and grasp of data are also particularly poor. Many charity directors are not effective at data management, and 25% of university non-executive directors say they do not have enough data to do their jobs effectively. We would question whether it is possible for directors to do their jobs to an adequate standard without a supply of data and the understanding of how to use it.

There is also a tendency for independent directors—and indeed, all directors—to look the same. Most independent directors in business are older, often retired or nearing retirement from executive posts. In 2019 the average age of male non-executive directors of Financial Times (FT)-100 companies was 61.5; the average age of female NEDs was 57.9.[9] Diversity is a problem in other sectors too. In contrast to student bodies and academic staff, who come from a wide range of backgrounds, we found that university boards are heavily oriented towards white males: 60% of board members are male, and

94% identified themselves as white British. In sport, despite drives towards improving sports participation among women and BAME groups, the proportion is much the same: 65% male and 93% white British.

In charities and the NHS the genders are more closely balanced, but in both cases more than 90% of trustees we surveyed were white. By contrast, only 59% of NHS doctors are white, and 41% identify themselves being from another ethnic group, an issue which has been starkly illustrated by the fact that a disproportionate number of doctors and nurses who died after contracting Covid-19 came from BAME backgrounds.[10] And while 41.9% of NHS directors we surveyed are female, this is still quite a small proportion when we consider that three-quarters of all NHS staff are women.[11] Similarly in sport, despite claims to be committed to promoting disabled sport, only 5.4% of directors have a disability. There is a question, then, as to how well these boards can truly connect with and represent the needs of the people and societies they are meant to serve.

<display box begins here>

Key Findings from the NHS

over 20% do not believe it is possible to be effective given the mandate of the NHS

16% of directors believe their organisation has no long-term strategy

66% of non-executive directors spend at least forty days a year in the role of which, over 50% spend at least one day a month monitoring performance, and only 9% spend at least one day a month on strategy

over 30% of directors indicate that board meetings last six hours or longer

22% of non-executives do not visit their Trust to familiarise themselves better

30% of directors say that NHS Trusts are risk averse

40% of non-executives fail to bring access to networks and resources

48% of non-executives fail to provide an effective bridge to the outside world

only 63% of directors rate the quality of relationships across the organisation as good or better

30% of directors consider the board not to be innovative

only 76% of directors think the board can effectively balance short-term pressures versus long-term objectives.

Finally, and alarmingly, 20% of NHS trustees we surveyed told us that it is simply impossible for them to be effective; the demands made on them are too great because the mandate of the NHS is too wide. Trustees of charities are even more pessimistic; only 74% rated their board's ability to deal with the challenges they faced as only good or better, while 26% rated it average or worse. In higher education the percentage who rated their boards as good to excellent rose to 87%.

We would question, however, whether even these figures are realistic. Are boards as good as their members think they are? Do independent directors recognise the reality of the problems that confront them, or are they blind—wilfully or otherwise—to the crisis that confronts them? We argue that in many cases they are, and that the crisis is much deeper and more immediate than even the evidence from our study suggests.

Evidence comes from a mismatch between the views of the people we interviewed, the results of the survey on factual questions, the many examples of governance failures and the results of the broader survey. Our interviewees, all of whom occupy senior positions in governance, spoke over and over again of boards struggling to keep up with the tidal wave of workload imposed on them, of dysfunctional boards and chairs, of breakdowns in relationships between chairs and CEOs, of lack of information and the often crippling inability to make decisions on an informed basis. The replies to questions about time spent, length of meetings, training, strategy days and so forth demonstrated a very unsatisfactory situation. The number of scandals in every sector is clear evidence of a serious failure of governance Yet many of the people we surveyed seemed to think that all was rosy in the garden. Yes, they said, there are problems; but when nearly three-quarters of charity board members and nearly nine out of ten university board members think their board is 'good to excellent', when we compare this with the picture painted by many of our interviewees, and the objective evidence of scandals in every sector then we can see that something is badly wrong. As we shall see in more detail in Chap. 2, the 'problems' boards think they are facing are masking a much deeper crisis of governance—a crisis of competence and a crisis of confidence—beneath.

Over and over we found cases where boards are out of touch with reality. A good example is universities where the answers by council members gave to the questions about the most important challenges facing the sector are at odds with the actual pressures facing institutions and the consequent failures. Board members are insufficiently skilled or trained, knowledge of the organisation and its environment is poor, performance is not properly evaluated and relationships with key stakeholders are weak. What makes the matter worse is that independent directors themselves are often unaware of this; they don't know what they don't know. That means their ability to serve people and make a positive impact on society is heavily compromised.

And in the face of the coronavirus pandemic, that lack of ability could be disastrous, for stakeholders and for the institutions themselves. The social care sector is a good example of this. With council run services slashed to the bone and many private sector care institutions already on the brink of insolvency, the sector now faces an existential crisis. If institutions begin to fail in large numbers, then large numbers of vulnerable people could be left homeless and without the care they so desperately need. Another tragedy is coming, unless boards get to grips with the challenges they face and drag their organisations out of the crisis.

Key Findings from Higher Education

82% of directors spend twenty days or less on their role each year; 23% spend ten days or fewer
79% of directors indicate that board meetings last three hours or less
over 50% of non-executives are recruited through the nomination committee
only 58% visit faculties and colleges to familiarise themselves with operations
only 75% of non-executives think they have the necessary data to do their job effectively
only 76% of directors rate their board as good or better in its ability to handle awkward or sensitive discussions
only 72% of directors believe that the views of the non-executives are aligned with the vice-chancellor
over 20% of directors believe that a cohesive culture does not exist among members at council level
only 44% of chairs effectively deal with non-performing or disruptive members of the board
only 63% of chairs have effective relations with external stakeholders
over 36% of directors say that the council is risk averse

Everywhere we looked, we found a governance system that is creaking at the seams. Observing the role of boards in government departments, the Kakabadse Report commented that 'departmental boards as collective governance bodies are identified as delivering less value than, say their private sector equivalents… The emergent view from numerous civil servants is that most boards are less productive then they could be.'[12]

The annual reports from London Business School/Harvey Nash paint a picture of corporate boardroom governance that is changing, but slowly, and not quickly enough to keep pace with events. For example, despite the fact that Brexit had been a topic of discussion for months, if not years, very few boards had done any planning for a possible Brexit scenario before the referendum.[13] Our own review of the effectiveness of sports boards is confirmed by other research including a study conducted by Birkbeck College and the consulting firm Moore Stephens in 2018 which described among other things a lack of training and evaluation and failure to replace non-performing board members. In that survey, 20% of respondents felt that fellow board members did not have the training and skills to be effective.[14]

Key Findings from Sports Organisations

62% have less than three years' experience as a non-executive director

over 30% of boards have between six and nine members

over 40% of boards have four non-executives or fewer

46% of non-executives typically spend ten days or fewer per annum in the role

only 56% visit operations to familiarise themselves with the organistion

87% of directors rate board competency as good or better

19% of boards do not have a strategy-only meeting

over 35% of directors believe key stakeholders have a strong influence on the management of the organisation

only 55% of chairs effectively deal with non-performing or disruptive members of the board

only 76% of boards effectively monitor the performance of its members

89% of directors rate their board as good or better in its ability to handle awkward or sensitive discussions

46% of directors rate their board as risk averse

Again, we must be careful not to be unfair to all independent directors. As we shall see in more detail in Chap. 2, they face a formidable array of challenges. Charities are competing for resources in an age when costs are rising but both public grants and private donations are flat or declining. They also struggle to recruit qualified staff—given that they can rarely afford to pay competitive wages—which means staff and volunteers often lack requisite skills and management falls short of the highest standards of professionalism.

In higher education, the introduction of tuition fees means that universities are now under increasing pressure to demonstrate value for money; UK universities are also facing increasing challenge from overseas universities and the UK's place as one of the pinnacles of higher learning may be under threat. The UK still has twenty-eight universities in the world's top 200, but many of these are sliding down the rankings.[15] The bulging deficit in the university pension scheme, the Universities Superannuation Scheme (USS), is also a headache that will not go away. Academic staff have already launched strikes over the issue. Instances of racism, sexism and extremism by tiny but highly visible groups of students have also made headlines in recent years, and are a growing problem for university governors.

Like charities, sports bodies are also competing for declining resources and they too struggle to recruit skilled professional staff (and, of course, many sports bodies are also charities). The problems of all of these groups almost pale into insignificance beside those of the NHS. The organisation's remit is vast, covering everything from community health to emergency medicine along with huge commitments to teaching and research. The NHS also has to cope with the rising health demands of an ageing population and the vagaries of government policy in an era where secretaries of state for health seldom stay in post for more than a year. And, right across the spectrum of institutions, the ordinary challenges of running organisations in a volatile, uncertain, complex and ambiguous world have been magnified, first by the challenge of Brexit and then, following hard on its heels, the global pandemic. The old certainties have over overturned, and we face a chaotic and highly uncertain world.

What Is to Be Done?

This book is divided into three parts, each structured around one of three overlapping themes: where we are now, where we need to be and how we can get there.

Part I defines the problem. The next chapter describes the crisis of governance in more detail, looking at the underlying causes and then at the damage that is being done to society, laying out the imperative for change and suggesting areas where independent directors can make a real difference and have positive impact. In Chap. 3 we argue that solving the crisis requires a greater understanding of the concept of *independence*. Independent directors govern organisations, but they are also the servants of those organisations; their purpose is to serve as well as control. They have a duty to the organisation, but also a greater duty to society and the people they serve.

We also examine the concept of *independence*, defining what true independence means and how it is a state of mind that directors need to cultivate. One of the main reasons for failure, we argue, is that directors are either not sufficiently independent, or do not exercise that independence even when they have it. There is a tendency to follow the herd, to keep quiet during important discussions and not speak out. Sometimes directors lack conviction—often because they have insufficient knowledge or data to work with—and sometimes as Kevin Carey suggested they are simply afraid to speak up for fear of going against the rest of the room. Whatever the cause, this lack of independence means their judgement is compromised and they go on to make poor decisions. We will discuss some of the barriers to independent thinking and how to overcome them.

In Chap. 4, we begin to segue into our second theme, where we need to be. Here we will take a closer look at how a culture of *engaged stewardship* can be created. Being truly independent helps directors to build that culture and contribute to it, enabling it to flourish and grow stronger.

In Part II, we present a picture of where boards and directors need to be in terms of thinking and mindset in order to have a positive impact on society. Rather than looking at the mechanics of the director's role—a mistake many policy makers have made up until now—we will focus instead on issues such as board culture and relationships between directors. Two of the most important attributes of the independent director are knowledge and experience. Chapters 5 and 6 look at these, showing how it is absolutely important for directors to have requisite knowledge—including financial literacy—to do their job. We will describe some of the gaps that our work has exposed, such as lack of skills in the digital economy.

Knowledge and experience are of course closely related, and we will look closely at the kinds of knowledge the independent director needs and where to find it. Where do you find the data you need? How do you interrogate that data to find out what it really means? And once you have it, how can you use it as evidence to add value to your organisation? We will show how the lack of knowledge can be harmful—perhaps fatally so—to organisations and how conversely requisite knowledge can help them chart their way through troubled waters. Once again, we must remember the endgame; knowledge and experience help organisations work towards their goals and meet societal needs.

In Chap. 7, we turn to the vital role of the independent chair. Unsurprisingly, there is a correlation between ineffective or domineering chairs and lack of independent director effectiveness. It is up to the independent director to make sure they truly are independent; but the chair's responsibility is to create and sustain a culture of independence and engage stewardship so that individual directors can do their job well. We explain how chairs create and sustain culture and enable independent directors to become more fully engaged.

Experience and knowledge count for little unless they are put to good use. As our research shows, many independent directors struggle to make impact, and a sizeable number feel they are unable to do so. Chapter 8 shows some of the impacts that a high-performing board can have in terms of creating real societal value, with examples from several sectors. There are barriers to impact, but we also show how these can be overcome. In this chapter, we come back to the fundamental purpose of why boards and directors exist; not to make money, not to perpetuate the organisation or their own position, but to act as good stewards and deliver the goods and services and value that society needs.

Chapter 8 concludes by describing the ideal position; this is where boards should be. So, how do we get them there? Part III offers practical recommendations for making boards more effective. Some of these are the responsibility of boards themselves, and we offer three recommendations for boards to consider for improvement:

- Improved board composition and diversity
- Improved certification and training
- Improved board evaluation and performance appraisal

These recommendations are important, because research has shown that in some sectors, up to 50% of independent directors are recruited because they are friends of the CEO or chair (and anecdotal evidence suggests the figure could be even higher). The Birkbeck and Moore Stephens study cited earlier suggests that large numbers of directors in sports organisations are co-opted rather than formally recruited and assessed. This leads to board where, as noted, directors tend to look very much like other, and often think very much like each other as well.

Training is a moveable feast; some organisations provide a lot, others provide little at all. The training gap needs to be closed, so that all board members are able to get up to speed quickly and have impact. Training also needs to be ongoing, and we discuss how training needs must be met over the course of the independent director's career. We look at particular types of training, both formal training programmes, in areas such as finance and digital skills, and more informal training through mentors, critical friends and so on. We also describe how evaluation programmes should work, explaining the benefits of evaluation and offering examples of best practice.

However, as noted earlier, independent directors need help and support if they are to do their vital and complex job well and have impact. Policy makers need to wake up and realise not only the value of the work that independent directors do, but also the nature of the crisis we currently face. If our system of governance collapses or even is seriously damaged, then society as a whole will suffer.

Every sector already has a code of governance, and for the most part these codes are fit for purpose, but the degree to which these codes are enforced varies from sector to sector; charities in the UK, for example, are regulated by the Charities Commission. And where regulators do exist, their powers are often limited. In health care, the Care Quality Commission can and does intervene where there is a risk of failure, but even there the interventions sometimes come too late. In other sectors, the regulators watch passively from the sidelines until institutions actually fail, and only then—too late—do they step in to pick up the pieces. We argue that a root and branch review of regulation needs to be undertaken in every sector to ensure that regulators exist and are fit for purpose.

We also argue that all independent directors should be paid, or at least be offered pay if they wish it. This will be controversial, and we acknowledge that the recommendation is not fully supported by our own research; many charity directors argued that they did not want to be paid. But we believe that suitable remuneration—provided it does not compromise the director's independence—is essential if we are to widen the pool of potential directors and attract people from diverse backgrounds, so that boards are no longer exclusively composed of middle-class, middle-aged white people.

Codes and compliance are important, but they are not the sole answer to the crisis of governance. We need to concentrate on creating that culture of engaged stewardship, where independent directors have the knowledge and critical tools they need to discharge their duties, and are allowed the freedom and independence that are so vital if they are to do their jobs well. In this way and no other, we believe, the challenges of governance in the twenty-first century can be met.

Notes

1. 'Boards in Challenging Times: Extraordinary Disruptions', Alvarez & Marsal/ Henley Business School, 2015, https://www.alvarezandmarsal.com/sites/ default/files/am_boards_in_challenging_times_research_0.pdf.
2. 'Most Charity Failures Due to "Trustee Cowardice", says RNIB Chair', Civil Society News, 24 July 2017, https://www.civilsociety.co.uk/news/most-char- ity-failures-due-to-trustee-cowardice-says-rnib-chair.html.
3. For more detail on some of these scandals, see Jamie Oliver and Tony Goodwin, *How They Blew It: The CEOs and Entrepreneurs Behind Some of the World's Most Catastrophic Business Failures*, London: Kogan Page, 2010; Stewart Hamilton and Alicia Micklethwait, *Greed and Corporate Failure: The Lessons From Recent Disasters*, Basingstoke: Palgrave Macmillan, 2006; Philip Augar, *The Bank That Lived a Little: Barclays in the Age of the Very Free Market*, London: Allen Lane, 2018; Peter Chapman, *The Last of the Imperious Rich: Lehman Brothers 1844–2008*, New York: Penguin, 2012.
4. https://www.telegraph.co.uk/news/2019/11/19/oxford-union-president- resigns-blind-student-dragged-debate/.
5. 'A Task for Which No One is Qualified', *Financial Times*, 10 April 2013.
6. 'The Uncomfortable Boardroom: The New Normal?' The Harvey Nash/ Alumni Board Report 2018/19.
7. *The Times*, Editorial, 9 July 2019.
8. Gerry Brown, *The Independent Director*, Basingstoke: Palgrave Macmillan, 2015.
9. 'The Female FTSE Board Report 2019', Cranfield University, https://www. cranfield.ac.uk/som/expertise/changing-world-of-work/gender-and-leader- ship/female-ftse-index.
10. 'Ethnic diversity in NHS Trusts', *British Medical Journal*, November 2016.
11. 'Narrowing of Gender Divide But Men Still the Majority in Senior Roles', NHS Digital 2018, https://digital.nhs.uk/news-and-events/latest-news/ narrowing-of-nhs-gender-divide-but-men-still-the-majority-in-senior-roles.
12. 'Is Government Fit for Purpose? The Kakabadse Report', evidence to the civil service effectiveness inquiry, Public Administration and Constitutional Affairs Committee, 2018, http://data.parliament.uk/writtenevidence/committeeevi- dence.svc/evidencedocument/public-administration-and-constitutional- affairs-committee/civil-service-effectiveness/written/79751.pdf.
13. Filipe Morais, 'Brexit—An Extraordinary Disruption—Reflections from the Boardroom', https://www.alvarezandmarsal.com/sites/default/files/am_brex- itreport-i_final_10-05-16-v2.pdf; 'Beyond Governance: How Boards Are Changing in a Diverse, Digital World', The Harvey Nash/Alumni Board Report 2016/17.

14. Birkbeck College and Moore Stephens, 'The State of Sports Governance: Are You Leading or Lagging?', www.sportbusinesscentre.com/wp-content/uploads/2018/03/FINAL-REPORT-the-state-of-sports-governance.pdf.
15. 'Oxford Stays Top as Britain Slides Down University Rankings', *Sunday Times*, 12 September 2019.

2

Challenges and Consequences

The complexities of governing even a relatively small institution in the modern world are immense, and it is frighteningly easy for an organisation to go downhill quickly if standards of governance slip. The case of Ardwick Green shows how it can happen.[1]

Ardwick Green

Ardwick Green is a Manchester-based charity providing grief counselling services to children who have recently lost a relative, especially in circumstances such as illness or suicide, or who have been victims of domestic abuse. It has a special focus on children living in deprived areas in Greater Manchester. As such, it provides vital service that cannot be easily replicated. Both the NHS and education system provide child mental health services, but these are heavily overstretched and oversubscribed. The charity has a staff of about twenty-five people.

In 2011, Ardwick Green underwent significant financial difficulties caused in part by a reduction in sources of funding. The board at the time was made up of contacts of the CEO of the charity. The independent directors were all very caring people and passionate about the services provided by the charity.

However, they were slow to recognise the challenges facing the organisation. This was due in part to a lack of understanding and challenge of the financial information being provided to them, in part to and a lack of involvement with the organisation outside of board meetings, meaning the directors were not fully engaged with the organisation and did not really know what

© The Author(s) 2020
G. Brown et al., *The Independent Director in Society*,
https://doi.org/10.1007/978-3-030-51303-0_2

was going on inside it. The result was an overspend in the financial year and a reduction in reserves to below £20,000. The situation was sufficiently grave that the vital services provided by the charity were under immediate threat.

In order to address the issues, a new CEO was put in place and new board members were recruited. Two of the trustees from the original board also continued in their role on the new board; it was deemed important that at least some people with experience of the organisation were retained. In order to identify the skills required on the new board, a skills review was undertaken across the board and the entire organisation. Trustees from appropriate backgrounds were recruited in to address gaps in areas such as business development, HR and marketing. The new trustees were also recruited from a variety of different sources and were subjected to a rigorous application process. Finally, all trustees were subject to a formal induction process to ensure that they understood their responsibilities and the organisation itself.

The new board contracted a new accounting service with the immediate goal of producing management accounts that were accurate and easier for trustees to understand. The board also recognised the need for much more direct links between the board members and staff to ensure that the board understood what was happening in the organisation on a day-to-day basis.

The new CEO and board reviewed services, funding streams and expenditure. Staff were directly involved and kept informed throughout the process. Despite the fact that wages were frozen and all staff lost essential car allowances as a result of the difficulties, the staff team remained committed to helping the new CEO and board with the review whilst maintaining high professional standards when providing the charity's services.

Following the review, with the help of a charitable organisation that links business people with charities, the CEO and board established a new mission statement and three-year business plan with strategic objectives. Targeted performance measures were established, and performance was monitored regularly by the board. The new board also identified that more active links with local businesses were needed in order to diversify funding streams, and the chair successfully applied for a grant to fund a business development worker for one year.

The accountant who produces the management accounts now attends every board meeting, and trustees have direct contact with staff members on a regular basis. Each staff team provides reports directly to the board on a regular basis. The board also established a service user panel to ensure that the board was getting direct input from service users when reviewing services and considering future service requirements.

CEO	Head of Services
• Founder passion v. governance professionalisation • Maintaining relationships and listening to others • Local vs National vision, strategy and skill sets	• Operational insight, knowledge and know-how of social services sector • Understanding funding streams and core services of the charity • Budget allocation and reports for the Board
Chair	**Trustee**
• Driving engagement with trustees • Leading the board for contribution • Holding accountability of the CEO	• Realistic belief in values and mission • Aligning governance role and financial awareness • Having a pulse on social engagement within organisation and its stakeholders

Fig. 2.1 Engagement and independence priorities at Ardwick Green 2010–13

As a result of the changes, the financial resilience of the charity has materially improved and the impact of the work undertaken by the charity (measured using outcome-based methodologies) has materially increased (Fig. 2.1).

The case of Ardwick Green shows clearly how board failures can bring an institution to the brink of collapse, but equally, it shows how swift preventive action by a strong board can rescue an institution and put it back on a sound footing. Sadly, this doesn't always happen. Not every story has a happy ending. As noted in Chap. 1, the list of scandals, failures, disasters and collapses is seemingly endless, and, every time, it is people inside and outside the organisation who suffer the damage.

Rather than compiling a grim list of failures, let us take two examples and look at them in turn. In particular, we should note the role of the board in the failure, and the consequences for people and society.

The Impact of Failure

In 2008, the Healthcare Commission (an ancestor of today's Care Quality Commission) investigated the high mortality rate at Stafford Hospital, run by the Mid-Staffordshire NHS Foundation Trust. Exactly how many unnecessary deaths occurred during the period 2005–08 is still a matter of dispute, but some press reports put the figure as high as 1200. The chairman of the Trust, Toni Brisby, resigned and the chief executive was suspended and ultimately left his post. A subsequent public inquiry in 2013 made the point that the Trust's independent directors (known in this case as governors) had failed in their duties during the period when the deaths occurred. It is worth quoting from the report at length (the italics are ours, for emphasis).

> The governors of a FT [Foundation Trust] theoretically play an important role in its oversight. Their power to dismiss the chair and non-executive directors potentially gives them considerable scope to influence the running of the organisation. It is clear from the experience of the Trust's governors, and from meetings the Inquiry had with governors at a number of other FTs of varying sizes that, in practice, there are numerous challenges facing them:
> <u>Weakness of mandate</u>: Apart from any governors nominated by local representative bodies, an FT's public governors are elected by a membership which is grouped into constituencies in a variety of ways. *The membership is by definition a self selecting group and is not necessarily representative of the community from which it is drawn...* While this may be inevitable under this type of structure, and has value in enabling local conditions and needs to be recognised, it is important that governors are accountable not just to the immediate membership but to the public at large...
> <u>Potential lack of authority and experience</u>: Governors are a disparate group from a wide variety of backgrounds. While they are a valuable source of information about local views, *they are unlikely to be able to assess fully the competence of the board or effectively monitor its performance unless they have adequate support, for which they are currently almost entirely dependent on the board itself.* Pursuant to the obligation of FTs to provide appropriate training, *steps need to be taken to enhance governors' independence and ability to bring to light and challenge deficiencies in the services* provided by FTs....
> *There appears to be a lack of clarity and consistency around what the governors' role is and how it is to be performed.* The Inquiry has encountered a wide range of practice, from a role not far removed from a hospital visitor, to something almost approaching the challenge expected to be undertaken by non-executive directors. Much seems to depend on the leadership given by the organisations' chairs and chief executives.[2]

In other words, the scandal happened in part, the report says, because the governors were not able to adequately carry out their duties and had no idea of what was going on inside the organisation for which they were responsible.

The second example is the charity Kids Company, which ceased operations in 2015. Kids Company derived most of its funding from the Department for Education. Civil servants began to express concern over how the charity was spending the grant money it received, and rumours also began to circulate about sexual misconduct in the charity's offices. Although the allegations were never proven, they caused a loss of fundraising revenue from other sources and increased the financial pressure. The DfE then decided to pull the plug, and in 2015 the grant was withdrawn. It then emerged that the charity had no financial reserves and was on the verge of collapse. The government agreed to provide a tranche of emergency funding on the condition that both the founder and CEO, Camilla Batmangelidjh, and the chairman, Alan Yentob, stepped down. Kids Company was then wound up.

The parliamentary commission of inquiry into Kids Company had harsh words for its trustees, its independent directors. Had they done their duty, the charity would have managed its finances in a prudent manner, accumulating reserves and spending its grant responsibly. Again, it is worth quoting the commission's report at length (again, the italics are ours).

> *Primary responsibility for Kids Company's collapse rests with the charity's Trustees.* Whether these allegations prove true or malicious, if the Trustees had not allowed the charity's weak financial position to persist for so long, Kids Company would not have been so vulnerable to the impact of the allegations. *The Board failed to protect the interests of the charity and its beneficiaries, despite its statutory responsibility to do so. Trustees repeatedly ignored auditors' clear warnings about Kids Company's precarious finances.* This negligent financial management rendered the charity incapable of surviving any variance in its funding stream; when allegations of sexual misconduct emerged in July 2015 and threatened to impede fundraising, the charity was obliged to close immediately.
>
> The Charity Commission's guidance requires Trustees to 'make decisions solely in the charity's interests, so they shouldn't allow their judgement to be swayed by personal prejudices or dominant personalities'. *Kids Company's Board of Trustees lacked the experience* of youth services or psychotherapy necessary to interrogate the decisions of the Founder-Chief Executive. *This approach left the Trustees unable to defend the reputation of Kids Company and thus to discharge a prime obligation of the good governance and leadership of any organisation.* It is essential that Trustees of all charities ensure that some members of the Board have experience of the area relevant to the charity's activities, in addition to the necessary skills, and that *all Trustees have the appropriate attitude towards responsible governance.*[3]

The collapse of Kids Company, like so many other scandals in public, private and third sectors, was eminently avoidable. But the board lacked the experience and knowledge to do their job, and were in effect not competent to govern the charity. To put it another way, they lacked the knowledge to be independent thinkers and ask the questions that needed to be asked about how the charity was being run. Without good governance, without proper oversight and scrutiny, the defects in management at Kids Company went undetected and the charity's collapse became inevitable.

The impacts of both these cases were considerable. The death toll at Stafford Hospital was appalling; twelve hundred lives lost, twelve hundred grieving families left to wonder what had happened and why. The reputation of the NHS itself was severely tarnished. The failure of Kids Company put employees out of work and meant that children who depended on the charity were left unsupported. Each case was a tragedy. But perhaps the most appalling thing of all is that these tragedies were created by human incompetence.

The first step to resolving the crisis of governance is to understand clearly the challenges institutions face and be realistic about their problems. Too many organisations fail, or come to the brink of failure, because through either ignorance or wilful blindness, independent directors put their heads in the sand and fail to see what is really going on around them. We need to be clear about the problems we face.

And, as we have already said, the challenges of governance are complex and difficult, and the pressures on independent directors are increasing. Some of the problems they face are generic. In the course of our research, many of the same issues cropped up over and over again in every sector: lack of resources, strategic challenges, coping with uncertainty and managing relationships with the executive team came up time after time. But every sector also has its own particular challenges, depending on the nature of the activity in which organisations engage, the risks they face and levels of resources.

Specific Governance Challenges by Sector

Business

Business is of course a very broad category indeed, and encompasses everything from small and medium-sized enterprises (SMEs) to global giants, but all face similar problems and challenges in governance.

In the corporate world generally, there are two types of risk: *business risk*, which will only affect the company itself, and *industry risk*, or risks faced by the entire sector. Business risks include issues such as:

- loss of key clients or contracts
- getting pricing strategy wrong and losing sales and profits
- failure of quality control systems
- failure of financial or information systems and data breaches

- loss of key personnel, either members of the management team or technical staff whose skills will be difficult and expensive to replace
- changes to organisation and restructuring, which can produce uncertainty be damaging to culture and morale
- the challenge of meeting customer expectations, especially when those expectations are prone to fluctuation and change

And finally, there is the age-old problem of corruption and malfeasance by employees or other stakeholders.

Industry risks include issues such as the continuing impact of globalisation and how it is changing the landscape of many industries. Retailing, for example, has been transformed by the rise of online platforms such as Amazon and Alibaba. The impact on high street retailing has been massive, and that impact is now beginning to spread to shopping malls. Coupled with globalisation, technological changes can render a company's existing products or services obsolete, or at least provided competition from unexpected directions, as Uber and Airbnb have done in the taxi and hotel markets.

Geopolitical events can affect companies in other ways. We have already mentioned Brexit, but in addition there are issues such as the introduction or reduction of trade barriers; some parts of the world are negotiating free trade deals, while others are erecting protective walls. At time of writing, a proposed free trade deal between the European Union and the South American trading block Mercosur is under threat thanks to Brazil's failure to deal with the problem of deforestation in the Amazon, which could have an impact on the global climate. Fluctuations in exchange rates, which are often linked to political events, can cost a company heavily if it is trading or sourcing material and components from overseas. Changes in law and regulation can restrict the company's activities or force it to develop new strategies for compliance. And finally, of course, there is always the threat of competition.

Despite the SARS outbreak in 2003 and despite repeated warnings from the World Health Organization and other scientific bodies, the risk of a global pandemic had pretty much disappeared off the radar screens of most companies. Despite the obvious risks to the health of employees and to global supply chains—and, as it turned out, to the ability of many businesses to stay open at all—most firms ignored the issue and very few had a disaster plan in place to cope. Having been caught flat-footed by the rapid spread of the pandemic, many businesses argued that this was a 'black swan' event that they could not have been prepared for. In fact, like most so-called black swan events, the pandemic had long been foretold, but businesses preferred to think of plagues as something that belonged to history, impossible in the modern day. This particular form of wilful blindness has come back to haunt them.

How these risks present themselves depends on the company, its size, its products and services, and its customer base. No company is immune to them, and no independent director is immune either. One of the most high-profile casualties of recent years was Sir Richard Broadbent, chairman of the board of Tesco, who was forced to resign in 2014 after a financial accounting scandal which saw a £420 million black hole open up in the company's accounts and several executives facing criminal charges.[4] The Tesco case is reminiscent of the fall of Dutch supermarket group Royal Ahold, which had expanded rapidly in the late 1990s. Accounting 'irregularities' at several of its overseas subsidiaries caused the company's collapse in 2003.

Royal Ahold is an example of a board that failed to exercise oversight. The CEO, Cees van der Hoeven, was given a free hand to do whatever he wished, and the board merely nodded along.[5] The collapse of Lehman Brothers in 2008 was another case of the board failing to scrutinise the actions of the chief executive, Richard Fuld; famously, only two of the independent directors on Lehman's board had previous banking experience.

Too often, independent directors remain silent when they should speak. A study by management consultants McKinsey & Company found that more than 60% of non-executive directors make no comment on corporate strategy papers and simply nod them through.[6] The same study also found a strong link between board engagement and corporate performance; that is, companies where the board had a culture of scrutiny and challenge by independent directors tended to show superior financial results. Sometimes directors see the problems but feel constraints and are unwilling to speak up; sometimes they come under pressure from shareholders and feel unable to resist (indicating they are not sufficiently independent; and sometimes, as in the cases of Tesco, Royal Ahold and Lehman Brothers, the board seemed to have no idea what was going on.

When boards fail to meet the challenges they face, the consequences can be severe. Corporate scandals and collapses destroy value on a massive scale. They reduce shareholder value, which in turn has knock-on effects such as reducing the income flowing into pension funds, and this in turn has downstream consequences for pensioners, now and in the future. In the aftermath of the Deepwater Horizon disaster in 2010 and the ensuing oil spill in the Gulf of Mexico, there were concerns that BP might collapse under the weight of costs to clean up the spill and fines imposed by the US government. Had this happened, British pensioners could have been in serious trouble. Every major pension fund was invested in BP, and some funds may not have survived the loss of these large investments.

One of the myths about business failures is that the only people who suffer are fat-cat shareholders. Nothing could be further from the truth. Corporate breakdowns cost all of us. When companies collapse, they stop paying taxes, meaning government has less revenue to spend on vital social services, health services, defence and policing and so on. Society as a whole becomes less secure. Collapses also cost us directly, too. The UK government spent £45 billion to bail out Royal Bank of Scotland in 2008, and taxpayers are still paying for this.

Failures also lead to job losses, sometimes on a very large scale. The *Retail Gazette* estimates that 164,100 retail jobs will have been lost by the end of 2019, while another report predicts a staggering 900,000 retail job losses by 2025.[7] Some of the people who lose their jobs will find work in other sectors; many may not. When jobs are lost, families lose their income, meaning they may be unable to pay mortgages or rent, or even put food on the table. Children may find their educational prospects are stunted and they can no longer get into the university of their choice, or even go to university at all. Futures are lost, hopes and dreams die, and families are condemned to poverty. The consequences could have been mitigated, if only the directors had done their job and governed the company well.

Charities

We have already touched on some of the challenges facing the charities sector. The competition for resources continues to dominate the thinking of many charity boards and managers. Overall giving by individuals in the UK rose slightly last year, but the Charities Aid Foundation warns that fewer people are making donations; those that do donate are giving more, but this well may eventually run dry.[8] Many charities are heavily reliant on contract income from other sources, usually government or from grants by foundations. The latter have also increased in value, but at the same time the demand for income has increased even faster, in part because of severe cuts to local government funding over the past decade.

Charities also have to guard their reputations closely. The public hold charities to a higher standard of account than businesses, and expect them to be cleaner than clean. The Oxfam scandal in 2018 damaged many other unrelated charities as well, and may be one of the reasons why fewer people are now making donations.[9] As for Oxfam itself, the decline in donations hurt not only the charity but, by extension, the people in developing countries who desperately need its services. Oxfam's ability to carry out its mission has been impaired.

Charities also struggle to attract staff and volunteers. Low wages are an issue for a former, finding time in their already pressured lives deters the latter. And the inability to attract high-calibre staff means charities are often lacking in vital areas such digital skills—at a time when digital delivery is becoming increasingly important—and professional, competent management.

All of these things mean that charities are struggling to meet the challenges that face them, at a time when their services have never been more badly needed. Overstretched and underfunded, local authorities and the health service are increasingly relying on charities to deliver services for them, from nurses and care coordinators funded by the Heart Foundation to charities taking over local libraries. If charities collapse, then many of the services on which society depends could collapse with them. We saw above, with the cases of Ardwick Green and Kids Company, how damaging these collapses can be.

Are charity boards up to the challenge? Our research suggests that many charity trustees are pessimistic. Only 74% of trustees we surveyed rated their own organisation as good or excellent for board competence; over 20% were concerned that there was no effective overall strategy, and 33% believed the board was risk averse. Over 20% felt that there was no long-term strategy. Among the failings we found were lack of evaluation or monitoring of board performance, lack of data with which to analyse performance, and lack of commercial acumen and experience on the part of board members, meaning they were unable to act as effective independent advisors.

Key Challenges for Charities
- Competition for increasingly scarce resources
- Maintaining reputation
- Attracting staff and volunteers
- Regulations
- Digital skills shortage
- Lack of professionalism

Higher Education

As noted, the introduction of tuition fees in the UK has put universities under pressure to deliver value for money and provide high-quality education. With fees at £9250 per annum and living expenses to pay on top of this, many students will end up with a debt of £50,000 or more by the time they finish their undergraduate degree. Unsurprisingly, they want something for their money, and are becoming more vocal about asking for it.

The Augar Review, which recommended a reduction in fees to £7250, sent shockwaves through university councils. Twenty per cent of universities already face financial difficulties, and if the Augar Review's proposals are accepted, the financial pressures will increase considerably. Brexit also poses an unquantifiable threat to research funding—most universities derived at least some of their research funding from EU programmes—and research staff, especially if UK governments continue the policy of restricting free movement from Europe.

Pensions are another major challenge for universities. The Universities Superannuation Scheme, the pension fund for academic staff, is badly under-funded with a deficit of £6 billion and proposed changes to the pension scheme have been poorly handled; in 2018, more than 42,000 academic staff went on strike to protest the changes.[10] Further strikes followed in 2019.

Research funding is another critical issue; there are fewer sources for fund-ing than formerly, and much of this funding is being invested in a handful of elite universities, leaving the rest to go begging. More generally, we found that university councils lack the capacity to cope with change, that they lack inter-national focus at a time when international competition in higher education is increasing, and that they are not adjusting to the challenges of the digi-tal world.

Now, the cracks are beginning to show. Many universities are declining in the world rankings, meaning they will find it harder to recruit foreign stu-dents.[11] Some UK universities are already struggling, and some have already been forced to merge. More mergers may well follow in the next few years, and outright failure or collapse of some struggling institutions is a distinct possibility. Cost cuts mean there is a threat to the quality of education that students receive, and also to the support that vulnerable students—for exam-ple, those with disabilities or struggling with mental health—receive while they are on campus. The purpose of higher education is to allow people to develop and realise their full potential, and to make a contribution to society. Failure to deliver high-quality education to those who want it is a broken promise, not only to students but to society itself.

Yet, despite the formidable challenges faced by universities, we found a remarkable degree of complacency on the part of independent directors. Too often, university councils appear to be in denial about the problems they face, or simply do not recognise that the problems exist. There is a worrying lack of engagement. Most councils meet six times or fewer per year, and most meet-ings last no more than three hours. Eighty-two per cent of council members spend twenty days or fewer per year attending to their duties. Thirty-five per cent currently have no other independent director role, meaning they lack experience of the post. Forty-two per cent never visit faculties or colleges of their university to meet staff and students. Too many council members are not engaging with their organisations, and as with businesses, this is bound to have an effect on board performance.

In part, as one interviewee commented, this may be down to the culture of universities themselves. University councils tend to be large, as they are required to represent a wide range of stakeholders including staff, students, the university senate and so on, and this can make them unwieldy. The majority of council members are part of the university. 'That creates a culture of stewardship, a culture of "we're all in it together", and that can be very good', the interviewee said. On the other hand, independent members of the council can easily get drawn into that culture and lose their independence.

Some council members did express concerns. We found that over 35% thought their council was risk averse, and 25% felt they lacked enough data to adequately monitor performance. Another 28% believed that the views of the independent directors are not aligned with those of the vice-chancellor.

Other concerns expressed included lack of shared vision and purpose, lack of an effective chair, not enough attention to strategy, insufficient adherence to codes of governance and lack of opportunities to challenge the vice-chancellor and his objectives. Ten per cent doubted whether the contributions they made at council meetings were effective. And yet, council members themselves seem to take a remarkably *laissez-faire* approach to their role.

Key Challenges in Higher Education
- Providing value for money and maintaining quality
- Capability to cope with the pace of change
- The Augar Review and the prospect of reduced student fees
- Pension fund deficits
- Concentration of research funding in a small number of universities
- Student loan book
- Lack of international focus
- Adapting to a digital world
- Loss of overseas students, especially from East Asia, in the aftermath of the pandemic

Health Care

As we noted in the previous chapter, the very broad mandate of the NHS makes governance difficult, to say the least. More than 20% of the trustees we surveyed said they believed effective governance was impossible. It is not only the vast size of the NHS itself that complicates governance, but the complexity within it. Individual NHS Trusts can employ up to 20,000 people across multiple sites with income of more than £1 billion, but that is only the beginning. As our interviewees explained, delivering health care in any given locality involves interaction between GPs and several different trusts including perhaps an ambulance trust, a hospital trust, a community health trust and a mental health trust, as well as local authorities and other stakeholders who are not part of the NHS. 'There is a particular governance challenge in overseeing a set of activities that are very dependent on other institutions and other public services over which you have no control', said one.

Other interviewees spoke of constant interference in the workings of the board by outside agencies including regulators such as NHS Improvement, the Department for Health and even cabinet ministers. One former chair reported that regulators had insisted on controlling some appointments to the board, and described how a minister of state intervened to insist the Trust purchase specific kinds of equipment. NHS Improvement had also insisted the board establish more committees, adding significantly to the workload of overworked and underpaid independent directors.

Government funding for the NHS has increased, but the demands on the service have increased still faster, thanks in part to an ageing population with more complex health care needs. Much progress has been made in fighting illnesses such as heart disease and some forms of cancer, but in their place have come 'new' diseases such as obesity and dementia.

Although preventive health could play a much larger role in combating lifestyle diseases like obesity, in practice the NHS has little alternative but to commit the bulk of its resources to treatment rather than prevention and research. The squeeze on resources means that care quality is sometimes endangered. A culture of targets enforced by government has also changed the nature of health care delivery, not always in positive ways.

Staffing issues are also becoming an increasing problem. There is a chronic shortage of GPs in many parts of the UK, and also a shortage of nurses; the latter has been exacerbated by the difficulty in recruiting nurses from overseas following the Brexit referendum. According to *The Times*, one in ten diagnostic posts in cancer treatment is vacant, and staff are also having to make do with outdated equipment; as a result, cancer survival rates are lower than in most other developed countries.[12] Brexit has also contributed to staff shortages in care homes, and more generally there is an acute shortage of care home beds with many private providers struggling to survive financially. Funding by local authorities has reduced by 50% over the past ten years due to central government cuts in expenditure. All this, of course, is happening at a time when a rising population of elderly people is putting more and more strain on the care system. According to Age UK the number of older people who do not have access to the care and support they need is now over 1.4 million. There have been a number of inquiries and reports, but so far the government has failed to come forward with a plan for social care, despite the fact that the predicted social care funding gap by 2025 is £3.56 billion.

Past lack of investment in the NHS is also coming home to roost. Respondents to our research programme speak of problems such as deteriorations in the fabric and infrastructure of hospitals, and failure to invest in new technologies. These problems, along with staff shortages, are contributing to a deteriorating quality of service generally. Long waiting lists and frequent cancellations for many hospital procedures are evidence that many NHS Trusts are failing to cope with patient demand. Data from the Estates Returns Information Collection (ERIC) in 2018–19 shows that there is a backlog of maintenance in NHS Trusts of £6.5 billion, of which £3.4 billion represents issues that are 'high risk to patients and staff'. Even attempts to modernise and improve service are running into problems. In 2018 the North West London Clinical Commissioning Group (CCG) came under fire for spending £66 million on fees to management consultants, who providing a modernisation plan which would cost £1.3 billion to implement, at a time when the CCG already had a large deficit.[13]

Our survey found high levels of pessimism amongst trustees. Over 40% felt that government influence over how NHS Trusts are managed was very strong, and the clear inference is that they felt this interference was hampering board effectiveness. Perhaps related to this, 76% felt their boards were too focused on short-term pressures, and 30% felt their board was insufficiently innovative. We found that 30% felt their board was risk averse.

We also found evidence of a real lack of engagement in some trusts. Forty per cent of those we surveyed failed to bring access to their own networks and resources to the board, and 48% failed to engage in relationship-building activities which might link the trusts more closely with its stakeholders and the outside world; 18% lacked commercial experience or acumen. Thirty per cent stated that when the organisation runs into difficulties, they do not step forward to help. Surprisingly, 10% said they felt unable to make an effective contribution to the board. We suspect the real figure may be far higher, and once again, this lack of engagement can only be damaging to the performance of the NHS. We strongly suspect that we have seen some of the consequences of this lack of engagement during the pandemic crisis, particularly around issues like lack of equipment and PPE. When the crisis is over, an inquest into these issues will be necessary, and that inquest must extend to include the role of boards.

Key Challenges in Health Care

- Too broad a mandate for the NHS
- Balancing achieving quality against limited resources
- Ageing population
- Delivering against targets
- Demands of modern-day diseases and lifestyle issues, for example, obesity, dementia
- Coordination with local authority services, for example, care homes for the elderly
- Funding innovation in life sciences

Sport

The picture in sporting bodies is more dismal still. Despite various attempts by governments and other bodies to stimulate a growth in interest in sport among the public, including the 'legacy' of the 2012 Olympics, sports governing bodies report a picture similar to that in charities (and many of these organisations are charities) including declining levels of funding, heavy reliance on government funding and lottery grants, and increasing competition between sports for declining levels of resource. Even sports which perform well in terms of competitions or medals won can have their funding capriciously cut.

We referred to some of the problems in sporting organisations in Chap. 1, including the ongoing corruption saga at FIFA, problems around doping in a number of sports and the sexual abuse scandals in youth football. The case of cycling is worth considering in more detail. Allegations of doping among cyclists have been around for a long time, but cycling in the UK seemed to be an exception to the rule. The all-conquering cycling teams at the Beijing and London Olympics and the extraordinary feats of Team Sky, who won the Tour de France with Bradley Wiggins and Chris Frome, seemed to show that cycling was a clean and well-governed sport.

Since then, allegations of poor medical record-keeping have dogged Team Sky, while the UK cycling team has been the subject of repeated allegations of verbal abuse and bullying, especially of disabled and female riders. Cycling remains a popular sport in Britain, but the fallout from these scandals is a real threat to its future, precisely at a time when more people should be taking up cycling, both for health reasons and to reduce the number of cars on the road.

Serious problems of governance can be found all across the sports sector. Our research found problems with lack of accountability, unclear governance and lack of skills and experience to sort out the mess. The survey results in this sector make for grim reading. Far too many directors and trustees responded to our questions by saying, 'don't know'.

In part, according to some interviewees, this is because of a confusion over the nature and purpose of sporting organisations. At times they can be called upon to act like a business, but many, especially the smaller ones, are organised as charities. Some spoke of a lack of diversity, and of board's recruiting directors 'who they think will give them a less challenging time'. Some people become directors of sporting organisations because they are passionate about the sport, but that too can compromise independence. 'If you're a fan of the sport, you really need to be able to separate yourself from that in order to provide check and challenge', said one interviewee.

Engagement levels are often poor. Ninety-two per cent of those were surveyed said they had board meetings six times a year or fewer, and 73% reported meetings lasting four hours or fewer. Forty-six per cent devoted less than ten days a year to their role as independent director. Nineteen per cent reported that their board does not have a 'strategy day', leaving an open question as to how strategy is made in these boards—is there a formal strategy at all?—and outside experts are rarely invited to board meetings to give advice. Ten per cent of chief executives were reported to have little dialogue with their boards, meaning communication between boards and executive teams in such cases is low, and 14% reported that they do not get enough information to assess performance or make effective decisions.

What makes this worse is that there is clear evidence of a lack of experience for the role, and of trustees and directors being appointed on an ad hoc basis. Sixty-two per cent of respondents had less than three years' experience in their role, and half had no other similar board position, meaning their experience is limited in the extreme. Only 26% were selected through a formal process conducted by a nominations committee, and 68% reported that they did not think the process of recruitment was extensive. More than 10% had no induction training.

What emerges, then, is a picture of inexperienced and untrained directors making decisions based on inadequate information, without enough discussion or debate to explore the issues thoroughly. Without effective governance, the door is open for scandals to continue to happen.

Key Challenges in Sports Governance

- Lack of resources
- Dependence on lottery/public funding
- Competition for declining resources
- Lack of accountability
- Unclear governance at lower levels in sport
- Lack of appropriate skills and competencies
- Rebuilding grassroots sports and sports participation in particular after the coronavirus pandemic

We could go on; there are clear challenges for governance in many other sectors too, government, further education and the police to name just a few. But the examples given above show the nature of the crisis in governance. On the one hand there are common problems such as lack of engagement by directors, lack of knowledge of how to govern, achieving targets with increasingly limited resources and so on.

But on the other hand, every sector also has its specific challenges. Businesses are—usually—better resourced than organisations in the public and third sectors, but businesses have to deal with a complex and changing business landscape, balancing the need to make a profit with the need to meet the demands of stakeholders. Charities, on the other hand, have to carry out their missions while operating on wafer-thin margins, sometimes unable to attract the best talent because salaries are so low, and always they must jealously guard their reputation, which are often their only real asset. Higher education needs to shake itself out of its rut and realise that here too, the landscape is changing; tuition fees, technological advances and growing international competition all pose a threat. NHS Trusts, locked into the complex mosaic of the medical and social care system, need to rethink how they can best deliver care, for example, concentrating more on preventive medicine and less on treatment. Sport organisation needs to become more professionally managed and, especially, more transparent and better governed if they are to attract more people to participate in sports and avoid further scandals. An understanding of the nature of these specific challenges and the skill and experience to deal with them are among the things every independent director needs.

Codes of Governance

But where do they turn for help? How are they to understand what their duties are and what phrases like 'independence' and 'engaged stewardship' actually mean? The usual starting point is the codes of governance, which exist in every sector. These codes stress the role of the independent director in ensuring good governance. Increasingly, too, they make directors personally responsible for the organisations they serve. Financial penalties and legal sanctions can now be handed out if directors, governors and trustees are deemed to have failed in their duties. NEDonBoard, the professional organisation of non-executive directors in the UK, summarises the position as follows:

> Directors may bring about personal liability, both criminal and civil regarding their omissions or acts in their manner of directing the organisation. Any individual can potentially be fined according to summary conviction and/or be sent to prison for as long as six months. Also, a director may be held negligent where he or she may be personally liable for a certain transaction or business contract concerning an additional third party.[14]

Thus far, instances of independent directors being punished are fairly few and far between. In the UK, Angela Burns was fined and banned from acting as a non-executive director in 2018 for 'failing to act with integrity' at two mutual societies, while overseas, Malaysian regulators banned the directors of Golden PLUS and delisted the company from the stock exchange for accounting irregularities.[15] The Charities Commission in the UK has banned a number of people from acting as trustees, usually because of financial irregularities in their personal or professional life, and in 2016 the Commission banned all trustees of the Anatolia People's Cultural Centre for financial irregularities and suspected links between some members of the organisation and terrorist groups.[16]

There are other examples of directors being banned, usually where criminality has also been proven, but on the whole the threat of punishment has remained just that, a threat. However, we should not assume this will always continue to be the case. In most countries, governments and the public alike are demanding more accountability from boards. Independent directors who fail to discharge their duties should expect to be sanctioned in some way.

This means in turn that independent directors need to know what is going on inside their organisations, and this is true whether that organisation is a charity, a university, an NHS Trust or a business. Ignorance is not considered an excuse. In the case of the Anatolia People's Cultural Centre, the Charities Commission concluded that most of the trustees did not know about either the financial problems or the potential connection with terrorism, and therefore were guilty of neglect. Independent directors often rely heavily—too heavily, we believe—on the executive team to provide them with information. In the previous chapter, we noted complaints by university governors that they do not have sufficient information to do their job. To a large extent, though, the onus is on governors themselves, to make sure they get the information they need and can understand it.

In the final chapter of this book, we argue that the role of the regulator should be reviewed. In particular, regulators should be given greater powers to intervene before disasters happen, not merely step in to clear up the mess and hand out punishments afterwards.

Be that as it may, most codes of governance limit themselves to explaining the purpose of governance and the role of the independent director. We provide two examples here, the Principles of Corporate Governance promulgated by the Financial Reporting Council and reviewed in July 2018, and for contrast, the Principles of Charity Governance issued by the Charities Commission. Other codes tend to look very much the same, with similar structures and principles.

Principles of Corporate Governance
Financial Reporting Council, July 2018

- A successful company is led by an effective and entrepreneurial board, whose role is to promote the long-term sustainable success of the company, generating value for shareholders and contributing to wider society.
- The board should establish the company's purpose, values and strategy, and satisfy itself that these and its culture are aligned. All directors must act with integrity, lead by example and promote the desired culture.
- The board should ensure that the necessary resources are in place for the company to meet its objectives and measure performance against them. The board should also establish a framework of prudent and effective controls, which enable risk to be assessed and managed.
- In order for the company to meet its responsibilities to shareholders and stakeholders, the board should ensure effective engagement with, and encourage participation from, these parties.
- The board should ensure that workforce policies and practices are consistent with the company's values and support its long-term sustainable success. The workforce should be able to raise any matters of concern.

Principles of Charity Governance

Charities Commission of England and Wales, 2018
    Principle
    The board is clear about the charity's aims and ensures that these are being delivered effectively and sustainably.
    Rationale

- Charities exist to fulfil their charitable purposes. Trustees have a responsibility to understand the environment in which the charity is operating and to lead the charity in fulfilling its purposes as effectively as possible with the resources available. To do otherwise would be failing beneficiaries, funders and supporters.
- The board's core role is a focus on strategy, performance and assurance.

    Key outcomes

- The board has a shared understanding of and commitment to the charity's purposes and can articulate these clearly.
- The board can demonstrate that the charity is effective in achieving its charitable purposes and agreed outcomes.

    Recommended practice
    Determining organisational purpose

- The board periodically reviews the organisation's charitable purposes, and the external environment in which it works, to make sure that the charity and its purposes stay relevant and valid.
- The board leads the development of, and agrees, a strategy that aims to achieve the organisation's charitable purposes and is clear about the desired outputs, outcomes and impacts.

    Achieving the purpose

- All trustees can explain the charity's public benefit.
- The board evaluates the charity's impact by measuring and assessing results, outputs and outcomes.
    Analysing the external environment and planning for sustainability
- The board regularly reviews the sustainability of its income sources and business models and their impact on achieving charitable purposes in the short, medium and longer term.
- Trustees consider the benefits and risks of partnership working, merger or dissolution if other organisations are fulfilling similar charitable purposes more effectively and/or if the charity's viability is uncertain.
- The board recognises its broader responsibilities towards communities, stakeholders, wider society and the environment, and acts on them in a manner consistent with the charity's purposes, values and available resources.

To repeat, these codes tell us what the independent director should do, but they do not tell us *how* to do it. Statements like 'the board recognises its broader responsibilities' are useful reminders that boards and directors need to consider all their stakeholders, not just the few that are deemed most important or that make the most noise. But what does that responsibility look like in real life? What is it that boards and directors actually do, in order to govern their organisations well and make a positive impact on society?

Making Positive Impact

Thinking Strategically

For a start, they need to think more strategically. All independent directors are responsible for the strategic direction of the organisation. They do not implement strategy, but they work with the executive team to decide the organisation's direction of travel. One of their particular responsibilities is to ensure that the organisation's strategy is aligned with its stated mission. Indeed, one our interviewees went so far as to say that this was the board's primary mission; all other activities were subordinate to that.

This sounds simple, but in the complex and fast-changing world we inhabit, keeping strategy aligned with the mission is seldom easy. Economic uncertainties are everywhere. At time of writing the American and European economies are beginning to slow, and there is concern that another global recession may not be far away. If this happens, private and public spending may be squeezed still further. Consumer demand will lessen, but demand for some key public services may well increase. On top of this, there are new political uncertainties as old trading blocs break down and protectionism is on the increase. Brexit represents a massive political risk for the UK economy and society, but it is not the only one.

And there are other risks that we seldom think about. So fixated are we on economic and political risks that we seldom stop to think about other, more deep-rooted changes that are going on around us. Technology is tearing up the rules of the game. The rise of robotics and artificial intelligence is changing the landscape in which we operate, and the nature of organisations themselves. But how many boards are fully aware of these changes, and have a strategy for dealing with them? The Harvey Nash/LBS report we cited in Chap. 1 suggests that while many companies are indeed aware of the challenges and confronting them head on, there is a long tail of companies that are engaging with these challenges only a half-hearted fashion, or not at all. Our own research at Henley confirms the same picture in the public and third sectors.

This must change. Independent directors must attempt to understand these trends and the range of possibilities the future could hold. When the organisation's strategy is no longer fit for purpose, the independent directors must be prepared to say so. They must also be able to argue the case for a new strategy, one that *will* meet the organisation's needs, and back up their case with evidence.

Fiscal Responsibility

When a corporation or a charity collapses, it is often because it has run out of money. This should not happen, but it does, with alarming regularity.

Scrutinising the organisation's finances and making sure that money is being used well, effectively and for its proper purpose has always been one of the duties of an independent director. Today, the pressure on finances is increasing in many sectors. Businesses are cutting costs and squeezing budgets, increasing the pressure to do more with less. The financial pressures on the National Health Service will be familiar to anyone who reads the British press. 'The big debate for most boards', said one person we interviewed, 'is whether the financial targets they have been asked to deliver are achievable, and whether the board is able to sign up to them.'

In charities and sports organisations too, we found a common pattern of lack of financial resources, meaning that these organisations struggle to meet their existing remit on a daily basis, let alone expand or take advantage of new opportunities.

Independent directors do not intervene in the running of the organisation, and they do not manage its finances. What they must do, however, is ensure that those resources are used as efficiently as possible. That means supporting the executive team with advice on issues such as financial strategy, but also scrutinising accounts and ensuring money is used wisely and well; and checking for any signs of malfeasance.

Most organisations will have a finance and audit committee as a sub-committee of the board of directors—in many sectors this is a legal requirement—and this committee has front-line responsibility for examining and approving budgets and spending plans. But responsibility does not end there. All independent directors must be aware of the organisation's financial position and must be prepared to scrutinise the accounts—even if they have already been approved by the finance committee—and to Questions whether those accounts give a true picture. We cannot stress the importance of this too strongly. Lack of financial literacy and ignorance of financial management on the part of the board has been the downfall of more than one organisation.

People Matter

We are all familiar with the clichéd slogan, 'people are our greatest asset'. In this case, the cliché is very often true. People determine the culture of the organisation, and culture in turn shapes the leadership's ability to get things done. A strong enabling culture leads to innovation and quality of service, but a weak or toxic culture can drag any institution down. We can see evidence of weak culture in many organisational failures: Lehman Brothers, Kids Company and Stafford Hospital among them.

Many of the organisations we surveyed cited lack of human resources as being a challenge of equal magnitude to the lack of financial resources. Charities in particular struggle to recruit people with the skills and experience needed to manage in complex environments (they also struggle to recruit trustees with the right skills and experience). Even in the biggest and best-funded charities, salaries tend to be lower than in the private sector, and this is a particular problem when recruiting to senior management positions.

The same problem can be found in health care. One of our interviewees spoke of a hospital he had visited where there was a permanent vacancy rate of 20% among nursing staff. Staff shortages mean increasing pressure on existing staff, forcing them to work longer shifts with potential consequences for the quality of their work. The physical and mental health of staff can suffer as well.

Independent directors who neglect the culture of the organisation and are not aware of the stresses that staff undergo are putting the organisation and themselves at risk. They *must* be on top of these issues, and they must also consider the changing nature of work itself and how this will impact on their workforce. Much has been written about Generation Z and changing work patterns, and it is quite clear that younger people have different expectations of work, and working hours in particular.[17] Artificial intelligence is threatening to be a game-changer in many sectors. Service delivery in sectors such as health care is increasingly being delivered online, which means organisations need to think differently about whom they employ and what skills they seek.

Here again the challenge for the independent director is to not merely accept the status quo—'this is how we've always done things'—but help the rest of the board and the executive team to imagine a different future. As work changes, so organisations will change too, and the independent director will play a vital role in making a successful transition to new models and modes of working.

Coaches and Referees

'I'm not just there to give orders to my chief executive', said one interviewee, 'I am there to advise her as well.' A good board of directors provides specialist skills and expertise in a variety of areas relevant to the organisation's needs. The composition of the board (which we will discuss more fully later in the book) needs to reflect the particular challenges that face the organisation. These could include areas like digital skills, experience of operating internationally, expertise in sectors such as law, property management, personnel development and training, intellectual property and patents, and many others. Any of these areas of high priority need to be reflected in the composition of the board with independent directors recruited for the experience they bring.

We can take strategy as an example. The executive team is also responsible for strategy, but the executives need the collaboration of independent directors to make strategy work. The executive team often—usually—face considerable short-term pressures and immediate demands on their time. In the words of management guru Henry Mintzberg, they are involved in 'firefighting', and have little time to consider the long term.[18] Freed from the pressures of day-to-day management, independent directors can concentrate on the long term and ensure that the organisation has a strong strategy and continues to follow it.

As well as working with the executive team, however, independent directors must also scrutinise their actions and hold them to account, acting simultaneously as coaches and referees. One of our interviewees described a situation in which the executive team were discovered to be concealing evidence of poor performance from the board. Clearly, in this case, the board needed to call the executives out and demand a full and truthful account.

The problem is that boards are often ill-equipped to do so. In particular, they lack diversity. There are no enough directors from different backgrounds or with different mindsets to ensure a diverse range of views and experiences. Too many boards of directors look the same; even worse, too many of them think the same.

Society and Community

In many sectors, private and public, stakeholders have become more active and more vocal. These groups can range from students protesting about tuition fees, to activists demonstrating against fracking or new airport runways, to community groups demanding to have say in local health care provision or protesting against the closure of community hospitals. Groups such as Occupy and Extinction Rebellion have had a huge impact on public opinion, and social media has made it much easier for such groups to organise and become active.

The independent director can also provide a valuable sounding board and conduit for relationships with stakeholders. The challenge for directors is to see both points of view. They are stewards of the organisation and have a duty and responsibility to it, but they also have a duty to stakeholders. When stakeholders come forward with their own agenda, independent directors need to stop and listen, and if they feel that the stakeholders have a point and may be right, or partly right, then they have a moral duty to represent that viewpoint to the board.

This is particularly true of concerns raised by employees, with the Financial Reporting Council's Code of Corporate Governance advising that companies should have directors with particular responsibility for employee engagement.[19] In some countries such as Germany, employee representation is already built into the corporate governance structure, with employee representatives serving on boards. Here, NHS Foundation Trusts also have staff trustees, and some charities have followed this example.

However, the responsibility of the independent director also extends more widely, to communities and to society itself. Given the financial and operational pressures many organisations face, then can be forgotten. Charities, for example, need to constantly remind themselves that their duty is to serve the community, not perpetuate themselves. Businesses could usefully do the same. Reminding the board and the organisation as a whole that the mission is not about 'us' but about 'them', the stakeholders we serve, is one of the most important duties of an independent director, and cannot be neglected. Enshrining that point of view in board culture is one of the key components of the idea of 'engaged stewardship' (see Chap. 3)

Risk and Reward

We saw earlier how many independent directors believe their boards to be risk-averse. We also saw cases where board took little account of risk or did not understand the risks, and crashed. Perhaps it is the memory of what happened in these cases that makes directors averse to risk, or perhaps it is the fear of sanctions by regulators; either way, this is a real problem. Running an organisation requires a certain level of risk, and too little risk can be just as dangerous as too much.

Different sectors have different perceptions of risk; in the NHS, patient safety is a primary risk, while universities face a significant risk if they fail to provide high-quality education. In the commercial sectors, risk can include things like market risk but also health and safety to both employees and customers.

There is also the issue of risk to reputation. The public tolerance of risk is low, and even a single incident can cause a major scandal, as the sandwich chain Pret a Manger discovered when a mislabelled food item caused the death of a customer. Tolerance for health and safety risk is also declining, with initiatives such as 'zero harm' spreading from the steel industry into other sectors as well. Also, new kinds of risk are emerging. The introduction of the General Data Protection Regulation (GDPR) has both highlighted the risks that organisations face when using data, and increased risk levels by ramping up penalties for those that fail to comply or experience data breaches.

Independent directors must scrutinise their organisations closely, partly to protect themselves and their own reputations, but also because they have a duty of care. They are responsible for the organisation, and if things go wrong and harm is done, then blame will be laid squarely at their door. They are responsible for ensuring that their organisation is compliant; to take GDPR again as an example, they must ensure that any data breaches are reported and investigated. More widely, they need to ensure that organisation is managing risks proactively and correctly. They should look at the broader environment and try to identify risks that the organisation might not be aware of, or which it is insufficiently prepared for. Once they have identified these emerging risks, they must bring these to the attention of the board and press for action to be taken.

Another example where risk enters the picture is takeovers and mergers. These are not just a corporate phenomenon; charities and sports organisations merge and acquire each other too, and we have seen several mergers of universities including the University of Manchester and University of Manchester Institute of Science and Technology (UMIST) in 2004, and the more recent merger of the University of Wales with Wales Trinity St David and Swansea Metropolitan University. Here the challenge for independent directors is to ensure that due diligence is properly carried out and risks assessed.

Sometimes in cases of merger or acquisition, the takeover is the pet project of the CEO and the executive team. They may have staked quite a lot of their own reputation on this project, and are determined to make it happen. But if the independent directors believe the risks are too great, then again, they have a duty to make their views known. Conflict between the executives and the independent directors is always unfortunate, and can be damaging. In such cases, the directors must weigh up whether the damage caused by the conflict will be exceeded or outweighed by allowing an unwise takeover to proceed.

What Must Be Done

Who ensures that all these tasks are carried out? Who checks to see whether the organisation has a clear strategy, and the financial and human resources to carry it out? Who is the guardian of the organisation's values and culture? Who understands the risks the organisation faces, and identifies these risks and ensures appropriate action is taken?

The answer in every case is the independent directors, who are the true stewards of the organisation. They must have the experience, the skills and above all the truly *independent* cast of mind to guide the organisation in the right directions. The task that faces us now—all of us, government, institutions, society—is to ensure that every organisation has these stewards, these independent directors, to watch over them.

In Part II of this book we will talk in more detail about the kinds of skills and experience that are needed in order to make a positive impact. First, though, we will examine the concepts of 'independence' and 'engaged stewardship'. What do these words really mean? As we will show in the next two chapters, they are not rules that can be written down in a code of conduct. They are an attitude, a cast of mind that needs to be cultivated and a culture that must be zealously guarded and protected.

Notes

1. Thanks to Nada Kakabadse for contributing this study. Ardwick Green is not the real name of the charity.
2. http://webarchive.nationalarchives.gov.uk/20150407084003/http://www.midstaffspublicinquiry.com/sites/default/files/report/Volume%202.pdf.

3. https://publications.parliament.uk/pa/cm201516/cmselect/cmpubadm/433/433.pdf.
4. https://fortune.com/2014/10/23/tesco-chairman-resigns-after-420-million-accounting-scandal/.
5. Stewart Hamilton and Alicia Micklethwait, *Greed and Corporate Failure: The Lessons from Recent Disasters*, Basingstoke: Palgrave Macmillan, 2006.
6. https://www.mckinsey.com/business-functions/strategy-and-corporate-finance/our-insights/high-performing-boards-whats-on-their-agenda?
7. https://www.retailgazette.co.uk/blog/2018/12/164100-retail-job-losses-expected-2019-woes-set-worsen/; https://www.theguardian.com/business/2016/feb/29/uk-retail-sector-predicted-to-cut-900000-jobs.
8. Charities Aid Foundation, 'UK Giving 2018', https://www.cafonline.org/about-us/publications/2018-publications/uk-giving-report-2018.
9. https://www.reuters.com/article/us-britain-charity-philanthropy-idUSKBN1I11X2.
10. *The Times*, https://www.thetimes.co.uk/article/university-lecturers-to-strike-as-students-sit-summer-exams-2jmmxlsbx.
11. 'Oxford Stays Top as Britain Slides Down the World Rankings', *The Times*, 13 September 2019.
12. Editorial, *The Times*, 13 September 2019.
13. https://www.theguardian.com/society/2018/jul/21/nhs-trust-wastes-million-on-flawed-financial-advice-london-north-west.
14. https://www.nedonboard.com/what-are-the-potential-liabilities-for-a-ned/.
15. https://www.fca.org.uk/news/press-releases/fca-bans-angela-burns-acting-non-executive-director-fines-failure-declare-conflicts-interest; https://www.theedgemarkets.com/article/finally-golden-plus-be-delisted.
16. https://pulse.assent1.com/press-release-charity-removed-and-trustees-disqualified-following-terrorism-investigation/.
17. https://www.visioncritical.com/resources/the-everything-guide-to-gen-z.
18. Henry Mintzberg, *The Nature of Managerial Work*, New York: Harper & Row, 1973.
19. https://www.frc.org.uk/directors/corporate-governance-and-stewardship/uk-corporate-governance-code/25th-anniversary-of-the-uk-corporate-governance-co.

3

Independence and Value Creation

One of the foremost criticisms aimed at trustees and governors in the two cases studies we saw in the previous chapter, Stafford Hospital and Kids Company, was that they were not sufficiently independent; that is, they did not challenge the executive and act in the best interests of stakeholders. This is a critically important point. In every sector, from charities and health care to sport and business, directors *must* be independent. Without independence, they cannot have real positive impact on their institutions and society. This chapter will show why independence is so important.

It is for that reason that we chose the term 'independent director' to embrace a wide range of roles including non-executive directors of businesses, trustees and governors. The term 'non-executive director', widely used in the UK—in the USA the title 'independent director' is preferred—has negative connotations; 'non-executive' can be seen to imply an inferior status to executive directors, or a lack of responsibility. 'Independent director', by contrast, stresses the responsibility of directors to do what it says on the tin: to be independent.

The Nature of Independence

What does 'independence' in this context mean? Codes of conduct often state that directors should be independent in terms of having no vested interest in the organisation. For example, the FCA's (Financial Conduct Authority) Code of Corporate Governance defines independence as follows:

© The Author(s) 2020
G. Brown et al., *The Independent Director in Society*,
https://doi.org/10.1007/978-3-030-51303-0_3

Circumstances which are likely to impair, or could appear to impair, a non-executive director's independence include, but are not limited to, whether a director:

- is or has been an employee of the company or group within the last five years;
- has, or has had within the last three years, a material business relationship with the company, either directly or as a partner, shareholder, director or senior employee of a body that has such a relationship with the company;
- has received or receives additional remuneration from the company apart from a director's fee, participates in the company's share option or a performance-related pay scheme, or is a member of the company's pension scheme;
- has close family ties with any of the company's advisers, directors or senior employees;
- holds cross-directorships or has significant links with other directors through involvement in other companies or bodies;
- represents a significant shareholder; or
- has served on the board for more than nine years from the date of their first appointment.[1]

The emphasis here is on avoiding conflicts of interest, but that is far from sufficient. Two-thirds of the directors of Carillion were deemed to be independent, but they did little to prevent the company's collapse in 2018. In the words of one professional observer, 'when you have a situation where fund managers seem to know more about the financial state of the company than the board does and are actively trying to short it, then non-executives are in trouble. How they did not pick up on this—and try to do something about it—is shocking.'[2]

The Carillion case shows that true independence is a state of mind, a set of behaviours and, indeed, a culture which should permeate the entire board. It is not something that can be regulated for; it is something that needs to be aspired to and cultivated.

There are several dimensions to independence. First, it means independent *thinking*, the ability to take a considered view of any situation, not conforming to the idea of others but using one's own judgement and experience. Second, it means making a contribution to a *shared purpose*, for example, by contributing one's own knowledge and values, or by scrutinising the actions of executives to ensure they are in line with the organisation's purpose. Finally, it means having a strong set of moral values and the courage to apply those values without compromise.

Three Dimensions of Independence

1. *Independent thinking*. Rather than accepting what they are told, independent directors analyse any given situation using their own intellectual abilities and judgement, against a backdrop of their own experience. They think for themselves. When they feel information is missing or inadequate, or when the figures they are given don't seem right, they ask questions and demand answers. If their answers do not resolve their concerns, they say so, politely but firmly.
2. *Independent values*. They match their own values to that of the organisation they serve. That does not mean they are blindly loyal to the organisation. Rather, they are critical friends, reminding the organisation what its values are and helping it fulfil its mission and serve the interests of its stakeholders.
3. *Independent principles*. They have a strong set of ethical principles and are not prepared to compromise those principles. They also have the moral courage to do the right thing, come what may.

The first point, the independent mindset, is absolutely vital. Without it, there is a danger that board members will fall into patterns of groupthink, agreeing with each other or with the chief executive on every substantial issue. This means nothing gets challenged and nothing gets changed.

'I take it, gentlemen, that we are all agreed on the next item on the agenda', the legendary chairman of General Motors, Alfred P. Sloan, once told his board. Every head nodded in agreement. 'Then I suggest we postpone this item until the following meeting', Sloan said, 'so we can go away and think of some reasons to disagree.' Sloan was right. Debate, discussion and scrutiny are essential to good governance and to good management. Sometimes it may even be necessary to play devil's advocate in order to ensure there is a proper debate. Without an independent mindset, true debate is not possible.

'If the word independent means anything', said one of the opinion leaders we interviewed, 'it means that you bring to bear on a board a perspective that is independent of the full time executives and independent of anybody else, that you have thought yourself and that contributes to the well-bring of the organisation.' Others spoke about a 'sense of freedom' to articulate one's views, even if one is the only person in the room holding those views. 'I never minded not thinking the same way as everyone else', said one respondent, although this person stressed that it is important to express one's views in a non-confrontational way, contributing to debate rather than starting an argument.

Independent thinking is also a matter of judgement. 'It's one thing to be independent', said another respondent. 'It's another thing to be independent and effective at the moment of decision, or at the moment of debate.' Knowing *when* to challenge is as important as knowing *what* to challenge.

Secondly, independent directors are the guardians of the organisation's purpose. It is their task to make sure that its strategy and operations are aligned to the organisation's mission, and that it is truly serving its stakeholders and creating value. 'Being independent in the board is having the interests of the organisation at heart', one interviewee told us. Another said:

> You want a shared commitment to the success of the organisation, and beyond that you want the diversity of perspectives on what it will take to succeed. You want people who are able and willing to do enough homework to be informed and then able and willing in the board meetings, even sometimes when it's difficult to raise a perspective that may not be comfortable.

And finally, independence means having a distinct set of values and a strong moral compass of one's own. Independence as moral values energises individuals not just to raise questions and issues but to follow them through with determination, even if this makes one unpopular with colleagues.

Being an independent director requires courage, to speak one's mind and say and do the right thing. It also requires the experience and intelligence to realise what the right thing is. Too many organisational failures are the result of directors knowing that something was wrong, knowing that something needed to be done, but sitting on their hands. Afraid of upsetting people, afraid of retaliation, afraid of not being believed or listened to, they kept silent when they should have spoken, and other people suffered as a result.

However, there is much more to independence than avoiding scandal or failure. On the positive side, independence is part of the process of creating value and having positive impact. This is the reason why independent directors exist; to ensure the organisation carries out its mission by delivering positive value to its stakeholders. Figure 3.1 shows the process of value creation

$$I \times C \times E \times A = V$$

I - Independence
C - Confidence
E - Engagement
A - Alignment
V - Value

Fig. 3.1 Delivering value

and how independence is the bedrock, the foundation from which value creation begins. Without the independent thinking, values and principles described above, it is difficult if not impossible for a director to have real positive impact.

Independence and Value Creation

Important though it is, however, independence is only part of the value creation process. Let us look at the process as a whole and see how the pieces fit together.

Independence

'There are lots of layers of independence', commented one interviewee, illustrating the point that independence can take different forms depending on the organisation, the sector it is in and the nature of the challenges confronting it. Nonetheless, there are certain pre-requisites for independence, assets that a director must have in order to achieve independence.

Foremost among these is knowledge, both functional knowledge (strategy, marketing, finance, etc.) and knowledge of the sector. Prior knowledge is essential for two reasons. First, independent directors need knowledge in order to understand and interpret the information and evidence they are given about their organisation, to compare its position to other organisations around them and to call the executives to account if needed. Second, as we saw in Chap. 2, independent directors also have an important role as advisors to the executive, and their own prior knowledge and experience are a vital resource for the executive to draw on.

Experience and reputation are also critical assets. 'You want someone who really understands and has credibility within a sector on the board', said one respondent. Another commented on how useful it is to have someone who knows a sector well but actually comes from outside of it, in order to give greater diversity of thinking. A respondent from a charity offered this view:

> you're looking for what experience they'll bring to the board but you're also looking for the cultural fit. A number of our governors are service users or previous service users…so they have quite strong views about not wanting the great and the good who just want to be non-execs. They don't like those sort of people, they want people who share our values.

Prior experience and knowledge, however, will count for nothing if independent directors are not given the information and evidence they need to do their job. As our research showed, however, the question of which information and how much is a tricky one. Not enough information and the directors are effectively left blind, unable to challenge or scrutinise; too much, and there is a risk of information overload, with directors lacking the time or headroom to process everything they receive. There is also a question of selecting what information is necessary for governors to receive and what can be set aside. One interviewee summed up the problem as follows:

> The principle I would always advance is that a member of the governing body, as with the director of a company, has the right to know about anything going on in the company, except stuff that is personal to an individual. So they should have unfettered access to information. But of course in practice, there is so much information that if you throw everything at them, they can't pick out the important stuff. You have to have effective systems for giving the key information in a form which can be easily interrogated and comprehended. Having the right key performance indicators which are linked to a good, clear strategic plan with clear objectives and so on is an important part of constructing the environment in which you can have effective governance.

Confidence

Possession of evidence, and the skills and experience to interpret that evidence clearly, gives independent directors the confidence to raise important issues for discussion and to make their views known. It is important that directors are authentic, speaking from their own experience and being unafraid to speak the truth. A good board will have directors from different backgrounds to give a rich variety of perspectives, but those individuals will also have the confidence to speak with authority and without fear of consequences. A number of interviewees spoke of the importance of having people on the board who have no contractual obligation to the organisation and therefore are free to speak their mind.

This is easy to talk about, but it can be rather harder to do. 'It becomes quite easy to fall into a lax way of thinking that's linked to personalities and people, rather than the purpose of the organisation', one respondent commented. Another felt that his own personal circumstances and upbringing helped him to have the necessary confidence: 'I'm governed by almost tough rules that were part of my background and unafraid to speak.' A third described a calculation that goes through his mind: 'Am I prepared to sit here and see this happen, or am I going to speak out?'

Challenge can be a delicate matter. On the one hand, as Alfred Sloan knew very well, there must be space in the boardroom for disagreement. A recent report by Henley Business School on conflict and tensions in boardrooms commented that 'Healthy boardrooms are characterised as places where all board members are actively engaged in robust debate, and where they can air concerns, ask questions and challenge fundamental assumptions. Disagreements are openly discussed as part of a transparent exchange of information.'[3]

Benefits of Healthy Tension in the Boardroom

- Preventing 'group think'
- Encouraging constructive criticism
- Keeping board members engaged
- A tone that allows big decisions to be questioned and conflicting viewpoints expressed
- Resolving difficult issues
- Preventing passive aggression
- Stimulating ideas
- Holding executives to account
- Creating shifts in thinking
- Momentum

On the other hand, some directors take the imperative to challenge a little too literally. One of our respondents described an independent director whose method of challenge was sometimes quite aggressive, which was at odds with the culture of their organisation. This director eventually resigned and joined another organisation where there was a better fit between their style and the organisation's culture. Another interviewee commented:

> You have to be quite careful about how and when you make the challenge, and the terms in which you make it. There's a real risk that if you ask too many difficult questions, you will get pushed to one side, and the executive will regard you not as someone who's there to work with the team and get a collective view, but someone who's a pain in the neck.

Clearly, confidence needs to be tempered with respect and the ability to be a team player. Getting the balance right will depend on the characters and personalities of the individuals, and the culture of the organisation. Once that has been achieved, it becomes much easier for directors to engage in a purposeful manner with their organisations.

Engagement

Fully engaged independent directors understand the mission and purpose of the organisation, and will gear their efforts towards helping it meet that mission. Engaging with the organisation, however, means working not just for the best interests of the organisation itself but also looking out for the interests of its stakeholders and the people it serves. In the words of one respondent from the NHS, 'we are fiduciaries not just for the Secretary of State for Health, we are fiduciaries for the communities we serve. That means not just patients, but everyone who lives in our communities.'

'You are not there not to represent any special interests', said another interviewee. 'You are there to promote the very best for the charity, and do the very best for the charity.' A third respondent commented:

> I think our duty as a trustee is to do what is right for the charity... As independents, we're the custodians of the charity for the long term. That's our responsibility as trustees.

Engagement, then, can bring its own tensions. Directors will often have very strong views about governance and the organisation's direction of travel, and there will be times when those views conflict with those of the executive. It is important to ensure that directors and executives are fully aligned and share the same vision.

Alignment

Alignment takes two forms: alignment of *interests* and alignment of *purpose*. The first is relatively easy to ensure. People tend on the whole to join boards of organisations in which they already have an interest. In sport, for example, several respondents told us that people become directors of organisations where they already have an interest as a player or a fan. Charities also attract people who already have an interest in their cause, and one health care organisation told us that some of their trustees are also current or former service users. The same is largely true in business, where people tend to join boards of companies where they already have some background or experience and they therefore understand the nature of the industry.

Alignment of thinking can be more difficult to achieve. It is not just a matter of the independent director falling into line with the existing culture of the organisation, or particularly of the culture of the board. In many cases, that is neither possible nor desirable. The existing culture may be too passive or too unprofessional, or even actively toxic. A good independent director will seek to influence the culture of the organisation and the board in positive ways, to make improvements and promote more engagement and a more proactive and entrepreneurial attitude.

Alignment, then, is a two-way street. Directors will align their thinking with that of their colleagues on the board, executive and independent, but they will also seek to influence the thinking of their colleagues and make their own impact on culture, especially at board level. As one interviewee said, 'the culture of the board sets the culture for the organisation'. Another argued that the role of the independent director is similar to that of a critical friend:

> I like the term critical friend for the role of a trustee. I would argue that we are a friend of the charity, not a friend of the executive. We're there for the charity, but I think sometimes people lose sight of that and begin to champion individuals.

As this interviewee says, alignment does not mean becoming uncritical. It does not mean believing that the organisation and the people who run it are always right, or that they cannot be held to account. On the contrary, engagement and alignment require the independent director to be a critical friend to ensure that the organisation is governed effectively and meets its goals. 'Critical alignment' does not compromise independence; instead, it reinforces and strengthens it.

Value and Impact

Figure 3.2 shows how the value creation process works. Independence leads to greater confidence, and once directors are confident of their ability to make a difference, they are more likely to become fully engaged. Confident and engaged directors who are fully aligned to the organisation and its culture, and have both the evidence they need to do their job and the skill and experience to make use of it, can add a great deal of value to organisations, for example, by ensuring good governance. And when the whole board works together, creating a strong team and an equally strong partnership with the executives, value creation is magnified. It is then, as we shall see in Chap. 8, that directors and board start to make a real positive impact on society.

To show how independent directors create value, we conducted several case studies of organisations where independents have made significant

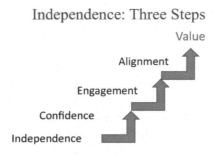

Fig. 3.2 The value creation process

contributions. All are discussed in greater detail later in this book, but for now let us look very briefly at the value independent directors can create.

University of Exeter

In 2002 the University of Exeter was performing well as an institution, but lagged behind many of its rivals. The university had never ranked higher than thirty in national league tables, student numbers and grades were modest, and research funding was about £10 million per annum. A large university council, with thirty-two members, met infrequently and did little more than rubber-stamp management decisions.

Starting in 2003, a series of reforms in governance led to a considerable strengthening of the council. A new model of governance called dual assurance was introduced, which assigned specific responsibility for areas such as infrastructure, fundraising, education and research to individual council members. New council members were recruited to fill specific gaps in capability, for example, digital skills and knowledge. The council now meets far more frequently and there is a much higher level of engagement by council members with the university. Significantly, council meetings have become places where challenges and debates are welcome and encouraged. The result is better decision-making all around.

The results have been dramatic. The university is now a member of the Russell Group of elite UK universities, and scores in the top ten in all major rankings. Student numbers have increased, and research funding has now risen to around £100 million per year. In a time when many universities face a future full of uncertainty and risk, Exeter's position looks secure.

England Hockey

In 2002 the English Hockey Association was closed down due to significant financial problems. The organisation had debts of around half a million pounds and there was no financial strategy in place to secure its future. Both the men's and women's national hockey teams were declining in performance. The organisation itself was run entirely by volunteers, including the board.

The new organisation, England Hockey, was established along much more professional lines, with an experienced chair and a board of directors modelled in part on corporate boards. The new board, which included three independent directors and three directors elected by the organisation's members, had much greater powers of scrutiny and could remove underperforming executive directors. After getting the organisation's finances on an even keel, the board set out to map the future for hockey not just in England but in the UK, becoming the national governing body for the sport.

The results have been impressive. Participation in the sport has increased across the country, more major tournaments have been staged in the UK, and performance by the national teams has improved. The men's team came fourth at the 2012 Olympics, while the women's team won bronze at the 2012 Olympics and a first-ever gold at the 2016 Olympics.

Ardwick Green

In 2011 the charity Ardwick Green lost part of its funding, leading to severe financial difficulties that threatened to impact on the vital services it provides. Governance was weak—trustees were former contacts of the CEO and not truly independent—and communication between board members and the executive were poor. The board did not receive vital information and was unaware of the financial problems until the crisis broke.

The CEO and all but two of the trustees were replaced, and new trustees were recruited with appropriate backgrounds to help the charity back on its feet again. After bringing in new financial reporting and control system to ensure the board was kept fully informed, trustees undertook a root-and-branch review of governance more generally. They gave the board a new focus on strategy, setting performance targets and monitoring these closely. The charity's finances are now back on an even keel, and the impact of the charity's work has increased.

London Ambulance Service

In 2016 the London Ambulance Service faced a crisis. There were staff shortages and the organisational structure was creaking at the seams. The board of directors were disengaged and communications between directors and executives were not working. More generally, communication throughout the organisation was poor. As a result of these failings, the trust had been heavily criticised by the Care Quality Commission (CQC).

Recognising that change starts at the top, the chair of London Ambulance Trust embarked on wholesale reforms of the board and then the structure of the organisation. Leadership and governance were brought together to create a collaborative, patient-centred culture where everyone knew the goal of the organisation and worked towards it. The transformation was swift and powerful. By May 2018, just two years later, the trust was rated 'outstanding' for patient care.

These examples show how directors and boards *should* create value, but as shown in Chap. 2, our research and prior experience shows that this is very often not what really happens. Many things happen to constrain and limit director independence, and these issues need to be dealt with and overcome. If they are not, then value creation will be hindered and impact will be limited.

Constraints on Independence

From our research it is clear that constraints come in four forms: *individual* constraints, *board* constraints, *organisational and sector* constraints and what we call '*issue-based* constraints' revolving around matters of reputation and performance. Any of these constraints can serve to limit director independence, and care must be taken to remove them; or, if that is not possible, at least reduce them to acceptable levels so the director is able to function effectively.

Individual Director Constraints

Individual director constraints stem from directors themselves and their relationships with their institutions. In particular, length of time served as a director comprises an important constraint. Unsurprisingly, staying on a board too long can lead directors to identify too strongly with the organisation and its executives and become 'domesticated' to the point where they will always defend the executives and never criticise them. In effect, they lose their independence and become swallowed up by the group.

Exactly when and how this happens is hard to say. In the corporate world, the UK code of governance states that directors should not serve more than six years (two three-year terms), although it accepts that in some cases a third term—nine years in total—is possible. It is important that boards not be comprised of the same old faces and new blood is brought in.

Our interviewees made this point as well. 'It is not possible to sustain independence over an extended period of time', said one interviewee. 'Individuals lose the edge, and the board needs refreshment so that different types of questions can be asked.'

The counter-argument is that it takes time for directors to gain experience and become effective. 'It does take much time to understand the board and the organisation', said the same interviewee. 'The danger [of excessive turnover] is continuity and loosing corporate memory.' Another commented that 'it's only about year six that you become able.' Clearly, not having enough time on a board—especially when coming into a new sector from the outside—is also an important limit on independence. New directors don't yet know what they don't know, and are therefore uncertain of what questions to ask. They may also feel nervous about making waves. As another interviewee put it, 'the newish appointees don't like to rock the boat and be seen as an outlier or a trouble maker...until they've got the kind of standing in the board to be listened to.'

In Chap. 1 we alluded to a shortage of qualified people to take on the role of independent director. One of the consequences is that those people who do have the right skills and experience are much sought after. Often they are members of two or three boards, or even more. As a result, as one interviewee said, 'they are spread too thin.' Multiple board duties leave them short of time, with the result that many directors don't prepare properly for meetings; in some cases they arrive at board meetings having not yet read the papers.

Overstretched directors also rarely engage with the organisation outside of board meetings. They may attend the occasional networking event, but they rarely undertake site visits or interact with employees and the rest of the organisation, simply because they don't have time. This means their knowledge of the organisation is limited, and that in turn restricts their ability to be independent.

Finally, independent directors may lack knowledge and experience of their sector. This is particularly true for universities and the NHS Trusts due to the complexity inherent in these organisations. There is a paradox here; as our research showed, these sectors desperately need people from outside the sector to provide diverse points of view and engage in scrutiny and challenge, and yet without detailed knowledge of the sector it is very difficult for independent directors to carry out these roles. How outsiders are inducted, developed and supported throughout their board service plays an important role in making them effective.

Board Constraints

Board dynamics, the interrelationships between members of the board and the relative power and position of each member, can also be an important constraint on independence. One of the most important factors is the relationship between the CEO and the board. Strong leadership in the form of an effective CEO with a strong track record of success is something that every organisation craves, for obvious reasons.

But if the CEO is too dominant, people begin to defer to him or her, and they stop asking questions. They shield themselves on past and current results and use them as defence mechanisms to disregard any contrary views that challenge their own decisions. Fred Goodwin at Royal Bank of Scotland, Terry Leahy at Tesco and John Browne at BP are all examples of CEOs whose record of past success meant that people stopped challenging them. Similarly, powerful vice-chancellors sometimes throttle independence on university councils. As one respondent told us bluntly: 'In fact any governor who showed real independence would probably be asked to leave the board.'

Similarly, a very charismatic CEO or one with a high public profile can also pose a constraint, as independent directors may worry that they cannot challenge someone who is famous or occupies a high position in society. Our research found that this is a problem that particularly affects some charities. Again for understandable reasons, charities will sometimes seek CEOs with a high profile in order to lobby for their cause and/or give more weight to fundraising efforts. Camilla Batmanghelidj, CEO of the children's charity Kids Company, was one such example. Batmanghelidj's public profile was immense, and she had won numerous awards including the CBE; in 2015 she was named one of the hundred most powerful women in the UK. The chairman of the board of Kids Company, Alan Yentob, also had a high public profile, but evidently he and the board were unable to exercise effective scrutiny over the charity's finances.

When relationships between the executives and non-executives on the board are not harmonious there is a lack of communication, and this in turn can result in a lack of information. Information asymmetry between the non-executives and the executives is a well-known constraint, preventing independent directors from scrutinising and raising questions confidently and effectively. 'In any organisation the odds are stacked in favour of the executive because they have more information and knowledge', said one of our interviewees, and another, from the academic sector, presented this picture of their own university council:

> The Vice-Chancellor knows infinitely more about their business than the council… The executive have a disproportionate power because they can reveal what they wish to reveal and keep hidden what they don't wish to reveal to predetermine the outcome of a discussion. It's very difficult for a non-executive director to get behind that, unless they come from the world of higher education. The council members need to spend a lot of time assimilating an enormous volume of paperwork (much more than in a company)… in an attempt to rectify the information asymmetry. They can't catch up with information built up over twenty years in one hour and then make a decision.

Apart from communication with the executives, lack of effective communication between independent directors can also pose a constraint. It is very difficult for a single individual director to raise issues of concern if they are perceived as not being shared by other independent directors. If directors do not speak to each other and share information, the result can be a form of 'pluralistic ignorance' where all are equally in the dark. It is important to have non-executives-only meetings to share concerns and ideas, but this practice is not used by many boards.

This lack of communication often has its roots in the cultures that individual boards build up over time (see below). Culture can pose other constraints too. For example, a culture of conformity sometimes emerges—especially when the board is insufficiently diverse in composition—where it becomes unacceptable to voice contrary views. Those who do so are shunned. Peer pressure to conform can be a very powerful force against independence; when people are frightened to speak out because of what their colleagues think of them, independence has been compromised. As one interviewee said:

> The social context in which directors operate is important. Do you want to be the difficult person and make life difficult for people on the board, given the implications for you in terms of social acceptance, not only on the board, might be significant?

Organisational and Sector Constraints

The nature of very large and complex organisations such as universities and NHS Trusts poses a real constraint to independence. The same is true in some areas of business, such as financial services, or companies whose products are very technical and therefore hard to understand. Several of our interviewees commented on the difficulties of having impact in such cases, and one felt that the only way to have impact was by being a member of a board committee that laid issues before the rest of the board, and therefore determined the agenda to some extent.

Cutting through this complexity is possible, but it takes time and experience and the acquisition of a great deal of specialist knowledge. Again, this is an issue where board development is very important. True independence only becomes possible once one has enough knowledge to be able to distinguish the individual trees from the much larger forest.

Who the organisation's stakeholders are and the power they are able to wield is also an important constraint. Football teams are a good example. Pressure from fans and the media exercises a very strong influence on the team's board, and very often their views are coloured by emotion and tradition rather than rational perceptions; evidence cuts less ice.

> Everyone's got an opinion on sport, which means there are always widely divergent, ill-informed views on every aspect of it which are then played out in the press. The press, the media, the divergent interests of people in the game, and the pure scale of the number of people who have an interest all constrain independence.

Other stakeholders create pressure in different forms. Organisations that have strong ties with government and politics are a case in point. Political stakeholders have strong imperatives to see their own agenda carried out. For elected representatives, failure to do so could lead to them being voted out of office, while officers and civil servants might see their career prospects suffer. Political agendas also change rapidly and unpredictably, piling on more pressure. It takes considerable courage to stand up in front of a political juggernaut and try to push back.

The pressure becomes even stronger if there is a single dominant stakeholder, able to impose his or her will on everyone else including the board. Examples include sports teams owned by a single individual, companies where the founder and owner sits on the board, or charities who rely on a single major donor. With so much power concentrated in their hands, these stakeholders can often claim to call the shots. Once again, it takes considerable courage to stand up to them and point out that 'owners' own the capital of an organisation, but they do not own the company or the team itself. Directors have a responsibility to other stakeholders as well.

Issue-Based Constraints

Reputational issues can pose real challenges for independence. In theory, the right thing to do when reputational issues come up is to be completely transparent, but this can pose an ethical dilemma; doing the 'right' thing might have negative consequences for the organisation and its stakeholders. One interviewee from the NHS describes the dilemma:

> In the NHS the stakes are just so high. You're dealing with life or death... with constrained resources, and things happen all the time that could damage the reputation of a trust or a career. So it's a constant balance; what is in the public interest? The public, patients and their families have a right to know when things have gone wrong. Equally, if you completely damage the reputation of a hospital in the public mind, that can be worse... and be less safe than being more circumspect, because patients don't won't to go there or doctors won't apply to work there and so on.

In situations like these, independent directors need to ensure they have first, a very strong moral compass, and second, a sufficient knowledge of ethics and ethical decision-making in order to advise the organisation on the best course of action. The pressure to cover up for the sake of the organisation can be very strong, and this pressure has led to many of the scandals in the NHS that were mentioned in Chap. 1. It is worth remembering that while in most organisations a scandal leads to a loss of money and destruction of value, in health care it can result in injury or death as well.

Another area where directors find it hard to be independent is when a CEO or other senior executive goes off the rails, for whatever reason, and ceases to do their job well or does something inappropriate. Dealing with this again has consequences. If the matter becomes public, the damage to the organisation could be serious, but keeping the affair hushed up also has its risks.

At Oxfam, failing to disclose the sexual abuse allegations against a senior staff member in Haiti eventually rebounded on the organisation, causing significant loss of reputation and revenue. At Uber, a culture of bullying coupled with instances of disregard for the law such as the 'greyball' cheat device, led to a rising tide of negative publicity. Again, the urge to protect the organisation at all costs can sometimes override true independence. It took a long time—arguably too long—for the board of Uber to finally make a decision and force founding CEO Travis Kalanick to step down.

How to Break Down the Barriers

In order to break down all of these barriers, boards need to develop and maintain a *culture of engaged stewardship*, where directors put the interests of stakeholders before those of the organisation or themselves and align themselves with the best interests of the organisation. In these cultures, the directors are seen as custodians of the organisations they serve, acting in the best interests not just of customers, clients and service users, but employees and society as a whole. Earlier we quoted an NHS Trust director who argued that his job was to serve not just the sick, but everyone in the community. The same is true of other sectors as well, including—especially—business.

In cultures of engaged stewardship, directors are encouraged, even required, to speak frankly and honestly and to challenge and stretch the executive and their colleagues. Individuals should feel empowered and have the confidence and knowledge to analyse and discuss the important issues facing the organisation in a fair and impartial way. Boards should be egalitarian places where everyone is equal and everyone is free to speak. We cannot overstress the importance of the role of the chair in ensuring this culture develops and is sustained, and we will devote a full chapter to the role of the chair later in the book.

Every sector has its own culture and its own ways of doing things, and understanding how things work can be a formidable barrier to a director working in a new sector for the first time. But here again, challenge and stretch are essential, and boards and chairs should not be afraid to push back against the prevailing culture to create open and honest spaces for discussion. And finally every director and every board need that strong moral compass we referred to earlier, to resist pressures to ignore or cover up bad behaviour and malpractice and to ensure that the right thing is done.

Easy to say, perhaps; not so easy to do, as many boards and directors have discovered the hard way. As a first step to showing how it can be done, let us look more closely at the notion of engaged stewardship and what such a culture might look like in practice, and how it impacts on the role of the independent director. In Part II, we will go on to look at how these cultures can be created.

Notes

1. *The UK Corporate Governance Code*, July 2018.
2. https://www.icaew.com/archive/technical/corporate-governance/roles/non-executive-directors/ned-articles/carillion-and-neds.
3. ICSA, 'Conflict and Tension in the Boardroom: How Managing Disagreement Improves Board Dynamics', Henley Business School, 2017.

4

Engaged Stewardship: Governance and Service

To better understand the concept of engaged stewardship, let us break it down into its component parts: engagement and stewardship. 'Engagement' means being involved with the organisation, understanding its purpose, committing to its goals and sharing its values. 'Stewardship' means governing the organisation in the best interests of its stakeholders, ensuring it is strong and sustainable so it can continue to meet stakeholder needs now and in the future.

As we saw in the first chapter, engagement is contingent on independence and alignment; without true independence, genuine engagement that creates value for everyone is not possible. Engagement instead becomes a narrow and warped shadow of what it should be, with directors engaging only for the benefit of a few stakeholders, or themselves. True engagement requires true independence. At the same time, we can argue that engaged stewardship is what gives independence its real meaning. Having an independent mindset is all very well, but thinking is not the same as action. Independent directors need to put their principles into practice; engaged stewardship is how they do so.

When we talk about engaged stewardship, then, we are talking simultaneously about independence. They are two halves of the same coin; neither can exist without the other. The following example of London Ambulance Service (LAS) shows how a culture of engaged stewardship can be created and sustained.

© The Author(s) 2020
G. Brown et al., *The Independent Director in Society*,
https://doi.org/10.1007/978-3-030-51303-0_4

London Ambulance Service[1]

When Heather Lawrence accepted the role as Chair of the London Ambulance Service (LAS) in April 2016, she knew that the trust had deep rooted problems and challenges. The trust had been failed on just about every possible parameter by the Care Quality Commission (CQC), the only exception being the care that paramedics were delivering, which was rated as good. On 27 November 2015 *The Guardian* newspaper echoed these failures with the headline: 'London ambulance service put into special measures. CQC inspectors express serious concerns after finding major incident protocols have not been amended since London Olympics.'

It is important to note that ambulance trusts only became part of the NHS in the 1970s, and had not always been regarded as an integral part of the NHS. Paramedicine was not recognised as a profession with a specific qualification. In addition, the organisation had historically an almost entirely male workforce, with a command and control leadership approach being applied somewhat indiscriminately. Under these conditions, a widespread culture of favouritism, racism, sexism, bullying and harassment developed.

> Up until 2012 LAS had a very big reputation. It is the only London wide organisation, and saw itself more as a part of the emergency services not the health service. My description of it would be the republic of LAS in an Eastern Bloc style of headquarters. (Heather Lawrence, Chair of the Board)

After the London Olympics in 2012 the organisation, which by its nature has a high staff turnover historically, experienced a 'spike' in leavers at both frontline and director levels, as many staff had postponed their decision to leave until after the Olympics. This led to continuous problems at the operational level, with staff shortages leading to an overall deterioration of the service. By this time, Dr Fionna Moore had been promoted from Medical Director to CEO of LAS. She drove an intense recruitment and staff development programme, including innovative solutions such as recruiting from Australia and New Zealand, and was able to stabilise the service. However, she left in December 2016, shortly after the appointment of Heather Lawrence as Chair of the Board. In a public statement the new chair commented:

> I want to sincerely thank Dr Moore for her years of service. Her leadership has helped steer the Service through a challenging period and in the last two years she has overseen one of the biggest recruitment drives in NHS history, the development of the advanced paramedic practitioners programme, an improved

fleet and focused on the personal development and recognition for everyone who works for the Service. (Heather Lawrence, Chair of the Board)

The stabilisation of LAS was, however, insufficient—the Service needed to come out of special measures and undergo a fundamental cultural transformation process.

A Fractured Organisation

The stabilisation of LAS was a short-term remedy. A fundamental cultural transformation was required to resolve several fractures that emerged in the organisation at multiple levels, namely:

- LAS-NHS system fracture. For many years LAS was perceived, both internally and externally, as quite separate from the rest of the NHS system. Its mission was to transport urgent patients mainly to Accident and Emergencies (A&Es). This fracture meant that the culture was very inward looking and isolationist.
- Board-committees fracture. Board committees worked in silos with little communication between them; information sharing was deficient and hence the quality of decision-making suffered.
- Board-executive fracture. The working processes between the board and the executive team were dysfunctional; independent directors tended to be too involved in trying to fix problems for the executive, and accountability suffered as a result.
- Executive team-general management/organisation fracture. Because of the fractures at the top, general management below C-suite were not well coordinated among themselves and consequently, communication right across the organisation suffered.

With fractured decision-making and poor communications, the organisation lacked a clear focus and a global sense of its own purpose. To fix those fractures, it was important to fundamentally change the beliefs, mindset, processes and routines of the organisation. To begin with, it was important to make necessary changes to the leadership, which included both board and executive team members.

Change Starts from the Top

Heather Lawrence, an experienced former senior NHS Chief Executive with an HR and change management background, recognised that change needed to start from the top. She undertook a 360-degree appraisal of the board and discovered that key critical competencies such as IT, digital and HR and workforce were lacking. With the support of head-hunters, Heather recruited two highly experienced independent directors in these key areas, and then went on to recruit two further highly experienced clinicians to the board. Heather also re-structured the board committees, creating, for example, a people and culture committee, chaired by one the new independent directors, and an infrastructure, IT and estates committee. Heather appointed Dr Trish Bain, an experienced NHS Trusts turnaround and quality executive, to over-see service quality improvement throughout the organisation. Additionally, Philippa Harding, a former senior governance director at Monitor and the Care Quality Commission, was appointed as interim director of governance improvement to help create a governance mindset, process and behaviour from top to bottom.

Another critical appointment was the new CEO, Garrett Emmerson, who joined in May 2017. He had tremendous experience, spending nearly thirty years in transport and local government, with his last role being Chief Operating Officer (COO) of Transport for London (TfL). The similarities between TfL and LAS are many. Both rely on complicated logistics, both require being responsive to major incidents, and they share many of the same key stakeholders in the city of London. Garrett had relevant knowledge and a strong general management background, but he lacked the understanding of the NHS clinical side and the integration of LAS with the rest of the system. Garrett commented:

> what is very different [from TfL] is the health sector involvement and the clini-cal side of the business. LAS was seen for a long time as primarily a transport related business of taking the sick and injured people to hospitals and so on. Today it's a very long way from that. Ten years ago we took 75% of our patients to A&Es, today it's less than 60% and the vision is to get it down towards 50% over the next few years. There is a much more diverse range of pathways avail-able to patients. (Garrett Emmerson, CEO)

Garrett continued to make changes to the top team, adapting it to the needs of the organisation and the challenges faced. He broadened the roles and provided support in terms of mentoring and coaching people into the new roles including managing people and the workforce, along with IT and digital. Executives and non-executives worked closely together and would challenge each other in areas where their expertise was on a common ground, particularly around digital and workforce issues.

Importantly, although they came to the organisation from different backgrounds, there was a high degree of convergence in thinking between Heather and Garrett. Both could speak their mind and challenge each other whilst bringing different experiences and skills to the table.

> Heather will challenge me very hard and very clearly and I will equally; I am not afraid to respond if I don't agree and we will get to a common place. And I think we have built a board of executives and non-executives that can do likewise. (Garrett Emmerson, CEO)

Fixing a Fractured LAS: Governance, Leadership and Culture

With the right people at the helm at both board and top team level, the LAS transformation focused on three intertwined elements: (1) the leadership approach; (2) improved governance from board-level down (i.e. how decisions are taken and how accountability works throughout the organisation); (3) a culture of collaboration, respect, responsibility and a patient-centred approach.

Leadership Approach

LAS has today a very clear vision that drives leadership behaviour. As Garrett explains:

> We have a very clear vision in our strategy in terms of what we want to for London and for the healthcare system in terms of being that integrator and joining up the world of frontline care. (Garrett Emmerson, CEO)

LAS had a history of command-and-control leadership which permeated the organisation. This was in part responsible for the unhealthy culture that developed. The relationship between the people in the organisation and senior leadership was too formal and structured. Indeed, senior leaders were often addressed by staff as 'sir', and not by name. The culture was very hierarchical, power-based and extremely formal.

Heather and Garrett set the tone from the top in terms of leadership behaviour. No longer was a command-and-control leadership style to be the dominant approach. In fact, this approach to leadership was found to be required only 10% of the time, that is, when the organisation had to respond to urgent and major incidents. Most of the time, the new LAS uses a collaborative leadership approach that enables communication and teamwork to find the best solutions for patients within the NHS system. A much more transparent culture and open-door policy exists today, and leadership is driving this throughout the organisation.

Improved Governance from the Board down

The interim Corporate Governance Director, Philippa Harding, was appointed with a clear mandate to restructure the corporate governance arrangements from the board downwards. Philippa brought enormous experience of NHS regulatory requirements and set out to fix internal controls and governance. As she was part of the executive team, she was able to explain to everyone why existing ways of working needed to change and what the benefits of that change would be. Independent directors became less involved in the day-to-day running of the business and the executive team took more control and became more accountable as a result.

What needed to change most was in fact not the governance structure, but the governance process. This included simple things such as improving the way board papers and reports were written, determining the appropriate level and quality of information required for board work, improving the sharing of relevant information between different committees leading to better integrated decision-making, improving the capturing of decisions in the minutes of meetings, and implementing reflection points at the end of board and committee meetings to identify what went well and what required improvement before the next meeting. Philippa believes this instils a greater learning culture:

> Having reflection points at the end of meetings to see how do we think the meeting went? How were the papers? Did we display the values of the organisation? Did we have the right papers on the agenda? Did we have to have everything that was on the agenda or could we have had something different? It's challenging ourselves at the top, so that people down the organisation feel it is okay to challenge all the way through. (Philippa Harding, CG Improvement Director)

Board engagement within the organisation is also much improved. Independent directors visit different parts of the organisation and talk to other layers of management to understand the issues faced, meet the workforce that is the pulse of the organisation and therefore have a much greater insight into board papers and discussions at committee meetings.

> We have added a new standing item slot, which is feedback from NEDs [independent directors]. We say: 'actually NEDs, please can you tell us about where you have been in the organisation?' We have allocated people to various sectors. (Philippa Harding, CG Improvement Director)

Not only do independent directors visit different parts of the Service, and hear in loco from different people, they also have their own specific strategy and briefing meetings, where they hear from a variety of people from inside and outside the organisation on specific topics. For example, the chair arranged for sessions on systems working in the NHS from experts in Sustainability and Transformation Partnership (STP) development.

> [every other month] there are informal sessions, which are not for decision-making. These sessions are either a full strategy session, in which case we might get people from outside the organisation to come and talk about a particular topic. We had recently the Chair of our Patient's Forum, an expert from NHS Improvements, and we had someone from another Trust come and talk to us on different topics. (Philippa Harding, CG Improvement Director)

A Culture of Collaboration, Respect, Responsibility and a Patient-Centred Approach

With changes in leadership and governance setting the tone for a culture of collaboration, respect and responsibility, there was also a need to make changes to a number of other cultural aspects.

Substantial changes were made to the diversity policy and its management in the organisation. Many individuals from the board and senior leader positions are now female and from ethnic minorities. At the time of writing, the new COO being appointed is from an ethnic minority, and is joining the director of estates, the ICT non-executive director, the people and OD director and many other senior leaders who are either female, or from an ethnic minority or both. Diversity considerations are now being enshrined in every process throughout the organisation and there is recognition from staff and trade unions that the diversity agenda has moved forward substantially.

The LAS board and executive team took the NHS-wide initiative 'Freedom to Speak Up' very seriously and drove it very hard throughout LAS. Twice a year the CEO goes in front of the 1800 staff and introduces the freedom to speak up guardian and the local champions. Staff also get to know the executive responsible and non-executive lead. As Garrett puts it:

> I felt that [freedom to speak up] was a really important tool for us to get a grip and drive forward rather than just saying, yeah, we have got a freedom to speak up guardian, you can go and speak to them if you want, and you will find the number in the phone book. (Garrett Emmerson, CEO)

The culture has also changed with regard to performance management. The previous command-and-control leadership style and culture led to performance management reviews, whereby staff would sit in front of the reviewer and attempt to convince him/her that they were performing well on all the relevant metrics. Today, performance management is now more focused on solving problems and using the process to support staff by shifting resources around to enable performance enhancement. There is also a reverse mentoring programme in place, which enables people to become more effective and to learn from other more experienced and senior people in particular roles.

In effect, the organisation culture has been transformed from a generalised command-and-control approach to a much more collaborative organisation, while retaining the ability to switch to command-and-control when circumstances warrant.

> When something big, bad or terrible happens as sadly it does from time to time, we have to be able to respond, we have to be in a clear command and control mode. We could have to, at a flick of a switch, set up a major incident response, and then you could be called in to be part of that team because, when you operate 24/7 it is inevitably about who is on call or on duty. It requires flexibility and adaptability from everybody on an almost permanent basis. (Garrett Emmerson, CEO)

Challenges Ahead: Embedding Change in a Difficult Environment

LAS was taken out of special measures in May 2018. It has achieved an overall rating of 'good' and achieved an 'outstanding' rating for patient care. The organisation has made great strides in changing its role within the wider NHS system as well as governance, leadership and culture throughout the organisation.

But LAS is on a journey that is far from complete. Heather maintains the ambition is to make continuous improvements and achieve more:

> We are on a journey that will take time. But LAS is more accountable and it's certainly patient centred. (Heather Lawrence, Chair)

In effect the organisation fractures are beginning to heal. The board and executive team have clear processes and can provide constructive challenge with clear lines of accountability where required, staff are increasingly aware of the LAS role as an integrator with the rest of the NHS system, and staff feel more confident and able to speak up, and to learn and support each other. But there are still challenges relating to sustaining performance and evolving the organisation further.

> The evidence is that if you have been in special measures, to sustain it you have to develop a methodology. There is a difference between getting it right and getting it embedded. (Heather Lawrence, Chair)

LAS needs to continue to evolve in understanding its pivotal role in the NHS system and the variety of patient pathways, developing further a patient-centred, collaborative culture and maintaining and improving the ability to respond effectively to major incidents. It therefore needs to continue to develop its workforce and effectively use digital tools and skills to enable collaboration and fast and appropriate responses to tackle rising demand. All of this is made all the more challenging by the macroeconomic environment, government budgetary restrictions and the demand for LAS services growing far faster than resources:

> The relentless growth in demand right across the health sector means that we are continually financially challenged to deliver more with less. It's probably double the percentage of growth that I have seen certainly in other public sector scenarios where you might be talking about 2 to 3% growth in demand. Here we are talking about 5 to 6% annually. (Garrett Emmerson, CEO)

Servants and Guardians

The case of London Ambulance Service shows graphically that the role of the independent director is primarily one of service. They are the custodians of the organisation, but they are also its servants. The work of Heather Lawrence and her board has been focused on making LAS fit for purpose, for one primary reason: so that it can better serve the community.

Directors are responsible for what happens to the organisation—legally and financially as well as morally and ethically—but their duty extends beyond the organisation and its managers to all its stakeholders, including the community at large. In the past, that has not always been the case. Independent director posts were often seen as sinecures, in the corporate world as well as in the public and third sectors. One turned up to board meetings four times a year, enjoyed a good lunch and went home again. A non-executive directorship was often seen as a way of rewarding someone who had given outstanding service in the past, or been to school with the chairman, or both. Unfortunately, that mindset continues to linger. As one of our interviewees said:

> A number of boards are constituted on the basis of membership by people that are semi-retired and who are collecting board memberships. That's what they do. They put together a portfolio of directorships, but they take on too many, and they don't give any one of them the attention it deserves. One of their boards might be in the arts, one might be politics, one might be sport, or whatever. And that means they turn up at meetings having not read the paperwork, and they just get through the meeting, do a bit of networking, go to the event or whatever. There is no mechanism for ensuring that the people on your boards are not spread too thin.

That attitude, as we have already seen, has led to some spectacular crashes and disasters, and will continue to do so if it is not rooted out.

However, change is in the wind. Boards are under increasing pressure to demonstrate value for all stakeholders, not just a return on investment to shareholders. For example, the Financial Stability Board Task Force on Climate-Related Financial Disclosures, published by the G20 group of developed economies 'require the board to design strategies that not only provide financial returns but also generate returns for society and the environment. For example, new business models are being developed to ensure the long-term efficient use of resources and energy.'[2] The Hermes EOS (Equity

Ownership Services) Corporate Governance Principles, published in January 2018 by Hermes Investment Management, open with the following statement:

> Companies aim to provide goods and services for customers and society at a competitive quality and price. This can only be achieved sustainably if they create and preserve value over time, not only for their shareholders but also for all stakeholders, society and the environment. Given this relationship, our overriding expectation is that companies be run not only for shareholders but with a wider purpose that benefits society. In turn, this will support the long-term interests of the beneficiaries of their shareholders, namely the savers and pensioners who rely on sustainable returns within an economy and a society that is capable of providing them and their families with a secure future.[3]

Among the principles laid out by Hermes Eos, along with remuneration, audit, protection of shareholder rights and management of social and environmental risks and opportunities, are board composition, independence and diversity, and board effectiveness and evaluation. It is worth quoting from the principles again, as these represent the 'new normal' in terms of societal and, increasingly, investor expectations.

> Boards should ensure that they comprise members with a diverse range of skills, knowledge and experience. These include leadership skills to move the company forward, good group dynamics, technical expertise to make informed decisions and sufficient independence and strength of character to challenge executive management and to hold it to account.

In the public sector, and even more so in the third sector, these pressures have of course been far stronger and been around for much longer. The pressure on charities, from donors and from the public at large, to be accountable and hold fast to their charitable purpose, has always been there (although a surprising number of charities forget or ignore this, and get into trouble), and in most countries there is strong pressure for public sector transparency and accountability.

What does this mean for independent directors? Put simply, it means they can no longer expect a free lunch. They must wake up to their responsibilities. If they do not, disaster could strike their organisations, and even themselves personally. As noted in Chap. 1, directors can be sanctioned, fined or even imprisoned if they fail in their duties.

That is the worst-case scenario, of course, and we hope that independent directors are not just doing their jobs because they fear reprisals if they do not. What we hope to see instead is the development of a real sense of pride and achievement. Being an independent director is one of the most important jobs in society, and without independent directors, many of our economic and social institutions would come apart at the seams. We would like to see independent directors do their jobs well because they know it is a job worth doing.

The Importance of Engaged Stewardship

In the previous chapter, we discussed the nature of independence and the constraints and barriers that can stop directors from having a fully independent mindset, or, at least, prevent them from expressing themselves in an independent way. These constraints show how important it is for a board to have a culture of engaged stewardship. Put simply, this means a culture where directors are enabled and encouraged to align themselves with the organisation and devote themselves to working in the best interests of it and its stakeholders. (The opposite, a culture where directors are disengaged, disinterested and put their own interests first, is a culture that can quickly turn toxic and lead the organisation over a precipice.) As noted, the concept of a culture of engaged stewardship is closely related to independence, and relies on directors having an independent mindset.

We argue that a culture of engaged stewardship is essential to any board in any organisation. Without such a culture, even the most independent-minded director, facing all these barriers—or even just a few of them—will struggle to have impact. Independent directors are only human. As our interviewees point out, they respond to pressure, just like anyone else. One respondent listed some of the pressures he had observed over the years:

> You may become too close to management, and therefore lose your independence in that respect. There's the issue of groupthink, which has a rather pernicious effect on the independence of individual directors. There are issues about whether independent directors can close the information gap in terms of information asymmetry with executive directors, whether they can devote sufficient time, and whether they have sufficient support and resources available to them to be able to do their job properly.

'There is a natural desire for people to want to fit in', said another director. 'They come onto a board and they're perhaps very conscious of their knowledge deficit and they can clearly see, and also they want to support management as well.'

This director also pointed out that external pressures can also play a considerable role. As an example, he described a remuneration committee considering whether to give the CEO a substantial pay rise. The directors on the committee know that if they refuse, the CEO might leave, which could mean a sharp decline in the company's share price. In this event, independent directors might come under pressure from shareholders to award the pay rise in order to protect the value of their investments.

In order to respond to these pressures, it is crucial to have a strong board culture that promotes and sustains independence on the part of its members. If the board culture is ineffective no individual director can exercise their role and independence to effect positive outcomes. Too often, when studying boards, the emphasis is on structure rather than culture. But as one of our interviewees observed, 'Structures are relatively easy to change. I think it's behaviours that are hard to change and it's the behaviours that make a difference.' Another said:

> It's not so much the individual but the culture. It starts with the fact that all directors have a fiduciary responsibility and that is about intellect. But its board culture that brings or prevents that sense of willingness to give those views without fear of upsetting somebody else, the chair or disagreeing with the chair.

A board with a strong culture of engaged stewardship can overcome many of the constraints we discussed in Chap. 3. In terms of individual constraints, it is down to the board to determine how long a director can serve, and when a long-serving director might need to move on. The board also has the freedom to set the workloads for directors and require them, by contract if necessary, to spend a certain number of days each year on their role and to be fully prepared for meetings. And finally, the board can also ensure that new members especially are given full training to enable to them to get up to speed and become fully independent as soon as possible.

As for board constraints, an independent board with a strong culture of engaged stewardship will be respectful of the CEO and the executive team, but will not allow past performance, reputation or charisma to affect their own judgement. Past performance is, after all, no guarantee of future performance, and there is plenty of research to show that organisations that stop and rest on their laurels put themselves at greater risk of failure; an independent board will push the CEO to attain more, and more still. The board will also put pressure on the executives to end information asymmetry, and will use their power to (politely) demand the information they need. The board will also encourage directors to work together and to be free to dissent and challenge.

Organisational and industry complexity is a huge challenge for boards, but a culture of independence will help boards to structure themselves in terms of lines of communication, committees and sub-committees and so on to ensure they gather enough knowledge to understand the complexity and come to terms with it. True independence and a culture of engaged stewardship means the board will also stand up to dominant stakeholders, becoming in effect the defender and shield of other, less powerful stakeholders who are still heavily invested in the organisation. Finally, the board will have the courage to make tough decisions about reputational issues and executives who step out of line.

Creating a Culture of Engaged Stewardship

What does a culture of engaged stewardship look like? 'It's a people thing', said one respondent. 'It's just talking a lot, being together in the right environment and having conversations which are not judging each other, actually working collegiately in the best interests of the organisation.' According to another:

> You have the interests of the organisation at heart, which is why you're there, and you're committed to its articles of governance and all those things, but you bring a perspective to bear that won't necessarily be held by the executive, and also won't necessarily be held by other members of the board who are appointed because of official positions.

The UK Code of Corporate Governance is silent on the subject. Other consultants acknowledge the importance of independence but do not fully define what board culture should be. As a first step, therefore, we have set out a list of some of the things our respondents thought were important features of a high-functioning board.

Features of a Culture of Engaged Stewardship

- Inclusiveness, a shared purpose of mission and values
- Effective board meetings
- The right balance between challenge and support during board meetings
- Shared behaviours
- Firmly established boundaries between executives and non-executives
- NED-only meetings
- Engagement with the organisation including 'thought visits', etc.
- An appropriate level and quality of information
- Effective board evaluations
- Ineffective or toxic board members are removed

Inclusiveness, a Shared Purpose of Mission and Values

In Chap. 3 we saw the importance of the notion of alignment with the organisation's mission and values, and many of our interviewees talked about the contribution of the individual director to a shared purpose. Independence and engagement can also be assessed by seeing whether and to what extent the perspective of individual directors is aligned to that of the rest of the organisation. Here is how some respondents see it:

> It is a contribution to a vision which is shared. It's worth reflecting of what the word independence means, as we all have the same vision and we all have a fiduciary responsibility.
> It's having the interests of the organisation at heart, which is why you are there.
> You want a shared commitment to the success of the organisation, and beyond that you want the diversity of perspectives on what it will take to succeed. You want people who are able and willing to do enough homework to be informed and then able and willing in the board meetings, even sometimes when it's difficult to raise a perspective that may not be comfortable.

However, our data shows there are significant weaknesses in this area. Figure 4.1 shows the average number of respondents across each sector who agree that individual directors make a contribution to a shared purpose. The data shows that most people in every sector agree that they do: most, but not all. The fact that 13% of charity directors do *not* agree, should be a warning sign in its own right. And secondly, do these figures tell the full truth? How are the respondents defining 'contribution'? How much of a contribution are they really making?

This is an area that needs more attention and discussion. Directors clearly believe that they have the best interests of their organisation at heart, but our investigation also showed that directors are not always fully aligned with their organisation. It is critical that the views of the executive, especially the CEO, and the independent directors are in synch. If they have different views about where the organisation is going, then one of two things is likely to result: (1) conflict in the boardroom or (2) independent directors passively accepting what the CEO wants; in which case, they quickly lose their independence.

Figure 4.2 shows further problems. Here we see evidence that some executive teams and some boards do not have a culture that promotes independent thinking and action among directors. Unpicking the data behind this figure, we find that the great majority of respondents, more than 90% in every sector, believed that independent directors make a positive contribution to debate,

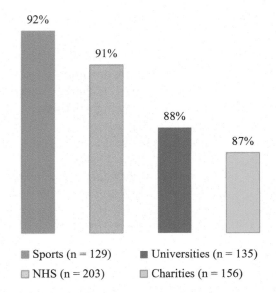

Fig. 4.1 Contribution to a shared purpose (% agree/strongly agree)

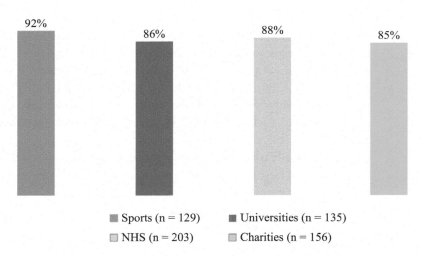

Fig. 4.2 Importance of a culture of independence (% agree/strongly agree)

and that they are given adequate opportunities to challenge the executive. However, somewhat fewer believed that the board has a culture that promotes independence and engaged stewardship, the numbers falling to 83% in charities and 78% in universities.

When asked whether a culture exists at executive team level that promotes cohesion among board members, the numbers fall still further, to 74% in both universities and charities and 80% in the NHS. In other words, anywhere from one-fifth to one-quarter of directors do not believe there is sufficient cohesion at board level. This matters, because without cohesion it is difficult to have alignment; what are we aligning ourselves to?

Figure 4.3 shows that many directors admit to facing constraints to independence. The figure for sports organisations is surprisingly low, and again we are entitled to ask if this is a true picture.

When asked about specific barriers, respondents cited issues such as management structure, lack of high-quality information, and complexity and the pace of change. Another constraint was that boards were dominated by a few key individuals who dominated proceedings, making it difficult for directors to make their voices heard. Dominance of the board by external stakeholders was also mentioned as a barrier.

The lesson we can draw from this is that culture and structure are related; a weak structure can contribute to an ineffective culture. Information sharing, transparency and equality, giving everyone on the board a chance to speak and to challenge, is absolutely vital, and board culture needs to promote these virtues. One of the important steps taken to strengthen board culture at

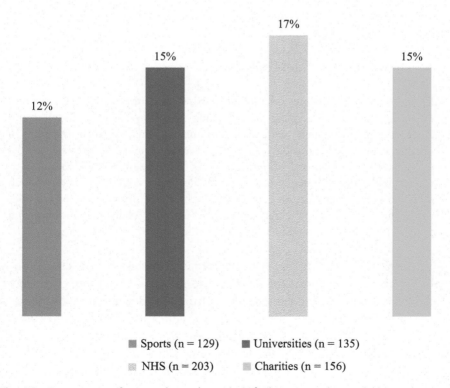

Fig. 4.3 Percentage of respondents that admit facing constraints to independence

several of the organisations we have discussed so far, including the London Ambulance Trust and Ardwick Green, was a structural change to link board and organisation more closely together, creating greater alignment.

Effective Board Meetings

What an 'effective' board meeting looks like will depend on the organisation, the challenges it faces and the make-up of the board itself. Interviewees told us that some board meetings have a friendly and collaborative atmosphere while in other cases there is more direct challenge. An effective board meeting, therefore, spans a wide range of possibilities.

Our observation is that effective meetings have two things in common. First, they allow the issues to be fully debated so that possibilities are aired, options compared and the best possible decision reached. If directors are not engaging, for whatever reason, and not contributing to the debate, then the culture of the board is compromised. Second, meetings need to yield results. Decisions must be made, strategies set and actions taken so that the organisation can move forward. Contentious issues may sometimes have to be referred to sub-committees or working parties, but agreeing to do this constitutes a decision in its own right.

The Henley Business School report 'Conflict and Tension in the Boardroom', to which two authors of this book contributed, sums up the issues as follows:

> Each board member brings their own expertise, roles, responsibilities, goals and agendas. They may even take pride in their own levels of independence and objectivity. Despite these attributes, they must ultimately work as part of a wider team that is responsible for the organisation's long-term interests.
>
> As such, effective boards should be places of harmony and collaboration as well as challenge and independence. Boards ideally act as environments in which each individual member can respect and incorporate the views of others and, when necessary, retain their independence and challenge fundamental assumptions.[4]

Ensuring that meetings are effective is one of the tasks of the chair, and we will come back to this issue in Chap. 7. The ability to contribute effectively to meetings is an important element in a culture of independence, and the people we interviewed—especially in the higher education sector—who said they felt unable to make a full contribution were also least likely to feel independent. We quoted earlier a respondent who said that anyone who did try to be fully independent would most likely be asked to leave the board. He was the most blunt-spoken respondent, but he was not the only one to express similar views.

As an aside to this, the 2019 Harvey Nash/London Business School report on boards noted a rise in off-the-grid decision-making. Nine per cent of board members who responded to their survey indicated that they 'often or always' took decisions outside of formal board meetings, and 22% had taken board-level discussions privately within the past year. The consultants at Harvey Nash who prepared the report expressed considerable concern over the practice of making decisions that are not minuted and not on the public record. While off-line discussions for the purposes of gathering information are acceptable, 'the final debate and decision must take place within [a board setting] to ensure that all members' voices are heard and decisions are not pushed through by just one or two individuals.'[5]

The Right Balance Between Challenge and Support During Board Meetings

Most directors believe the ability of their boards to handle difficult, awkward and sensitive discussions is good to excellent. However, a significant percentage of respondents do not agree. Both our own research and anecdotal evidence show that the ability of boards to raise and debate difficult issues is a critical part of effectiveness. Hard questions need to be asked, even if they make people feel awkward or uncomfortable. Yet, 24% of university directors in our sample did not believe their board encouraged raising these questions; 21% of charity directors felt the same, as did 17% in the NHS and 11% in sporting organisations.

A lot depends on how these awkward and difficult conversations are handled, and here again the chair has a vital role in ensuring that hard questions are handled in a diplomatic manner. One interviewee talked of a situation where things were going wrong:

> I wanted to have a relationship with the executive team that they would see me as supportive, rather than antagonistic, because a lot of what they were getting from the other members of the board … was antagonistic. There was a standoff between the board and the executive, with the chief executive saying, 'that is not your responsibility, the executive has to be given the space to do this and that.' In those circumstances, I felt the role was a difficult one because I didn't want to just pile in. But the board at the time just wanted to shout at the chief executive.

We also found widespread recognition that if the board *could* handle those tensions effectively, then there would be benefits. This view was particularly prominent amongst university directors, who were anxious to see a better quality of debate, better decision-making, better solutions for challenges faced, improved performance of the executive team and of the board, more forward thinking and better quality of relationships.

'It's no good sitting there and then someone speaks, and you say, oh yeah I was thinking that', said one respondent. 'That's your role, you've got to be proactive. There's got to be no fear of expressing your opinion, even if you risk the wrath of particularly a charismatic leader and their supporters.' An independent director from sporting bodies agreed:

> There are times where I'm just biting my tongue because you get in trouble for calling up on things. I tend to be quite direct and it doesn't do me any favours to be that way. But I refuse to change and I think that means I'm not a match for this sector and would fit better in another sector. But that shouldn't be the case when you're a moral person … There can be huge personal consequences for having a strict view on what's right and wrong.

Firmly Established Boundaries Between Executives and Non-executives

Boundaries between the non-executive and executive roles and the balance of challenge and support provided by independent directors are well-recognised sources of tension. Where and how the boundaries are established is an essential part of a board's operating culture.

Drawing that line is again part of the chair's responsibility, and, again, we will come back to this in more detail in Chap. 7. For the moment, the important point is that having these firm boundaries is an important part of the culture. On the one hand, the boundaries establish firm limits to the independent director's role; he or she must not interfere in the day-to-day workings of the organisation, which are the province of the executive team and management more generally.

However, the reverse is also true. The executive cannot—or at least, should not—attempt to exercise authority over the independent directors. Their freedom of action and thought must be preserved at all costs. This is in some ways similar to the freedom accorded to British civil servants to speak their mind and give frank opinions. As described in the Kakabadse Report on civil service effectiveness in 2018, civil servants see themselves as having a duty to tell the truth to elected representatives including cabinet ministers.[6] The report's authors noted that most cabinet ministers are highly appreciative of the work their civil servants do. Sadly, cases like that of Sir Kim Darroch, the British ambassador to Washington who felt compelled to resign after a perceived lack of support from politicians, reinforce the report's further conclusion that some ministers are suspicious and reluctant to engage with their civil servants.

Just as civil servants fight to protect their freedom to speak, so boards must also fight to preserve the independence of their directors. That independence is their safe space. It gives them a platform to speak out and to hold others to account. Take away that independence, and the culture of stewardship is compromised. The independent director's entire reason for being begins to erode.

Independent Director-Only Meetings

As well as formal board meetings attended by both executives and directors, it is important that the independent directors also meet from time to time without the executives present. As one interviewee put it:

> I see independence as [enabling directors] to talk about the performance of the executives separately. Occasionally that includes talking about the strategy without the executives present. And I think it is very important also that they are able also to talk about the performance of the chairman without the chairman present.

These private discussions are another safe space, where directors can speak freely and bounce opinions off each other and engage in—constructive—criticism without fear of hurting the feelings or the dignity of the executives. Directors need to be free to express their views and engage in dialogue. Of course, not all executives are happy with this. They object to being, as they would see it, talked about behind their back. Therefore, these discussions have to be conducted in a way that is diplomatic and respectful, with proper feedback to the executives at an appropriate time. The same goes of any discussions about the performance of the chair when he or she is not present.

The point was also made by several respondents that director-only meetings also serve as important social interactions, bonding exercises that allow directors to get to know each other and explore how each other thinks.

An Appropriate Level and Quality of Information

As already mentioned, the independent director is only able to exercise independence if they have access to unbiased, high-quality data and evidence. The next chapter of this book is devoted entirely to this issue, but for the moment let us simply reiterate that information and evidence gives directors the tools they need to do their job with confidence. Without information, they are effectively blind; possession of reliable information means they can scrutinise, monitor and advise the rest of the organisation in an effective manner. As we saw at Ardwick Green and Kids Company, the quality and quantity of the information independent directors receive can make the difference between success and failure.

Effective Board Evaluations

Board evaluation, both internal and external, is extremely important in ensuring not only that individual trustees are competent, but that the board itself is functioning as it should and that a culture of independence exists. Even high-performing boards—or those that imagine themselves to be high-performing—need to be reviewed, because as one interviewee said, there is always room for improvement:

> We've had an independent board evaluation carried out over the last two years. We came out of it very well, but there were recommendations, which we've implemented. I also carry out reviews of my trustees every year. I see them all individually. I get reviewed myself.

When asked about the benefits of evaluation, this respondent was forthright: 'It means the charity has been run to the highest standards and there is accountability.'

Unfortunately, there is still a large gap between desired standards of board review and what happens in real life. The Harvey Nash/London Business School report for 2018–2019 reported that although best practice says boards should undertake an external review every three years, 46% of corporate boards had not done so within this time frame. Almost a third of companies, 31%, had *never* undertaken an external review.

Our own findings were very similar. A majority of institutions do carry out regular evaluations—charities being a notable exception, where less than half of organisations do so—but these are usually internal evaluations; for example, in the NHS, most evaluations are not carried out by an external agency. We will discuss the role played by board evaluation in much more detail in Chap. 10, but one of the important benefits of evaluation is identification of those who are not pulling their weight; or even, perhaps, are pulling the organisation backwards.

Ineffective or Toxic Board Members Are Removed

Dealing with non-performing board members is of course a task for the chair, but the chair should not be left to do this alone. The chair needs the support of other board members, who must forsake whatever personal allegiances they might have to fellow directors, and instead think of the good of the company. Factionalism must never be allowed to creep into board discussions and relationships. To reiterate the point made at the start of this chapter, the independent director is the servant of the organisation, and must put the good of its stakeholders ahead of personal feelings. Failure to do so will compromise the culture of independence.

The Role of the Chair

As we have seen, the chair of the board is ultimately responsible for creating and sustaining a positive culture. Equally, a toxic chair can also be a potential destroyer of board culture. Several of our interviewees made this point very strongly.

> The buck stops with the chairman. If the culture isn't right it is the chairman's fault. The chairman can change it all.
>
> The Chairman has the responsibility to create, identify, build and nurture a proper group dynamic for the board composed by disparate people, to function in a unified way.
>
> Part of my job as chair is to create and maintain that culture of openness and supportive challenge where people can talk about things.
>
> The culture only changed when the chairman left.

How a chair goes about reinforcing or changing the culture of the board will depend on the board itself and the circumstances in which he or she finds it. If a chair inherits a board where there is no clear mandate for change, then it will be much more difficult to remove non-performing members or change ways of working. Alternatively, it may be that the culture is actually very effective, in which case the chair's task is to find ways of strengthening that culture and preserving it. To do either, or both, the chair needs to consider all the features of independence we described above.

What good chairs do will be discussed further in Chap. 7. For the moment, the key point to bear in mind is that the chair plays a pivotal role in supporting and sustaining the culture; but they do not play the *only* role. How individual directors respond to the chair, the relationships they build with the chair and with each other are also vital. In the end the chair is just one person; they cannot compel others to share the culture and vision they have set out. It is not just the chair but the board as a whole that ultimately establishes the larger culture of the organisation.

The Role of the Director

The task of the independent director has three parts. The first is scrutiny: ensuring that the organisation operates within the bounds of legality and complies with legislation and regulation; ensuring that the finances are in good order and that money is being used effectively and responsibly; developing strategies that are fit for purpose and that will take the organisation towards its goals and so on. We refer to this as the *monitoring role*.

The second part of the task is custodial. Independent directors are stewards of the organisation. That does not mean they 'own' it in any conventional sense (although in some structures such as public sector mutuals, independent directors may have notional 'shares' in the organisation). Rather, like a good steward, they are responsible for its well-being and good management, looking after the organisation's best interests on behalf of stakeholders. We refer to this as the *stewardship role*.

Finally, the third part of the task is support: backing up the executive with competent advice, making assessments of risk, better understanding of the environment in which the institution operates and generally acting as a kind of consultant to whom the executive team can turn if needed. We refer to this as the *resource-provision role*.

Of course, all three roles are interlinked. Monitoring is an important part of stewardship; like any good steward, independent directors scrutinise accounts and performance to make sure stakeholders are getting what they need. Resource provision is vital; a steward who stands by and does not support the organisation is failing in his or her duty. Our data shows that about 40% of directors in health services failed to bring access to networks and resources to their trusts, and about half failed to provide a bridge between the organisation and the outside world. Anecdotal evidence from interviewees suggested there is a similar problem in sport.

Remembering that all three are part of the same task, let us take a look at each role in turn.

The Monitoring Role

Monitoring is of course an extremely important function, and our research confirms what many earlier studies have already found, namely that independent directors coming from outside the organisation are necessary to monitor the actions and performance of executives, in the interests of stakeholders. Stakeholders themselves—providers of capital, customers and clients, service users—lack the time or capacity to monitor themselves, and rely on independent directors to provide this function for them.

Figure 4.4 shows respondents' perceptions of their own organisations and how effective directors are at the monitoring role. The numbers are the percentage of respondents who agree or strongly agree that monitoring is effective. Again, we see a very high figure for sports organisations, with the numbers then trailing off in other sectors down to charities, where one in five respondents did *not* feel that directors are effective monitors.

Some of the aspects of effective monitoring include willingness and confidence to intervene, asking the right questions at the right time and, ultimately, the courage to resign from the board if necessary.

Willingness and Confidence to Intervene

Despite the chair's efforts to create an effective board with the right culture and atmosphere, there will always be situations and issues which will challenge the independent director. We have discussed the importance of an independent mindset, but without the corresponding behaviour, the willingness to intervene, the mindset counts for very little.

Intervention requires confidence originating from values and beliefs, knowledge and experience and the support of the rest of the board, good information and data, good relationships and communication with other directors, engagement with people and stakeholders at all levels and, of course, an enlightened chair committed to a culture of independence. Here is what some of our interviewees had to say on the subject:

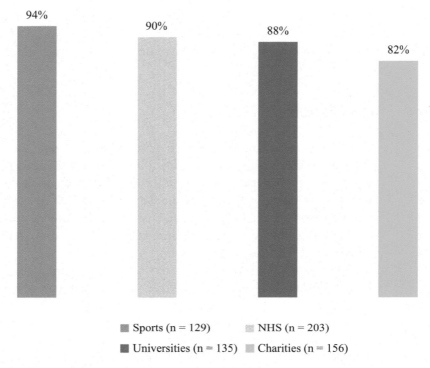

Fig. 4.4 Directors monitoring role effectiveness (% of respondents)

You can create a role but it depends how the person acts in that role and the perspective they bring to bear and their willingness to intervene.

Keeping it simple, and being focused, and having that curiosity and courage with chemistry to bind it all together.

Confidence to intervene effectively and in a way that is clear, not unnecessarily provocative or conflict generating.

As these comments make clear, the onus is on the individual; no one else can intervene for you. What is more, if individual directors are not willing and/or do not have the confidence to speak and ask questions, that can jeopardise the culture of independence.

Asking Questions

The art of asking penetrating questions in a sensible manner is a fundamental skill for the independent director. Time and again during the course of interviews, participants emphasised the fundamental importance of how questions are raised.

You need to have the right chemistry. It's not just what you say it's how you say it.

Despite their best intentions, directors sometimes frame questions in ways which are perceived as confrontational. They might use the wrong tone, or ask too many different and difficult questions. As a consequence, executives might become unhelpful, defensive or even outright hostile. None of this helps to preserve the culture of independence, as another interviewee pointed out:

> How do you avoid becoming the serial moaner and turning people off? It's the ability to ask questions in a way so that people won't get defensive. Or you get closer to the executive, have a chat with the executive in charge of risk or HR or whatever, and ask where they are spending their time, what's troubling them and so on.
>
> There are different board cultures. We expect the [directors] to challenge in the spirit of support rather than criticism, because otherwise you get antibodies. People get defensive. What you actually want to do is to create an environment where people can talk about things and reach better solutions.

Different contexts will require different questions and approaches. For example, in organisations where the product or service is produced/delivered by highly specialised individuals the independent director may have to ask for things to be explained in lay terms. There is no shame in doing so:

> The word challenge is inadequate. It's about inquisitive, intelligently framed questions—what have you done about this issue? But if you are challenging a nurse or a doctor as a lay member you can be out of your depth in terms of professional criteria. So you have to say, I don't quite understand that please explain it to me.

Overall, the ability to frame questions and then have a dialogue with the executive around them is an important part of the independent director's role.

Timing

Asking good questions is one thing, but knowing when to ask them and how to prioritise your concerns is another. Timing is important. Sometimes it is easier to ask questions when the issue is still developing, so that it can be explored in advance. It is also important to understand whether the board is prepared to back you or whether you have enough evidence to raise a critical issue or question. The effective independent director is able to read the board context and mood, look at the evidence and make a judgement of whether it is the right moment to raise an issue or ask a penetrating question about something.

> The effective independent director understands when to make his/her move.

Most importantly, the effective independent director will not attempt to address every single concern. One cannot, as one of our interviewees said, fight every battle that you want to. Instead the best course is to have an 'inquiry strategy', tackling the most relevant and important issues first and asking questions that might shed light on multiple aspects or problems:

> It's really important to be sensitive to context and to what is going on around the table, not to be over assertive or over interventional which can be counter-productive. It's always important to exercise judgment in sensitivity and that will sometimes mean that you will let minor things go.

In other words, independent directors have only limited amounts of time, and therefore they need to concentrate on addressing issues where they are likely to have impact and where they have the knowledge, evidence and support to make their case. When they are confident they can do so, they then need to ensure the issue is laid before the rest of the board. Often, the best course of action is to first discuss the matter with the chair and persuade him or her to include it in the agenda. Sometimes, though, the chair is part of the problem. In this case it is important to gain the support of other independent directors to compel a full discussion.

Resigning

In the course of our research, it was not uncommon to hear board members say that they have experienced being ignored or marginalised in the board-room, when they were raising a legitimate, well-informed case regarding a particular decision. When questions and active, intelligent inquiry make no headway and the board is not working effectively, then the independent director needs to decide whether to persist, or to take the nuclear option and resign:

> You have to express your opinion if you believe in it. Ultimately you can resign but you are bound, in my view, by corporate responsibility. You only threaten to this once, because if you do more than once and you don't follow through you lose all your credibility.

I was acting as co-sec with the chair and we tackled the issue head on with the senior trustees. The director said: 'it's just unacceptable, the chair is interfering with operational matters', etc. I then resigned and he was removed later.

This is not a decision to be taken lightly. The independent director has a fiduciary responsibility for the funds invested in the organisation, and resigning could be seen as an attempt to escape from responsibilities. However, if the situation persists despite reasonable attempts to address it, resignation may be the only way to send a signal to interested parties that something is not working at the top of the organisation.

The Stewardship and Resource Provision Roles

Stewardship and supporting the executive team mean a different set of responsibilities. Figure 4.5 shows how well respondents feel that directors are carrying out their stewardship roles. It is interesting to note that perceptions of effective stewardship are much lower than perceptions of effective monitoring, that is, the view is that independent directors make better monitors than stewards. Around a quarter of respondents in every sector except sport have doubts about whether directors are effective stewards. This finding raises concerns, which we shall come back to in a moment.

Bringing an External Perspective and Resources

Many respondents to our survey felt that a critical role of the independent director is to bring to the board an external perspective, as well as networks and access to resources not otherwise available:

All trustees have fiduciary responsibilities and need to be aligned interest in ensuring the success of the organisation. What the independent director brings is an external perspective.
   The independent person sits between the organisational purpose and the outside world's point of view. [The independent directors] make that bridge.
   The independent director needs an understanding of where the [organisation] is and wants to be. They need a good perspective on strategy and performance from the outside, and they then can challenge the executive.

Bringing different thinking and options to the table can be very beneficial. Sometimes, however, the exercise of this role, particularly in securing resources

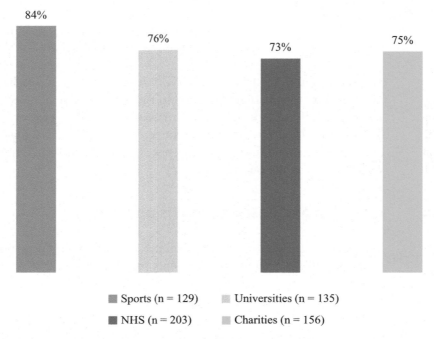

Fig. 4.5 The stewardship and resource provision roles effectiveness (% of respondents)

from external financing bodies (e.g. in the charity sector), has an impact on independence as it may make the board more dependent on that individual.

The independent director also fulfils an advisory and mentoring role, assisting the management with expertise and experience around particular areas of expertise or mentoring them through particular situations of dilemmas:

> Where I see independent directors working well is when they are playing their advisory role. They are able to bring to the board knowledge and experience, access to contacts and access to finance to complement their skills.

The effective exercise of mentoring and advice by the independent director is an important tool for building a relationship of trust and respect with the CEO and the executive. This allows vulnerabilities and tensions to be exposed and discussed. Independent directors who are good at supporting executives are often highly respected by the CEO and their advice is much sought-after. Commenting on this issue, one respondent added a warning note:

> A measure of a really good independent directors is when the executive thinks, 'what would X say?' when X is not in the room. That CEO respects your view

and advice. Of course, this can also create dependency from the executive on the independent director's views, which is crossing the boundaries.

Another said:

The man who dresses the king has no idol. He sees the king with nothing, just like anybody else. That is very important. That's why I think the confidante mentoring role is a great privilege.

The Role of Board Committees

Committees play an important role in board effectiveness. They are in some ways the workhorse of the board, harnessing the energies of small numbers of board members to focus on particularly important issues the board faces. The board as a whole needs to look at the organisation in the round and see the entire picture from the point of view of all stakeholders groups. Committees take a narrower focus and dig deeper.

What committees and how many a board should have will depend on many things, including the nature of the organisation and its business, the most important risks and challenges the organisation faces, and the size and composition of the board. The structure of the committee system needs careful attention. Too many committees, and the board can become overwhelmed with detail; too few, and important issues will not get the scrutiny they require.

One committee that is found nearly everywhere is the audit committee, which in smaller organisations is sometimes known as the finance and audit committee. The audit committee is responsible for overseeing the financial controls of the company and ensuring that financial resources are used wisely. This can include issues such as financial planning and forecast, ensuring that financial reserves are kept up to the required level, scrutinising the accounts and generally ensuring that the organisation's finances are in a healthy state.

Consultants Ernst & Young recommend that audit committees should have at least three independent directors, or two in the case of smaller companies, in order to be full objective. Among the duties of the audit committee identified by EY are as follows:

* Monitoring the integrity of financial statements and any formal announcements relating to the company's financial performance
* Reviewing internal financial controls and the company's internal control and risk management systems

- Monitoring and reviewing the effectiveness of the company's internal audit function
- Recommending the appointment of an external auditor and approving the terms of engagement of the auditor
- Reviewing and monitoring the external auditor's independence and objectivity
- Reporting to the aboard any matters concerning the above points where action or improvement is needed

Audit committees are some of the most hard-working board committees, and members have to be able to master a wealth of information. Their responsibilities are heavy and they need to be able to work together as a team. Needless to say, they need a great deal of financial experience and skills.

Another common type of committee, especially in the private sector, is the remuneration committee, or Remco. Their function is to determine levels of executive compensation from an independent perspective. Executive compensation needs to be fair and transparent; directors should be rewarded for their achievements, but that does not mean letting them simply name their own salaries. Needless to say, Remcos can come under a lot of pressure, from executives wanting pay rises and from shareholders and other stakeholders objecting to 'fat cat' levels of compensation.

There are many other types of committees, from permanent standing committees to temporary working groups. Some committees are only activated when needed, like the nominations committees who lead the search for candidates for key posts such as chairman and CEO, and sometimes for independent board members as well. Health and safety, human resources, safeguarding, ethics, fundraising, education, quality and IT/technology are just some examples of the kinds of committees organisations may need.

The reason for mentioning committees here is that serving on committees is one of the duties of independent directors. As well as being effective board members, they also need to be effective committee members and committee chairs. Boards rely on committees to gather information, set agendas and take decisions on key specialist points. For an independent director, how well they can contribute to committee work plays a big part in determining how much impact they have. When considering board roles, then, prospective directors need to look at committee structures and see where they can fit in and what role they can play.

Independent Director Qualities

What kind of person can carry out these roles? The role of independent director is capable of almost infinite variation, depending on the size of the organisation, its structure, culture, the nature of the sector and host of other variables. There is a danger of being too prescriptive; as we shall see in Chap. 9 when we come to discuss recruitment and selection; it is important there is a good 'fit' between the director, the board and the rest of the organisation.

That said, our research suggests that there are some particular qualities that are essential to fulfil the role of independent director. These centre mostly around soft skills and human qualities, and especially personal integrity.

A Strong Sense of Ethical and Moral Behaviour

Effective independent directors have a strong sense of ethical and moral behaviour and are not willing to compromise those principles and values. In the words of one respondent, 'the independent director is the guardian of the ethical issues.' Others described independent directors as the conscience of the organisation. One of the most important themes to emerge from the research was the notion of independence as comprising, at least in part, an ability to distinguish between right and wrong, founded on strong personal moral values. Here are a few comments from interviewees:

> It's about developing wisdom in people so that they understand what's right and wrong. It's about a moral sort of framework, I think.
>
> That's how I have worked throughout my career. The office clerk is as important as the Chief Executive. The cleaner is just as important. So I am independent.
>
> You obviously need some evidence base, or you need some reason to question something and challenge it. But if you raise something in a board you have a moral obligation to follow through.
>
> The way I have always put it to people who work with me is: 'if you're worried about the ethics of what we are doing or attempting, raise it'. It's a virtue ethics approach. You think about how you are going to flourish and what the questions are and how you can live a good life. There are always grey areas and the best thing is to surface them and debate them.

Feeling Comfortable with Complexity

We have discussed the need for experience already, but our research also high-lighted the need for independent directors to be familiar with complexity. Large multinational businesses have no monopoly of complexity; many of the institutions with which directors work are incredibly complex with multiple, overlapping stakeholder groups, complex sources of funding, complex sources of internal influences and hugely uncertain operating environments.

Complexity for most independent directors is now a part of everyday life, and directors must have the ability to not only tolerate complexity but turn it to their advantage, for example, by exploring complex environments for opportunities others might have overlooked.

Committed to Learning and Development

Partly because of complexity and partly because of information asymmetry and the inherent difficulty of the role, independent directors must possess a curiosity and commitment to learning about the organisation:

> A good independent director immerses himself/herself in the organisation's affairs, become more knowledgeable and takes every opportunity to develop.

One chair summarised the qualities of an independent director as follows:

> Independence of perspective, confidence, capacity and time and skills to under-stand what being an independent director means; an analytical mind, emotional resilience and an ability to build relationships.

Where Boards Need to Be

Every board should have a culture of engaged stewardship, a culture that encourages an independent mindset but also puts the principles of indepen-dence into practice. Board members think and act independently; but para-doxically, they also think and act collectively, working together in the best interests of the organisation and all those who depend on it. That paradox of independence and collective decision-making and responsibility can create tensions, of course. Sometimes those tensions are creative, and are just what the board needs to galvanise it into action. Sometimes, if left to get out of control, they can be disruptive and ultimately destructive.

Managing an independent board with a culture of engaged stewardship is not always easy, but what are the alternatives? We have seen the results already: value destruction, harm to society, and even injury or death to innocent people. We *must* move forward. We must create board cultures with greater independence, more engagement, more and better stewardship. But how do we do so?

To answer that question we must constantly keep in mind the purpose of the independent director: to have a positive impact on their organisations and on society. The next question then becomes: how can they do so? To have true impact, directors need of course to have skills such as good communication, team working and so on, but much more importantly they need a mindset that will enable them to confront challenges and solve problems. In Part II of this book, we will look at how independent directors can gather the knowledge and experience they need to do their job before arriving at the final definition; positive impact, what it is, and how directors can achieve it.

Notes

1. This case is based on interviews with Heather Lawrence (Chair of the Board), Garett Emmerson (CEO) and Philippa Harding (Director Corporate Governance) and on publicly available information.
2. 'The Uncomfortable Boardroom: The New Normal?' The Harvey Nash/ Alumni Board Report 2018/19.
3. 'Corporate Governance Principles: United Kingdom', Hermes Eos, January 2018.
4. 'Conflict and Tension in the Boardroom: How Managing Disagreement Improves Board Dynamics', Henley Business School, 2017.
5. 'The Uncomfortable Boardroom: The New Normal?' The Harvey Nash/ Alumni Board Report 2018/2019.
6. Professor Andrew Kakabadse et al., 'Is Government Fit for Purpose?', Public Administration and Constitutional Affairs Committee, Civil Service Effectiveness Inquiry, 2018.

Part II

Independent Directors and Boards

5

The Importance of Knowledge

Throughout this book, we have stressed the importance of knowledge and how it is one of the constituent parts of independence. There are two kinds of relevant knowledge. The first is *requisite knowledge*, the knowledge and experience that a director needs in order to be qualified and fit to hold the post in the first place. The second we call *evidence*, the knowledge of the organisation and its people, culture and environment that are needed in order to effectively discharge those roles monitoring, stewardship and resource provision that we talked about in the previous chapter. This chapter will deal with pre-requisite knowledge, while the next will look at evidence and how to gather it.

What kinds of knowledge do independent directors need in order to be effective and make impact? They need basic professional skills, of course, and as cases like London Ambulance Service shows, they need experience and the ability to make change happen. Importantly too, they need a broad range of knowledge, including knowledge of things happening outside of their sectors, including events and trends in the broader environment. Ignorance, wilful or otherwise, played a major role in lack of preparedness for coronavirus because people mistakenly believed that major pandemics were no longer likely to happen. Board knowledge needs to be broad as well as deep.

Two examples will illustrate this. University boards are very much focused on what is happening in universities, and pay too little attention to what is happening in the wider world. As a result (and they are by no means alone in this), they are increasingly behind the curve when it comes to the digital revolution and its ability to transform their operations. The NHS has a vast and complicated supply chain which has largely evolved rather than been strategically designed, and the service lacks up-to-date knowledge of logistics and

© The Author(s) 2020
G. Brown et al., *The Independent Director in Society*,
https://doi.org/10.1007/978-3-030-51303-0_5

supply chain management. Bringing in more knowledge on these issues could have a transformational effect. Let us look at both these examples in more detail, starting with a thoughtful study by Richard Sergeant on technology and governance in universities.

University Technology and Governance: Is an Avalanche Coming?[1]

'For the last three years I have been on the University of Exeter governing body, the Council.' Unusually for most higher education governing boards, independent members of Council hold a specific portfolio of responsibility alongside an executive lead, in my case, for digital and technology.

During that time, I have worked with the council and executive to identify and respond to a rapidly changing technology landscape that has influenced pedagogy, research and administration. This year, the university will embark on the biggest programme of digital change ever undertaken. A hundred million pounds of capital has been allocated for investment among many other competing calls, including international expansion and the improvement of the existing physical infrastructure on campus. The expectations for 'digital' are that it will be a core enabling element of the effective provision of education services in the years to come.

And yet, higher education still stands out as one of the few sectors of human endeavour that has been changed little by the digital revolution sweeping retail, publishing, banking, transport and so many other sectors of the economy. Over the last thirty years, the internet has fundamentally changed the accessibility of knowledge, but the Victorians would still recognise our classrooms. More recently, real world artificial intelligence techniques offer the ability to automate and personalise assessment and pedagogy, yet tutors and lecturers still spend hours laboriously marking student scripts and providing written feedback.

The value of a degree has been falling for years, even as the cost to students has risen. Yet it is still the default choice and destination for half of those aged 17–30, with participation reaching record highs in recent years.[2] In 2013, Michael Barber, the Chair of the Office for Students, promised that 'An Avalanche Is Coming' for higher education.[3] Yet six years later, despite gathering clouds, the resorts, instructors and skiers of higher education look much the same as they ever did.

Here, I want to address how a governing body should think about digital in the context of a university. What the strategic place of technology is among competing priorities. And how a university council can best equip their university's executive to succeed in an uncertain future.

There are well-understood reasons why the university sector is conservative by nature. Three reasons stand out. First, the choice to study is often influenced, if not funded, by parents who will tend to gravitate towards replicating their own youthful experiences. The continuing ubiquity of the degree means that for many, university is still more an unquestioned assumption than a choice. Second, while information is more accessible, the availability of knowledge is not the predominant attraction of universities which provide, in addition, a ritualised gateway to adulthood and independent living, a social environment to develop friendships and networks, an accredited qualification that may be worth as much or more as the skills students acquire. And third, in the UK at least, the prestige of the institution, and the signalling value of a degree is strongly correlated with the age of the HE institution, not the quality of the tuition. Moreover, the lack of differentiation in degree outcome (most students end up with either a 2.1 or a first) means that there is little to set them apart aside from the reputation of the institution that they went to. This both makes it difficult for new entrants like NMITE and LIS to compete, and reduces the incentive for students to complain about teaching even as many universities use tuition fees to cross-subsidise research activity. The London School of Economics was poorly ranked in the 2018 teaching excellence framework, but it still managed to top the table for graduate earnings.[4]

In that context, and amid other such pressing concerns as resolving staff pension disputes, growing physical campus capacity and access to EU research funding under Brexit, a university's digital activity might be seen to be more a matter of hygiene than strategy. Does the Wi-Fi across campus work? Is there reasonable information on the university website for new applicants? Can students view recordings of lectures and access course notes digitally? Are we reasonably well protected from cyber-crime? The answer to all of these questions should be an emphatic 'yes'! But any university council should set a higher bar for mere adequacy, let alone competitive success.

Digital and technology now means more than the provision of infrastructure and hardware for students and staff. More also, than merely the efficient administration and automation of routine and manual tasks. Almost every service the university offers: admissions, enrolments, timetabling, lectures, assessments and student feedback, student counselling, research grant applications, performance management processes and expense claims are significantly enabled or inhibited by the quality of the digital service that surrounds them. Furthermore, any ambitions to add distance learning as part of the university service offer will succeed as much because of the quality of the platform students have to use, as the effectiveness of the course materials and tuition.

How should boards target and measure the effectiveness of university digital transformation programmes? The National Student Survey (NSS), and the Cubane functional benchmarking of efficiency for university professional services provide two core sources of data to derive programme performance indicators. Nevertheless, separation of the influence of digital is not straightforward, with several factors including digital plausibly driving the answers to questions such as 'feedback on my work has been timely', or 'the course is well organised and is running smoothly.'

There is no space to go into detail with an explanation of how boards should work with a university executive to drive a digital transformation, but I would suggest the following elements as a summary:

1. Appoint senior digital leadership reporting directly to the registrar of vice-chancellor
2. Focus on user needs, not technological requirements
3. Do the hard work to make digital services simple for their users
4. Allocate sufficient capital and resource funding
5. Ensure competitive compensation for digital staff
6. Establish the in-house capability to build as well as buy your digital services
7. Drive ownership for digital services from the academic faculty, not the IT function.
8. Consider incubating disruptive services in a separate company away from the university
9. Visibly reward academic staff that generate or promote effective digital innovations
10. Accept the necessity of funding and administering continuous iteration of digital services.

Will an avalanche come eventually? I believe the inexorable advance of change upon the HE sector is indeed coming, but that is likely to come at the speed of a giant snail rather than as a cataclysmic fall of snow and ice. Nevertheless, given the pace of change possible within such a large and conservative institution as a university, transformation should start today. Organisations such as Kodak, Blockbuster and Borders could all see transformation coming when it was years away, and still couldn't move fast enough to

avoid being overtaken. I believe over the next decade we will see higher education institutions going bust, and student satisfaction gradually falling.
Alternatives to university education such as apprenticeships will gradually
become more credible for more students. Policy changes such as lowering
tuition fees; breaking the link between tuition and degree accreditation; or
offering student loans to pay for apprenticeships would further acceler-
ate change.

Digital is neither a singular source of salvation for the sector, nor a nemesis
to dwarf other challenges such as Brexit, pensions and strengthening international HE competition. But Digital services are now pervasively important
and strongly linked to quality. Digital has traditionally been overlooked
because of the lack of familiarity that university boards have with technology.
Boards in retail, publishing and financial services sectors have long grappled
with the meaning of digital transformation for their own organisations.
Higher education now has the chance to do the same.

Reading Richard's report, it is hard to escape the conclusion that university
board, and boards in many other sectors, need to address this issue as a matter
of urgency. Boards need to think about how to upskill their members so they
can understand the digital age, take advantage of the many opportunities it
offers and avoid the equally numerous pitfalls that await the ill-informed.
Cost overruns and outright collapses of information systems projects are not
uncommon, especially in the public sector. With proper oversight from
trained and skilled board members these problems could have been avoided.

Supply Chain Optimisation in the NHS

Changes to the demographics of the UK population will result in an additional 1.1 million people over the age of sixty-five between 2015 and 2020 (a
growth rate of 12% p.a.), increasing demand for health care services. More
older people are and will be living with two or more chronic health conditions
for a number of years.

The need to be able to care for patients in the community either in their
own homes or through community care centres and GP services will present
significant logistical challenges. Patients may need their homes adapting for
reduced mobility, nursing care may need to be scheduled, medical consum-
ables, devices and pharmaceutical products will be required for their care and
comfort. The need to make life easier and more comfortable for the patient in
a cost-effective way will require considerable logistics planning and flawless
execution.

Within the hospital setting it has been identified in previous NHS studies that too much variation exists across the NHS organisation of 200 plus trusts. There are too many suppliers, too many products, too many people being able to order products, facilitated by a fragmented delivery system where significant volume still comes direct from suppliers. In addition, high levels of inventory spread across multiple stock locations within the hospital (often with little visibility of what is actually held), consignment stock for some high-value product areas and sometimes manual demand management results in high stock levels, waste and obsolescence. Hospitals often have an element of warehousing and transport within their estate which may put in additional handling or add time delay and transport costs, with little value added to the system.

Can a Professional Supply Chain Management Approach Make a Significant Contribution to This Challenge?

Retailers, automotive companies and technology companies have long recognised the importance the supply chain plays in reducing costs (10–20% is achievable) and also in improving customer service. Most of this has been driven centrally by companies with a clear supply chain strategy and a main board member responsible for the strategy and its execution in support of the wider business strategy. Our interviews with the NHS organisations show an absence of professional supply chain management capability at board level within NHS organisations. This is not surprising considering all the other priorities that exist in the system today.

The start of any good supply chain strategy is to support the NHS strategic plan which is currently being reviewed in the light of the increase in government funding committed to in 2018. From this a vision should be created to describe how the supply chain will look in ten years' time, and importantly, how it will support NHS plans. Having this vision will help the NHS decide what the building blocks might need to be, for example, how to design the supply chain into the community, how to leverage IT and technological innovation including bar code capability, demand forecasting and so on. Utilising industry experts and NHS knowledge should generate workable solutions, but will require local collaboration between several NHS organisations and local authorities who today provide different parts of the patient pathway. Perhaps the first step should be to take a region and produce a plan to quantify the benefits in cash terms and importantly how patients can benefit.

How Big Could the Prize Be?

Better patient experience and lower costs should be the output of a focused supply chain approach and an ability to meet the future needs of patients in the community. There is little transparency on what supply chain costs are today, but based on experience in other sectors it should be possible to get at a 10–20% improvement in costs along with better service levels. In an organisation the size of the NHS the prize likely to be worth hundreds of millions of pounds.

Knowledge and Experience

But for the NHS, the 'prize' is about more than money; it is also about lives. It is not yet clear whether or how supply chain bottlenecks directly contributed to the shortage of PPE and ventilators in the NHS, but logic suggests that more efficient supply chain management could have increased the speed with which vital equipment flowed to the front line. This issue too must surely be part of the remit of any future inquiry.

The point of both these examples is clear: boards need to broaden their knowledge base and bring in requisite knowledge from outside. That means recruiting people with different and diverse experience and skills sets.

Requisite knowledge stems from what the independent director has already done and learned in their career so far. In his book *The Independent Director*, Gerry Brown described how he drew on his experience as an executive in international logistics firms to carry out his duties as a director, even in firms that had no direct connection with the world of logistics. In Gerry's words, 'it is the expertise, the contacts, the networks and the professional and personal experience that independent directors have that makes them valuable.'[5] Gerry went on to break requisite knowledge down into several different types, *personal knowledge, professional knowledge* and *entrepreneurial knowledge*.

Personal knowledge and skills include things that are inherent in individuals: how to lead and motivate people, how to communicate and, especially, how to listen, and the all-important skills of empathy and sensitivity to others which are essential to good communication and relationship building. In terms of leadership, in particular, independent directors will often serve as leaders, of sub-committees and task forces and action groups, and they are also part of leadership of the organisation more broadly; day-to-day leadership is the province of the executive, but independent directors help to guide and steer the organisation, set its goals and determine its culture. All of these things are important tasks of leadership.

Professional and managerial skills come from a mixture of training and experience. How to determine strategy, how to structure and manage an organisation, how to analyse and solve problems are skills that can be acquired through a mixture of formal learning and practice. The same applies to board-specific skills like chairing meetings and managing sub-committees. Board members need to know how to chair meetings, even if they are not the chair; if they understand the functions and role of the chair, they will be able to work with their own chair much more effectively. Finally, entrepreneurial knowledge and skills include things such as vision, judgement and the ability to make decisions and take action, propelling the organisation forward (Table 5.1).

From this, is it clear that the independent director needs to be a person of considerable experience. This brings us to an apparent paradox. One of the problems of the current independent director landscape is its lack of diversity, and that lack of diversity is particularly apparent when it comes to age. According to the *Financial Times*, the average age of male non-executive directors in the UK in 2019 was 61.5; the average female age was 57.[6] The *Wall Street Journal* recorded that the average age of directors in US companies in

Table 5.1   Types of knowledge and skills required by independent directors

Personal knowledge and skills
• How to lead
• How to motivate people
• How to communicate
• Interpersonal sensitivity
• How to listen
Professional and managerial knowledge and skills
• How to make and implement strategy
• Technical knowledge
• How organisations are structured and function
• How to analyse
• How to solve problems
• How to chair meetings (important even if you are not the chair)
• How board committees are constituted and how they function
Entrepreneurial knowledge and skills
• Vision
• Judgement
• Conviction
• Decisiveness
• Commercial acumen

Source: Adapted from Gerry Brown, *The Independent Director*, Basingstoke: Palgrave Macmillan, 2015

2018 was 64, and like the FT, noted that the average age was rising with the passage of time.[7] The average age of independent corporate director in Australia in 2009 was 60, and that figure too has probably risen.[8] In India, legislation has been enacted to allow independent directors serve to the age of 75, and indeed longer if the board passes a special resolution to allow them to continue.[9]

We argue that to achieve greater diversity, more younger people need to be included on boards. But, runs the counter-argument, how can young people be expected to have the necessary experience and accumulated wisdom to serve as a non-executive director? To our view, this is a fallacious way of thinking. Wisdom and longevity do not necessarily correlate. In Gerry Brown's words again, 'no one is good at everything, and experience levels will always vary ... Depth and breadth of experience changes from person to person.'[10]

Further to this, we would argue that *what kind* of experience is just as important as *how much*. In terms of appointing younger directors, it is precisely their experience of being young that gives them fresh perspectives and new ideas that boards need if they are to avoid groupthink. Exactly the same applies to women, disabled people, and members of ethnic minorities. In other words, there are many different kinds of experience, and not all of them are the product of time. Indeed, when it comes to digital skills, it is likely that young people who have grown up in the digital age are more likely to have a broader range of skills than older people who came to the digital world later in life.

Assessing the importance of age can be clearly seen in the list of requisite knowledge and experience that came out of our research at Henley. Table 5.2 shows some of the most important of these.

Of these, only experience of complex organisations and environment is time-dependent, and even here, some people learn more quickly than others and have had different experiences of complexity. Anecdotally, we know of examples of highly effective independent directors in charities who are less than thirty years old, but who have had particular work and life experiences that make them comfortable with complexity. The rest are rooted in interpersonal skills and attributes such as empathy, flexibility of thinking, having a strong moral compass and so on which can be found in people at any stage of life. When it comes to recruiting independent directors, youth should be no barrier.

While the research identified key types of knowledge that independent directors *should* have, it also found that reality does not always correspond to this ideal picture. While independent directors generally have a strong sense of duty and are aware of the challenges facing their organisation, they are less

Table 5.2   Independent director knowledge and experience

- A clear understanding of what the role requires
- The capacity to be effective in the role
- Knowledge and understanding of ethics, in order to fulfil the duty of seeing things are done in an ethical and moral manner
- Experience of complex organisations and environments
- Knowing the challenges facing the organisation
- Knowing how to build relationships with other people and organisations
- Knowing how to adapt to working with people from other, diverse backgrounds
- Knowing how to adapt to changing needs and priorities
- Knowing how to put forward a well-articulated case for debate
- A diverse range of skills that adds value to the board and to the organisation

certain about what their own role is, and lack experience of complexity, leading to doubts about how effectively they can discharge their duties. There is a striking lack of capability to build relationships across all four sectors we studied, and, as Table 5.3 shows, charities are weak in many dimensions.

These are issues that urgently need to be addressed. Many independent directors are struggling to carry out their duties because they lack the necessary experience and knowledge. Let us look at each of these dimensions in a little more detail and try to identify its key features and also its wellsprings, how this knowledge is gained and gathered in the first place. Doing so should help us to understand more clearly the needs of organisations and boards in terms of recruitment, selection and training in order to make sure they have independent directors with the right range of requisite knowledge.

Understanding the Role

The lack of understanding of what the role of independent director entails is both understandable and unforgivable. Here is how one interviewee described the situation in her sector:

> As far as I'm aware there's no formal induction process. It's just a case of, right, you're on the board, that's it, off you go.

We found that most organisations do have induction programmes—although around one-quarter of charities do not—but even in those organisations that do have inductions, anecdotal evidence suggests that quality varies. Induction programmes are good at imparting what the organisation does and how it works, but they often fail to explain what the independent director's duties are.

Table 5.3 Director knowledge and experience to the role (% agree/strongly agree)

Director qualities	Sports (n = 129)	Universities (n = 135)	NHS (n = 203)	Charities (n = 156)
Have a sense of duty to see things are done both ethically and morally	97	98	98	97
Are experienced enough and comfortable with organisational complexity	95	92	92	78
Are aware of the challenges facing the organisation	98	95	94	88
Clearly understand what is required of them in the role	94	85	88	80
Have the capacity to be effective in the role	93	90	90	81
Are effective in building relationships	91	88	88	79
Have a diverse range of skills that adds value	95	95	95	87
Are effective in putting forward a well-articulated case for debate	95	88	90	81
Are adaptable/flexible to changing needs/priorities	89	86	88	73
Can easily adapt to working with people from different cultures/backgrounds	88	84	85	74
Effectively use their experience and expertise from working in other sectors	95	91	92	88
Have the necessary commercial acumen	81	84	82	63
Communicate effectively	94	91	94	84
Are truly independent	96	93	94	83
Total	**93**	**90**	**91**	**81**

It could be argued, of course, that induction programmes are the wrong place for doing this. It would be better, surely, if independent directors already knew what the role entailed *before* they joined the organisation, or even better, before they applied for the role in the first place. As we mentioned in Chap. 1, there is a wider ignorance about what independent directors do, particularly in the press. The Kakabadse Report on civil service effectiveness suggested that some cabinet ministers are not entirely clear about the role of their own departmental boards and, as a result, tend to ignore them.[11]

Clearly something needs to be done to inform independent directors more clearly of what is expected of them before they take up their posts, because throwing them into the deep end of the pool to see if they sink or swim is not working. Many do learn to swim, very quickly and sometimes quite brilliantly. But in other cases the independent directors are left to tread water until the company sinks, taking them down as well.

Effectiveness

It used to be said that leaders were born and not made. A wealth of research into leadership (and a healthy dose of common sense) tells us this is not so. Yes, some people are naturally better at leading than others, but personal ability to lead can also be enabled through coaching, mentoring and confidence building. Experience plays a role also; in theory at least, the more experience one has of leadership, the more effective they are at leading.

The same is true of the independent director. There is no magic spark that makes a good director, nor is there any mathematical formula that can be calculated or framework into which prospective directors can be put to measure their suitability. The needs of every organisation are different. What is more, given the nature of change and evolution, the same organisation may need different kinds of directors at different times in its lifespan. We need to forget about trying to find the perfect directors for organisation, and find instead the ones who can be effective.

That diversity of organisations also means that the nature of what 'effectiveness' is will change across time and space. We will come back to the nature of impact in Chap. 8, but the moment, it is important that independent directors *know* how to make an impact, and should go into the role in the first instance with a view to having impact and being effective. That can mean helping the board and the CEO with strategy, conducting reviews of operational frameworks, coming up with ideas for new markets or new fundraising channels, or a host of other things based on their own experience and knowledge.

A lot of this comes back to value alignment. 'I've chosen the organisations [where I am a director] on the basis of my own value alignment', said one our interviewees. 'The organisation must mean something to me, so I have chosen an organisation relating to young people and to the environment. But I have also chosen organisations where I feel I can be helpful to the CEO.'

Values are a starting point, but there is more to it than that. Everyone is unique; everyone has their own set of experiences, their own learning and accumulated knowledge and beliefs, their own point of view. Being effective means matching your own personal experience and knowledge to the organisation and then working out what impact they could have and how they would go about making it.

Knowledge and Understanding of Ethics

In Chap. 4 we noted that a strong sense of ethical and moral behaviour is an important quality of an independent director. Knowledge and experience come into play here in two ways. First, there is the knowledge of what exactly constitutes moral and ethical behaviour, and this, as our interviewees often pointed out, is not always easy.

> There are no utilitarian rules that will tell you exactly how to deal with every ethical situation. There are always grey areas. The best way of dealing with them is to surface them, debate them.

This particular interviewee raises an important point. Most people have an innate sense of right and wrong imparted through family background, education and experience, and this is usually good enough to get them through, most of the time. Most, but not always. Many ethical dilemmas have no clear dimension of right or wrong.

That brings us to the second reason why knowledge and experience are important. Prior experience of having dealt with similar ethical issues is a valuable resource to any board, but so also is good practical knowledge of ethics including some key concepts like deontology, utilitarianism and virtue ethics. All of these give independent directors a useful set of tools for analysing and breaking down these grey areas and charting a course of action.

Experience of Complex Organisations and Environments

In Chap. 4 we also mentioned familiarity with complexity as being an important quality of an independent director. This too is largely a matter of knowledge and experience. To the outsider, complex environments often appear confusing and intimidating. However, experience brings the ability to understand *why* these environments are complex and what makes them work. For example, to someone coming onto an NHS board for the first time, the health service is a frighteningly complex organisation working in even more complex environment, facing multiple stakeholders including the Department for

Health and local authorities. But to an insider, the organisation of the health service may make sense (after a fashion).

Of course, plenty of insiders complain about the complexity of the health service too, and we noted that in their responses they often used two different adjectives, *complex* and *complicated*. The two do not necessarily mean the same thing.

According to complexity theory, some things—organisations, environments, technology and so on—are *complex* because they need many different parts and elements in order to function effectively.[12] A computer or a smartphone are complex because the many different relays and codes are what gives them their processing power, enabling them to perform so many different tasks, often at once. Things which are *complicated*, on the other hand, have too many different elements for their function which are actually harming performance. For example, complex bureaucratic organisations can be simplified by taking out layers of structure and making them simpler, thereby also enabling them to be more effective. Knowledge and understanding of what complexity really means and how organisations work enables directors to distinguish the rightfully complex from the needlessly complicated.

Knowing the Challenges

It is important that organisations have people on their boards who have broad sector experience. There is no substitute for having worked at the coal face and understanding the sector from the inside. Some of our respondents, particularly from health care and sports organisations, made this point strongly. In health care, it was noted important to have knowledge of technical and medical issues on the board, while in sports there was criticism of directors who, although passionate about the sport itself, have lost touch with the grass roots and the people who volunteer and play the sport.

In business, too, sector experience is vitally important. Lack of experience and knowledge by the board has led more than one company to disaster. Earlier we mentioned Lehman Brothers, which had only two trustees with previous banking experience on its board, but in other cases too, like Nortel, the Canadian telecoms company which overexpanded and then collapsed in 2009, there was a fatal lack of experience. Many of Nortel's non-executive directors came from legal and political backgrounds and little experience of the sector.[13]

That said, boards do need other perspectives. A banking board of directors composed entirely of bankers will lose something in terms of diversity, as will a health care board composed entirely of health care professionals. Board urgently needs those different perspectives and fresh ideas, and should be humble enough to admit that outsiders are capable of understanding their business and can provide important views and advice. A balance must be struck between deep sector experience and broad experience of the wider world.

The requisite knowledge lies in knowing how to translate one's own experience and perspectives and turn them into something that the rest of the organisation can understand and use. Every sector, every organisation is different, but at the same time, many of the challenges organisations face have common elements, or at least common roots. The same problems tend to crop up over and over again. By applying their experience, independent directors can offer new ideas about how to analyse challenges and solve problems.

A good example is England Hockey, the sporting organisation established in 2003 to replace the English Hockey Association which had been wound up after incurring substantial debts. England Hockey has gone from strength to strength under two chairmen, Phillip Kimberley and Royston Hoggarth, both of whom come from commercial backgrounds (Kimberley was in the oil industry, Hoggarth sat on the board of a software company). Both were able to apply lessons from their commercial experience to running a sporting organisation. Recruiting business people to serve as independent directors on boards in the public and third sectors is not uncommon. We argue that the benefits could also flow the other way, and businesses should look seriously at recruiting experienced people from the public and third sectors onto their boards.

Knowing How to Build Relationships

Everything turns on relationships, everything turns on cooperation, everything turns on tolerance. You must be tolerant of your eccentric professionals, so long as their eccentricity isn't dangerous.

As this interviewee points out, building relationships within and outside the organisation is a key task of the independent director. Knowing how to build and maintain these relationships is an important part of requisite knowledge. Networking experience in some form is very important, but again, there is no especial need for that experience to come from a particular sector. Although there are variations in how networks function, these are as much as anything a matter of cultural differences; some sectors will be more formal than others, some already have established networking channels, others are more ad hoc. The task of the independent director is to find out how networks function in that sector and then apply previous experience and knowledge of network building to creating a new set of relationships.

Too often, we get it wrong. One interviewee described a particularly toxic situation:

> Relationships at all levels were poor. One organisation had taken the commissioning organisation to arbitration five times in the last four years. There had been a competition, so relationships were really poor, and in some organisations the boards had become tribal. Rather than taking a step back, they were so wedded to their organisation being right and their responsibilities to their part of the population, not the whole, that they lost sight of the purpose of health and social care on a population basis.

The same respondent described the difference good relationship management can make:

> In terms of building relationships, building networks, building trust we had to allow people the safe places to have difficult conversations and challenge, because any of the changes we wanted to make had to get through a public consultation. The health service the local authority would scrutinise these changes and possibly refer them to the Secretary of State.

But good relationships with these stakeholders meant higher levels of trust and thereby less of a chance of challenge.

Often, independent directors can bring their own previous networks from different sectors into play. For example, business leaders moving into other sectors as independent directors can call on their old colleagues to provide information and knowledge about common issues such as financial management, marketing, technology or data management. Health care professionals and academics often have access to scientific networks which technology company boards in particular could benefit from. Social media has contributed greatly towards wider and broader network building, and directors with good social networks can access many different sources of knowledge and wisdom.

It might also be worth looking at the recommendations for relationship management contained in the Kakabadse Report on civil service effectiveness, which looked particularly at the relationship between ministers and permanent secretaries, the chief civil servant in each department. The relationship is not exactly like-for-like, but the report made the point that the effectiveness of government departments is highly dependent on how well that relationship functions. The report mentioned several important aspects of relationship management:

- Deliberation, careful thinking and analysis about what ministers want and 'how to get onto the Secretary of States's wavelength';
- Investing in relationships, and very often making relationship building and maintenance the first priority;
- Offering challenge, but also being calm and 'creating a sense of meaningful consideration of the issues at hand especially when under pressure';
- Behaving in an authentic manner, and with integrity.

All of these are very useful pieces of advice for independent directors in any field of endeavour.[14]

Working with Other People

For all the talk of diversity, it is clear that boards only function well if people from diverse backgrounds recruited onto boards are made to feel part of the team. Whether they can work well in a board context depends in large part on how well the other board members are able to work with them.

Working with people from other cultures and backgrounds is not always easy if one has no prior experience. It is easy to fall into the trap of believing that other people think and reason in the same way as oneself, and that their life experiences have also been the same. Of course they have not; one of the reasons for recruiting people from different backgrounds onto boards in the first place is to take advantage of that diversity of experience. Good independent directors have the ability to understand and empathise with people from different cultures and backgrounds, and to learn from their experience and listen to their views without judgement or prejudice.

How can this knowledge be acquired? The best and simplest way is through exposure; living and working with different cultures, for example, or working with disabled people or people from disadvantaged backgrounds, or even working in organisations with a good ethnic and cultural mix. On top of experience, there are human traits such as emotional intelligence, empathy and the ability to listen impartially which can be cultivated.

Adapting to Changing Needs and Priorities

We live in times of change and flux, and knowing how and when to adapt is important. Experience plays a major role here. People who live and work in chaotic conditions are often very good at adaptation, because they must be in order to do their work well and prosper. An ability to analyse a situation and know when the current strategy is not working or practices need changing is also important, and again experience is essential in helping directors recognise when change has to happen; if you have been there before, then you are likely to recognise the signs.

Here again a mixture of sector experience and outside points of view are important. The outsider who comes from a completely different background may nevertheless recognise signs of impending crisis, based on their own experience, that the sector experts might have missed.

Putting Forward a Case for Debate

We have already discussed how important it is for independent directors to challenge the status quo and stimulate debate, but we also noted that you cannot win every battle. Independent directors need to learn to choose their fights. Knowing how to prioritise issues and pick the ones on which to take a stand is important. So too is knowing how to gather evidence to back up one's case, and how to present that case to board colleagues. As one of our interviewees says:

> Understanding some of the tactics of meetings and when you should intervene and all those things makes a big difference. These are skills you can learn, but almost nobody teaches them.

Failing formal instruction, independent directors need to fall back on common sense and on their ability to empathise with other people and work with them in a collegiate setting. Arguments need to be made firmly but diplomatically, and respect has to be shown for the views of others, even when dissenting with them. Once again, experience is important; the more one engages in board debates, the easier it is to know what to say and when.

Notes

1. Our thanks to Richard Sergeant for contributing this study of university technology and governance.
2. DfE HE Participation Rates (2017).
3. http://www.avalancheiscoming.com/.
4. https://www.bbc.co.uk/news/education-41693230.
5. Brown, *The Independent Director*, p. 20.
6. https://www.ft.com/content/b07f4610-e40b-11e7-8b99-0191e45377ec.
7. https://blogs.wsj.com/cfo/2015/06/17/average-director-age-creeps-higher/.
8. https://ro.uow.edu.au/cgi/viewcontent.cgi?article=1554&context=commpapers.
9. https://indiacorplaw.in/2018/06/age-limit-criteria-non-executive-directors-amended-sebi-listing-regulations-prospective-retrospective.html.
10. Brown, *The Independent Director*, pp. 20–21.
11. 'Kakabadse Report on Civil Service Effectiveness', 2018.
12. Kurt A. Richardson (ed.), *Managing Organizational Complexity: Philosophy, Theory and Application*, New York: Information Age Publishing, 2005.
13. Chapman, *The Last of the Imperious Rich*.
14. 'Kakabadse Report', 2018.

6

Engagement and Evidence

However knowledgeable and experienced they may be, independent directors are only able to exercise independence if they have access to unbiased, high-quality data and evidence about the organisations they serve. This is the 'engagement' part of the culture of engaged stewardship; working closely with the organisation and understanding the challenges it faces and what it needs.

Once independent directors have gathered evidence, then they have a powerful tool for driving change and creating real positive value for society. The case of 4global and its work with the England and Wales Cricket Board (ECB) shows what can be done.

4global[1]

Social value now sits at the heart of strategic investment in health, sport and physical activity, and rightly so. Every delivery and commissioning organisation should have a consistent, credible, accurate and up-to-date understanding of what good looks like and how to deliver it locally, accounting for different environments and opportunities.

Unlike other sectors, until now sport and physical activity have not had a comprehensive and representative set of data, collated in one place, which can be compared with other cross-departmental datasets on an individual level and at scale. For example, investment in youth employment leads to savings against crime. Both government departments involved understand the data, agree on the conclusions, and therefore from a national to local level are

© The Author(s) 2020
G. Brown et al., *The Independent Director in Society*,
https://doi.org/10.1007/978-3-030-51303-0_6

prepared to back the modelling with investment, knowing what the likely returns will be, every time.

4global is an international sports consultancy and sport intelligence agency which provides a range of services to government, local authorities, organising committees and sports governing bodies. Established in 2002, 4global Consultancy is involved in events, planning and strategic services, while the intelligence arm of the business offers unparalleled data services to clients.

Its sports intelligence service provides our clients—including local authorities, sports centres and governing bodies—with accurate and actionable insight and information management solutions. It has developed two sector-leading platforms, the DataHub and the SportsHub, which manage membership, offer data analysis and provide clients with a more detailed understanding of their service.

4global's team is passionate about the positive social impact sport can have on individuals and communities. As a result, it has designed a solution to ascertain the monetary value sport creates in terms of health, subjective well-being, crime and education. Through this, 4global can help reduce wastage in the NHS and police force, and have a genuinely positive social impact. The Social Value Calculator is a politically important project and offers an excellent example of the positive externalities that sport can bring about. In the UK, where 14% of deaths are caused by physical inactivity, the model can help raise awareness and help society and government deal with this issue.

'Sport and leisure provider budgets are being squeezed tighter and tighter', says Carl Daniels, Senior Sport and Leisure Manager at Carmarthen County Council. 'Using the DataHub we have established that seven of our facilities generate approximately £5m in social value every year, much more than we're being given to run those services. That is so powerful. In funding bids I'm able to show our exact contribution to health, crime, education and wellbeing and prove to the Council that extra investment will have a direct impact on the wider community.'

Carmarthenshire County Council is currently looking to build a £200 m Wellness and Life Science Village in Llanelli, incorporating new leisure centre facilities for the town. Daniels has used the DataHub's social value module to ascertain the value generated by the existing Llanelli Leisure Centre. As the project progresses, he will be able to conduct a health impact study to predict what social impact the new centre could have. 'Everything we do is going to be based on robust intelligence moving forwards, and being more informed can only make us more effective, which can only benefit our customers', says Daniels.

The England and Wales Cricket Board (ECB) is the national governing body of sport (NGB) responsible for the governance of formal and informal cricket across England and Wales. As part of its remit, the ECB uses funding generated through commercial and public funding to invest in the grassroots game and provide the greatest possible opportunity for people to play cricket.

The ECB's current strategic framework is called Cricket Unleashed and is built around five pillars: more play, great teams, inspired fans, good governance and social responsibility, and strong finance and operations.

4global's sector leading consultancy team has worked in partnership with the ECB over the past five years to identify the investment opportunities that will drive the greatest possible benefit for formal and informal players across the UK, including two high-profile projects that combine the use of cross-sector data and cricket-specific insight to plan effectively and efficiently:

- The ECB Insight Platform began with a full audit of all cricket facilities across Greater London, as well as consultation with cricket stakeholders from clubs and organisations across the city. It developed into a national strategic project across London and four other ECB 'core cities' that has provided the ECB with an understanding of national investment priorities and potential risk areas for the ECB team. All data stored is stored and updated using a bespoke software platform at www.ecbinsight.com, which allows data to be kept up to date on a daily basis.
- The Urban Cricket Centre investment programme is the flagship project within the South Asian Action Plan. With the initial objective to develop one to three pilot projects followed by a wider national network, the programme will provide fit-for-purpose indoor facilities across focus areas of the UK with a high number of potential South Asian participants. 4global is the insight partner for this project, providing a comprehensive and robust service to identify the optimal locations and facilities for new investment.

Bruce Cruse is Head of Participation at the ECB and leads a number of high-profile facility and participation programmes on behalf of the organisation. Speaking about the London project and wider collaborative working with 4global, he says, 'we were looking to improve strategic planning capability. 4global worked with us in a genuinely joint venture to develop the ECB Insight Platform, a bespoke and powerful tool that is now integral to what we do and used by the entire organisation in every stage of planning.'

Our partnership with the ECB demonstrates the benefits of senior teams at public bodies maximising the use of data and insight to ensure public funds are invested in the most effective and efficient way. The days of facility and programme investment being allocated on the basis of gut instinct are quickly disappearing, to be replaced by a transparent and effective methodology for deciding the 'what, where, why and how much'.

Boards across health, sport and physical activity have only been making strategic decisions based on their own success or failure and not the impact they have on the community or their performance against their peers in a true like for like way. Having access to strategic data and collaborating with broader initiatives allows board members to be informed to make focused decisions that will make a positive contribution to society as well as to the business. Too many decisions are made by proposed expert board members based on their previous experience rather than the current strategic position, profile and impact of their organisation.

Within a dynamic, unpredictable commercial and economic environment, using live sector-focused collaborative data means decisions can be made in an insightful way. Boards should be the inspiration for a company, but too many times we hear from further down the hierarchy that they are uncertain as to the goals and objectives of senior teams. Transparent use of data to drive a business from the top down makes the whole company not only measurable but accountable for its success, both internally and to the communities they serve.

Barriers and Walls

The 4global/ECB example shows what can be done once directors have data and evidence (as well as encouraging them to use professional sources to gather data where necessary). However, this is not always the case. Many things can obstruct directors in their quest for evidence:

- organisational complexity, meaning it can be hard to know where in the organisation to go in order to find reliable data;
- information asymmetry, meaning communication lines are constricted or cut off, and information which is intended for the independent directors never actually reaches them;
- the tendency by some CEOs to embezzle the data presented, holding back from the board and ensuring the chair and independent directors never see the full picture;
- lack of industry experience by the independent members, meaning they struggle to interpret and fully understand the data that does reach them.

All of these things can affect the flow and availability of reliable data, meaning that independent directors are hampered in their ability to raise questions and partake in discussions. We regard the lack of data and evidence as one of the most important barriers to the independent director in discharging his or her role effectively.

And, we must reiterate, when data is withheld from directors, deliberately or through organisational ineptitude, the institution and its stakeholders are at risk. Many organisations have failed because the directors were either kept in the dark or failed to act on the evidence they had. In 2017, an investigation into an accounting scandal at the American financial services firm Wells Fargo laid the blame squarely at the door of the board. An article in *Fortune* summed up the board's failings on three levels: failure to act on evidence already received, failure to respond to the crisis in a timely manner, and failure to inspire a new corporate culture that would put an end to corrupt practices.

On the first point, it transpired that the audit committee had been receiving reports of suspicious and unethical conduct for nearly fifteen years, but had failed to act on them; not until 2016 did the board finally set up its own investigation. The subsequent report 'sidesteps the board's systemic failures to properly assess the company's and the CEO's performance … and … the failure of its members to read all materials carefully, ask relevant questions and review outside sources of information'.[2] In other words, the board failed to gather evidence, or when evidence was presented, failed to heed it. The author of the *Fortune* article, American corporate governance expert Eleanor Bloxham, stops just short of using the phrase 'wilful blindness' in conjunction with events at Wells Fargo, but the implication is there.

'Wilful blindness' is of course the term used by Margaret Heffernan to describe the prevailing culture at Enron, when many senior leaders including some non-executive directors deliberately made sure they did not ask too many questions about what was really going on inside the energy trading firm.[3] Similarly, independent directors at the Italian firm Paramalat appear not to have noticed the large-scale accounting fraud going on almost under their feet. Some information was deliberately withheld from directors in both cases, but even so, directors should have had their own sources of knowledge. 'Corporate governance mechanisms cannot prevent unethical activity by top management', concluded one observer. 'However, they can at least act as a means of detecting such activity by top management before it is too late.'[4]

Our research project at Henley exposed many of the same concerns. Time and again during the interview process, participants provided examples which put 'data and evidence' at the centre of major governance failures. Boards were 'kept in the dark' by the executive, with no adequate data from which to challenge or support the executive proposals and numbers. Here are two responses by interviewees who had direct experience of these situations:

> Not only was the board not accountable for what was going on, it couldn't be accountable because it wasn't being given the right information and it was very hard to know where to lay the blame.
>
> I came across a case where there has been a very clear governance failure at board level where effectively the information had not been shared appropriately, where the organisation had a series of problems that were not brought to the board table, and where the board was not in a position to identify this.

Further comments suggest that lack of appropriate and truthful information is as a much a product of a corrupted executive as it is of a poor, unengaged and non-independent board:

> It turned out that the executive were colluding to keeping information from the board, who were completely reliant on only one source of information.
>
> Every big train crash has manipulated, inaccurate, inadequate data, about finance, student numbers or both.

However, despite arguments that the board cannot be held accountable if it does not have the right information, active boards with a culture of independence can perceive warning signs that the executive is not being transparent and will seek out ways to triangulate existing information or seek new sources of independent information, and take action.

> A high-performing governing body will have access to good data, with competitor information, comparative information so that it is able to challenge on the basis of data and information.

'Data', of course, means not just numbers and financial information. Vitally important though these are, the independent director also needs to assess 'soft' features of the organisation such as culture, staff morale and engagement, and leadership. Directors need always to have a finger on the pulse of the organisation, and very often the pulse can be found not just in numbers and statistics but also in human relationships. Both are equally important.

Given the importance of data and evidence, we should then expect that most boards will pay close attention to this issue and will make the provision of evidence a key priority. Or should we? In fact, the findings from our research make for rather grim reading:

- 44% of sports Independent directors and 42% of university Independent directors do not often visit operations and talk to other layers of management.
- 31% of charity Independent directors and 29% of university Independent directors do not have regular updates from other employees/experts (other than the C-suite) before the board.
- 13% of Independent directors at universities do not have an effective dialogue with other fellow directors to cross-check concerns and information.
- 17% of charity Independent directors and 15% of university Independent directors do not work with other directors to ensure appropriate action is taken at board level based on available evidence.
- 25% of university Independent directors and 22% of charity Independent directors do not believe they are given all necessary information on the agenda to be effective at board meetings
- 22% of charity Independent directors and 13% of university Independent directors do not agree that the CEO is open and transparent in ensuring all information is made readily available and shared.

It would appear, then, that many organisations have work to do in ensuring their independent directors have access to the data they urgently need; and that directors themselves need to take responsibility and become active agents who go out and acquire data, rather than waiting for it to come to them. Here are some of the things they need to do and issues that need to be addressed.

Visiting Operations and Talking to People

Especially in complex institutions, independent directors must become familiar with the organisation and all its various elements. This cannot be done sitting at home. Directors need to get out into the field, visiting operations and talking to employees and other stakeholders at different levels, in order to gain an unfiltered perspective of things like culture, staff morale and operational issues. Many of our interviewees made this point, talking too about the steps they took to gather more evidence. Here are some examples:

Information asymmetry is much bigger in universities than in the NHS, and therefore chairs and independent directors must visit and talk to people.

Independent directors need to go out and visit the whole range of operations.

I devised a partnership with independent directors to visit every department in the NHS trust throughout the year.

> We expect all of our independent directors to go out in visits, to find out more about a division. We expect our independent directors to go around services, and we have a programme of visits.

This discipline by independent directors allows them to not just reduce the information asymmetry vis-à-vis the executive, but also to increase their own knowledge and gain the confidence to put relevant and grounded questions to the executive.

Once again, this can be easier said than done. As two of the interviewees mentioned, some boards have organised programmes of visits. They organise groups to tour particular sites or departments, or arrange for visits by individual directors, often several times per year. This is easy if operations are relatively concentrated, for example in a local hospital trust or a university campus. For multinational businesses and overseas aid charities, visits become rather more complex and expensive. Directors of an aid charity working in Africa, for example, really need to see the charity's operations on the ground, but travel to and from remote locations can be costly and even dangerous.

The best practice model for evidence gathering, in our view, is the dual assurance model at the University of Exeter (which will be described more fully in Chap. 8). In this model, each executive function has two leads, one a member of the executive team and the other an independent director from the university council. This obviates the danger of having all information channelled through the vice-chancellor/CEO, who can then act as an information gatekeeper. Instead, directors are obliged to go out to different parts of the university, meet with faculty, staff and students and hear their views. Armed with sufficient knowledge, the council lead then sits down with the executive lead to discuss and analyse what they know, before reporting jointly to the council.

More commonly, especially in smaller organisations, there is no formal or organised plan for visits. In these cases it is up to directors to organise their own visits. Some organisations will be supportive and encourage directors to undertake independent visits and make sure doors are open to them. Others, where the relationship between board and executives has broken down, may try to put obstacles in their way. Directors will also have to organise these visits in their own time, and quite possibly at their own expense. Nevertheless, this must be done, and in such a way that the directors are able to see and hear what is really happening, not just what the executives would like them to think is happening.

In eighteenth-century Russia—this is not quite the non sequitur it seems, by the way—Empress Catherine the Great used to go on tours of the countryside conducted by her chief minister (CEO), Grigori Potemkin, to reassure herself that her subjects were well cared for. Once a tour had been organised Potemkin would build brand-new model villages along the route of the tour and bring in healthy, well-fed peasants to pose as their inhabitants. Seeing them, the empress was reassured that her people were happy, and she never saw the reality of the harsh poverty that existed in the countryside. Once the royal entourage had passed, the villages were knocked down and the peasants were sent home again. The term 'Potemkin villages' came to be applied to any sham or deceit designed to make people think the situation is better than it really is.

Former World Bank president James Wolfensohn encountered similar problems when making field visits to Africa. After several visits, 'he realised he was only being shown successful projects, smiling villagers, and grateful government officials.' He realised that in order to discover what was really going on, he needed to get away from his guides and get out into the field on his own.[5] Wolfensohn was an executive, but exactly the same principle applies to independent directors; make sure you are seeing what is really there, and not a Potemkin village.

Bringing Other Employees or a Third Party to the Board

Broadening relationships within the organisation also enables the independent director to find other sources of knowledge. Who are the subject area experts on issues like IT and digital, or marketing and publicity, or health and safety, or any of a dozen issues the board needs to consider? Going directly to these people enables directors to bypass any potential information bottlenecks around the CEO and senior executives.

Informal conversations are a good way to gather information, but it is also perfectly acceptable for the board to invite these professionals to present formal reports. Care has to be taken here; the professionals are likely to be busy people with much to do, and requests for information should be made in such a way that does not give offence to senior managers or look like the board is interfering in the organisation. On the other hand, a diplomatically framed request for a report will often be met with a very positive response; people will be pleased that the board is taking an interest in their work and respects what they do. Several of our interviewees already follow this practice:

We have certain agenda items where people with professional responsibility in different parts of the organisation will come and report to trustees.

Don't rely on the CEO to present all of the papers on the board, bring in the people who are actually writing them.

In some cases, it may be necessary to bring in an external expert to advise the board. Auditors, for example, should report to the full board and not just the finance sub-committee. Other advisors can be called in to make up for expertise the board lacks. We particularly recommend this practice on issues such as digital and technology, where the landscape is changing rapidly and knowledge quickly goes out of date. Experts on legal issues such as GDPR can also be very useful.

Also, if the board has doubts about a particular decision or direction the executives are taking, an outside expert's view can be sought to provide reassurance; or alternatively, evidence that will help to pressure the executives into thinking again about their course of action. The experts bring dispassionate perspectives and allow the board to see levels of detail and nuances that may not always be provided by (or apparent to) the executives.

More generally, board can use consultants as a source of expertise and knowledge on an ongoing basis, although cost will be an issue especially for smaller organisations. Care must be taken to use consultants wisely and not overuse them, remembering always that the consultant is there to advise the board and not the other way around. The partnership between the England and Wales Cricket Board and the consultancy 4global is an excellent example of how consultants can add value to a board.

Getting to Know Other Independent Members

It may seem obvious, but one of the best sources of evidence and knowledge can be found among fellow independent directors. We have already discussed the need for good relationships among the boards, and knowledge exchange is one way in which those relationships bear fruit. If directors have a suspicion or a concern that something may be wrong, discussing the issue with fellow directors and drawing on their knowledge is a good way to crystallise thinking and decide on a course of action. Our interviewees recommend this kind of dialogue as a way of learning:

People don't know as much as you think they ought to know, given the responsibilities they have. They only know more if they take the trouble to learn what is going on, and speak to other independent directors.

It is important to know who in the board holds certain information.

Through these inter-board discussions, evidence can be cross-checked and made more robust. Then, if necessary, a case can be developed and put to the executive to answer.

Triangulate the Data

Again at risk of stating the obvious, information needs to be triangulated and verified:

> I wanted to verify what I thought, and make sure it wasn't just me putting two and two together and make it five. You always need a second source, or a second way of verifying.
>
> You need to try different ways and means to validate and triangulate beyond what you're told.

Fundamentally, this means doing homework, checking facts, checking the validity of data sources, getting second opinions and trying to put together a complete picture of what is really going on. Doing so means getting out and talking to people: fellow directors, executives, junior managers and employees, stakeholders, peers in other organisations and so on, in order to make sure the narratives we have heard are the real story, or whether someone has made a mistake; or worse, someone is deliberately creating a false impression in order to deceive the board. It is important to gather data; it is even more important to validate it and make certain it is real evidence.

The Custodians of Data

A question that arises frequently is: who is the guardian of good data? In most places the chair attempts to fulfil this role through his or her relationship with the CEO, perhaps aided by the organisation's secretary.

> One of the huge responsibilities is to ensure that the other independent trustees actually do have the information about what is happening. This involves strong

interaction on agenda paperwork and information between meetings, and ensuring that as many directors as possible are engaged in sub-committee work.

To take universities as an example, there was agreement among those we surveyed that the role of the registrar (in effect, the company secretary) should have a contract that gives him or her an operational line to the vice-chancellor, the CEO, but also a strategic direct line to chair of council. This means that if the registrar has any concerns about information that is going to the council, they are in a position to raise these concerns with the chair. The registrar is seen as the keeper of the university conscience, the go-to individual when things are not functioning well. The role requires someone who is highly experienced, knowledgeable and respected within higher education and that particular university, and is therefore able to deal with both the vice-chancellor and the chair of council.

In theory this should work, but in practice as we saw above, a quarter of university directors do not believe they get enough information to be effective. In part this is their own fault. As we also saw above, 42% of university directors do not visit operations or engage in dialogue with employees. But we also heard complaints about over-mighty vice-chancellors controlling the agenda, in effect interfering with that strategic relationship between registrar and chair. All independent directors must be able to access the information they need, and if they cannot, then they must make their views known to the CEO. However, there is no guarantee that the CEO will listen.

CEO Attitudes

The attitude of the CEO towards transparency and sharing data with the board is critical. Some CEOs are protective of anything that can represent a threat to their position, while others have a tendency to present only success stories to the board, withholding less positive aspects of performance:

> In a very small number of cases the executive are trying to actively manage the information flow to the board, restricting the conversation. To be frank, they don't particularly want active challenging input from non-executives.
>
> A lot depends on whether the vice-chancellor is open to debate and challenge, or whether he/she wants to manipulate the council and information.

The relationship between the chair and the CEO is critical for ensuring that good data is available and acted upon. This relationship needs to be cordial but not too cordial; some chairs are dominated by their CEOs, while others simply become too close to them and lose their independence.

> The chair and chief executive had become so close that at no point did the chair really challenge the CEO. He just accepted the CEO's version of events.

While much responsibility for making this relationship work rests with the chair, like any relationship it is also a two-way street. CEOs need to be prepared to work with chairs and boards and see the relationship as a partnership rather than a zero-sum game in which each tries to win power at expense of the other. A good CEO knows that the board is there to help and support them, rather than knock them down. If the CEO refuses to work with the board or tries to undermine it, the board is entitled to ask why and to question the CEO's motives. Sometimes a secretive or uncooperative CEO is merely trying to protect their own position; but sometimes, as examples such as Wells Fargo, Enron and Parmalat show, something more sinister is going on.

Acting on Evidence

Having gathered evidence, it is then incumbent on the independent director to act on that evidence in an appropriate manner. Independence means very little if it is not followed by action.

Taking action is not always easy, especially if the independent director can expect challenge or opposition from the executives. It is important to harness the power of the board. The most obvious way of proceeding is to raise the issue with the chairman and press for action.

> We got evidence, and went to the chairman and said, 'you can't ignore this. It's too damning'.

In more complex cases, the independent director may need to build a coalition of fellow directors in order to come to a joint position and be willing to act collectively.

> In one of the companies I thought there was an issue of going concern in terms of our liquidity position. I was able, as the chairman of the audit committee, to involve other independent directors, have a separate discussion with them and go through the numbers and the mind-set of management.

More complex still are cases where the independent director can expect opposition from fellow directors. The task then is to present the evidence fully and use it to persuade others to change their minds. Persuasion rather than confrontation is the key. If the case is strong, the power of the evidence should be enough to persuade other independent directors to come around.

If they fail to do so, then it may be that something else is influencing them and they are not truly independent. The independent director then faces a dilemma; back down and stay silent, even though they know there is something wrong, or continue to speak the truth as they see it. The former means the director is in effect letting bad things continue to happen, which makes them part of the problem rather than part of the solution. The latter may be difficult and painful and may ultimately lead to the director exiting the board. The path of independence is not always a rosy one; even when the evidence is overwhelmingly in favour, the way can still be strewn with thorns.

Alternatively, it may be that the case is not as strong as the director thinks it is, in which case there is a possibility that the other directors are right. Perhaps they have evidence of their own that proves the opposite case. A good independent director is also one who has the integrity to admit mistakes and to consider the facts again.

Evidence and action lead to impact, and every independent director should be seeking to make a positive impact on the organisations they serve. We will come back to impact in Chap. 8, but first we need to stop and consider the most important member of the board, the first among equals, the chair.

Notes

1. Our thanks to Chris Phillips for contributing this account of 4global and its work.
2. Eleanor Bloxham, 'Here's How Wells Fargo's Board of Directors Just Failed Customers', *Fortune*, 14 April 2017, https://fortune.com/2017/04/14/wells-fargo-fake-accounts-2/.
3. Margaret Heffernan, *Willful Blindness: Why We Ignore the Obvious at Our Peril*, New York: Bloomsbury, 2012.
4. Rezart Dibra, 'Corporate Governance Failure: The Case of Enron and Parmalat', *European Scientific Journal*, June 2016, https://eujournal.org/index.php/esj/article/viewFile/7580/7307.
5. Ron Ashkenas, 'How to Overcome Executive Isolation', *Harvard Business Review*, 2 February 2017, https://hbr.org/2017/02/how-to-overcome-executive-isolation.

7

The Role of the Chair

At the heart of the culture of engaged stewardship sits the chair. More than any other individual, it is the chair who creates and sustains that culture and sets an example of independent thought and action for other directors to follow. Being a chair is a balancing act, requiring diplomacy and tact as well as an independent mindset and no small amount of willpower. Chairs also serve as bridges between the board and the executive team, and their relationship with the CEO can often make the difference between organisational success and failure. A good CEO-chair relationship makes the organisation stronger. The result is superior performance, more value creation and greater social impact as the organisation carries out its mission.

Equally, a bad chair can quickly erode a culture of independence and hamper the board's ability to discharge its responsibilities, and a poor relationship between chair and CEO means dissent, confusion, lack of direction and lack of control, and opens the door for scandal and failure. A weak chair will surrender authority to the CEO and executive team, or to stronger-minded characters on the board, or both; an overly strong chair may dominate the board and stifle debate. In each case the result is the same: the loss of independence, leading to poor decision-making, the destruction of value and negative impacts on society.

It is time to put the spotlight on the chair, examining the qualities that make a good chair and the role they play in building and sustaining that culture of independence. Given how many qualities and competencies are expected of them the ideal chair, like the ideal director, might seem to resemble a superman or superwoman. In reality chairs are human and fallible like

G. Brown et al., *The Independent Director in Society*, https://doi.org/10.1007/978-3-030-51303-0_7

145

the rest of us, making it all the more important that chair have the full support of a harmonious board.

There are many examples of good chairs making a real difference to organisations and society. The transformation of England Hockey is one such case.

England Hockey: From Greek Tragedy to Gold Medal[1]

England Hockey is the national governing body for the sport of field hockey in England. As chairman of England Hockey from 2002 to 2015, Philip Kimberley led the board and the organisation through the complete rebuild of the organisation. He took it from a position of bankruptcy to being recognised as one of the best-run governing bodies in British sport. Under his stewardship, the organisation was set on the road to its highest ever participation figures. England Hockey was awarded the right to host major events including the 2018 Women's World Cup and won medals in all the sport's major international tournaments, including a first Olympic medal in twenty years.

Background

England Hockey was formed on 1 January 2003 to replace the defunct English Hockey Association (EHA) suspended in 2002 due to its significant financial problems. The EHA had originally been formed in 1996 to combine the functions of the separate governing bodies for men's, women's and mixed hockey. According to the long-standing chief executive, Sally Munday, the EHA was at 'rock bottom and the governing body was on its knees'. It was a volunteer-run organisation with elected volunteers on the council as committee members. The EHA was on the verge of bankruptcy and the national stadium at Milton Keynes was a white elephant. At the time organisation owed £500,000 and had no strategy or financial controls to improve its circumstances. The cost of running the stadium was one of the factors that led to the demise of the EHA. At that time there were two organisations, EHA and World Class Hockey, the latter running the elite side of the game but not living up to the notion of 'world class'.

International success was fading. A steady decline in British performances in Olympic competition was evident after 1996. The women's hockey team had relative success with silver medals at the 1998 and 2002 Commonwealth

Games and a gold at the International Hockey Federation's second tier Champions Challenge event, 2002, but not at the Olympics. After five unsuccessful Olympic Games, losing 2-0 to Korea in a must-win battle in the chase for fifth place in the qualifying tournament in 2003 in Auckland and not then being able to win a spot at the Athens 2004 Olympic Games was the last blow. Team morale and the self-belief of the players, coaching staff and the governing body were indeed at rock bottom.

Birth of England Hockey

In 2002 the new board of England Hockey was formed and led by executive chairman Philip Kimberley. Phillip had a distinguished international general management career with Burmah Castrol PLC. Sally Munday, the development director, who had previously held the position of regional manager in the old EHA, had the task of reviving the declining organisation which had experienced a loss of 60–70% of its funding.

The organisation was saved from bankruptcy by a £500,000 interest-free loan from businessman, Stewart Newton, on the condition that the board was completely restructured along corporate lines. This was not quite achieved in the first instance, but the board consisted of a mix of executive directors and non-executive directors, the latter elected by the membership. 'We had quite a small, compact board being run in a corporate style which gave us an advantage over a lot of other sports. …it meant that we could put in place stuff that other sports took ten years to put in place' (Finance Director).

Following the demise of the EHA, England's international hockey was for a time managed through a separate limited company called World Class Hockey Limited, funded entirely by Sport England. In 2005, the chairman managed to re-integrate the elite World Class Hockey back into England Hockey and put in place a performance-determined strategy. He also appointed two young coaches who could learn fast: Danny Kerry who became head coach of the England women's team and Jason Lee as England men's team head coach.

Game-Changer

Kimberley's first action was to appoint a financial director and a hockey director. Further, he recruited an Olympic gold medallist from the GB Team at Seoul 1988, David Faulkner, as performance director. Together with his directors, Kimberley spent time writing a performance plan. Additionally, a new governance structure was put in place and in 2003 the England Hockey organisation was born. Sally Munday joined the new board in 2003. She was development director from 2003 to 2009 and became the CEO of England Hockey and chief operating officer (COO) of GB Hockey, the national body for the sport, in 2009.

The true game-changer for both England Hockey and GB Hockey came on 6 July 2005, when London was named as the host city for the 2012 Olympic Games. That presented an opportunity to grow the sport and nurture a culture of performance. The first task was to win back the trust of grassroots hockey by building bridges with the hundreds of clubs in the UK. Towards this end the CEO and chairman engaged with people at all levels of hockey.

Kimberley developed the concept of the Great Britain Hockey Business and Performance Framework, a legally binding document signed in 2006 by the three home nations: England, Scotland and Wales. The framework was built around an underlying structure called Great Britain Primacy. All three nations committed to putting the GB Team forward to achieve Olympic success. While UK hockey is organised by separate bodies for each of the home nations, the UK is required to enter a combined team to the Olympics. By 2009, the benefits of this strategy were evident as England men became European champions. The women's team equally performed well, winning a bronze at the 2012 Olympic Games in London.

England Hockey has become the national governing body for each Olympic cycle since the signing of the framework agreement. The Great Britain Hockey Business and Performance Framework Agreement has been one of the most significant factors in the rise of Team GB over the last ten years. A new level of commitment and understanding between the home nations was developed, putting athletes at the very centre of the programme thus maximising chances for success at the Olympic level. It is the GB Team that competes at top level events such as the Olympic qualifiers, Champions Trophies and, of course, the Olympic Games.

Revitalising Governance

In the lead up to the London Olympics, the Board decided that the position of executive chair should become a part-time role and that a full-time chief executive was needed. Sally Munday was appointed the CEO, and the executive chairman moved into a non-executive chair's role.

In 2013 the Board introduced three independent directors replacing certain membership-elected Directors. The Board now consists of three independent non-executive directors, three membership elected non-executives and five executive directors. The executive consists of CEO, finance, commercial, development and performance directors. On the board, only the independent chair receives a small remuneration. The rest excluding executive directors are all volunteers who give their time for free.

Of the twelve voting board members 25% are women and the board is moving towards a 50/50 gender balance. The board also has two female observers. The board is designed to allow the non-executive directors to vote out the executive directors. These efforts resulted in the GB women's hockey team winning the gold medal in Rio de Janeiro in 2016.

> The board works out what skill set it needs, so we do a skills audit. We recruit against the job description and they're appointed for three years and can serve a couple of terms. The board is not very political. It's focussed on strategy and delivering the strategy and it's reasonably good at staying at high level strategic stuff and doesn't get too bogged down in the detail, which it leaves to the executives (Finance Director).

Change of Guard

Philip Kimberley stepped down in 2016 after twelve years as chair, and England Hockey appointed Royston Hoggarth as its new chair. Royston had held the position of non-executive director and chair of the audit committee for Intercede Plc, a leading software business, and chaired the board of IPSL Limited. 'He's not dissimilar in business experience to our previous chair. They're both very much business people but very different personalities' (CEO). The current chair is 'enthusiastic. ... The number one priority was getting somebody who would be a good chair of meetings, who could conduct the meetings and bring the best out of a good group of people and I think he does that well' (CEO).

When Royston arrived, England Hockey had already mapped out their journey from 2015 to 2018. This was largely driven around major events such as hosting the Hockey World Cup in 2018. England Hockey is now moving into a different era as Royston has allowed the organisation to almost reinvent itself again. 'The new Chair has absolute clarity on the line between the strategic responsibilities of the board and the operational responsibilities of the executive team. He's very respectful of that' (CEO).

On Reflection

As the national governing body of the sport, England Hockey has to work through conflicting concerns, trying to grow the sport, win medals and improve visibility.

> England Hockey is also the custodian of the governance and the enforcer of regulations. England Hockey may award a club a grant to develop their facilities and then fine them for breaching regulations. As a governing body, England Hockey is located between being the facilitator growing the sport as well as regulator of the sport… So, we're reporting against five objectives: international success (basically winning medals); increasing participation in the sport; growing the visibility of the sport (broadcast and people attending live events); enhancing the infrastructure of the sport (making sure that we've got the right facilities, coaches, volunteers to enable us to deliver the growth); and being a proud and respected governing body, and a big part of that is about how we manage the integrity of the sport (CEO).

Qualities of a Top-Performing Chair

The examples of Philip Kimberley and Royston Hoggarth show how much difference a good chair can make. But what makes a good chair? As with independent directors more generally, the answer lies not so much in what they do, but in who they are; the mindset and approach they bring to the board, and the extent to which they are prepared to engage with both the board and the CEO. Even more than with other directors, engagement matters here. A chair who cannot and/or will not engage can cripple a board.

What makes an 'outstanding' chair depends to some extent on circumstances. For example, different qualities may be needed of a chair during times of crisis compared with times when the organisation is relatively stable and successful. Different organisational cultures also require different styles of chairing; for example, some boards are more comfortable with confrontation than others. The size of the board might also require a different style and approach.

However, there are common features that are found in outstanding chairs across a wide range of organisations. The Henley research project identified several of these including humility, listening skills and emotional intelligence; high moral standards; a systematic and evidence-based approach; and knowledge about the organisation and its sector.

Humility, Listening Skills and Emotional Intelligence

Respondents to our research questions depict effective chairs as having 'no ego' and a humility in the way they are willing to learn and listen to board members. They lead by example, have no fear of being confronted and are ready to admit to being wrong. These characteristics allow them to persevere patiently and work through difficult tensions and situations without trying 'quick fixes' or jumping to conclusions. 'The chairmen should not impose his/her experience on the CEO or the board', one interviewee said. The bad chair emerged as being just the opposite.

Listening skills are seen as particularly important: 'The good chairman listens, the bad one speaks.' Emotional intelligence, the ability to empathise with other people and see other points of view, is particularly important. Chairs are the servants of the board, and their task is to bring together diverse points of view and ideas and synthesise them, rather than imposing their own views on the board or the CEO.

High Moral Standards

The high-performing chair has been described as possessing high moral standards which will not be compromised under any circumstances. However, the values of the chair must be aligned with the values of the company, and a mismatch between them can be harmful:

> You start with organisational values, because if there isn't a fit with the values of the chair, than that person should not be the chair.
>
> The organisational ethos endows you a certain value set, and endows you with what you bring to the board.

High moral standards give the chair a strong basis from which to make difficult decisions, particularly on issues that might be ethically fuzzy or 'grey'. Knowing the right thing to do, no matter how much pressure is being heaped on their shoulders, is a priceless quality in a chair and enables them to exercise decisive leadership in times of crisis. In particular, it gives them the foundation from which to challenge the CEO when immoral or ethically dubious behaviour has been uncovered. A strong moral compass was also described as a source of inspiration for board colleagues, who often take their cue from the chair and adopt a similar moral position. This creates a virtuous circle where the chair and the board support and reinforce each other.

Systematic and Evidence-Based Approach

We discussed evidence in Chap. 6, and everything we said there about independent directors and evidence applies even more strongly to chairs. The chair must seek evidence on which to base their own views and decisions, but the chair also needs to insist that other directors do their bit and gather evidence for their own arguments. If a director takes a position on a certain issue, the chair is entitled to challenge that position and ask what evidence the director has to support it. That same challenge also applies to the CEO; if the latter recommends a particular strategy or course of action, the chair is entitled to ask what evidence has led to this decision. One interviewee described the work of the chair as requiring 'patience and working through, being systematic and evidence-based'.

Knowledge About the Organisation and Sector

'The chair really needs to understand the sport or the business which he/she chairs', said one interviewee, and another added, 'having deep knowledge of the business/charity is critical.' The chair needs to have a deep level of understanding of the organisation and its sector, the nature of current and future challenges, how tensions might emerge, the features of the dominant culture, and the key stakeholders and how they behave, along with a host of other factors. This is not to say that the chair must necessarily be an 'old hand' in the industry; good chairs can come from very different backgrounds, but if they do come from outside the sector, they should nevertheless still have a good working knowledge of that sector and the key players. They should have experience of discussing and formulating strategy, as well as understanding of the difficulties of implementing strategy in real life, and finally they must of course be good team leaders.

Chairs and Culture

How chairs carry out their task of creating and sustaining a positive culture of engaged stewardship varies widely depending on the personality of the chair and their own style and approach. The nature of that task, however, tends to be the same in nearly every organisation, and requires patience, openness, support and encouragement for directors to be free and independent. Some of the opinions of our interviewees are worth quoting:

The buck stops with the chairman. If the culture isn't right is the chairman's fault. The chairman can change it all.

The chair is the most important figure on any board. If the chair carries out his/her functions in a conscientious and intelligent way, then I think it makes the world of difference to the board and to the role of independent director. The chair of the board is actually very key to the governance of any organisation and they can make or break an organisation all the way down.

The chair has the responsibility to create, identify, build and nurture a proper group dynamic in order for a board composed of disparate people, to function in a unified way.

Part of my job as chair is to create and maintain that culture of openness and supportive challenge where people can talk about things.

Sustaining the culture requires a great deal of hard work, and this is even more true if cultural change is required. If a chair inherits a board where there is no clear mandate for change, for example, then it can be even more difficult to remove non-performing members or change ways of working. If the chair arrives during or following a crisis then wide-ranging change will be required, and will need to be enacted quickly. Our research identified a number of steps chairs need to take in order to build, change and sustain a culture of engaged stewardship:

- Assess the board culture by gathering evidence
- Create shared purpose, values and behaviours
- Establish boundaries between executives and non-executives
- Promote independent director-only meetings
- Have one-to-one meetings with the CEO
- Ensure there is an appropriate level and quality of information
- Lead board meetings effectively
- Deal with or remove non-performing or toxic board members
- Use external board evaluations effectively

Let us look at each of these points in a bit more detail.

Assess the Board Culture by Gathering Evidence

Effective chairs place importance on board culture from day one. They seek evidence to establish a robust understanding of the existing board culture and where changes are required. Instead of bringing pre-conceived ideas of what works best, the effective chairmen recognise that each board and organisation are unique and therefore what works elsewhere might not be effective here. Therefore the chair collects evidence and forms a judgement about board culture by talking extensively with key employees and other stakeholders and learning about the organisation:

> I went around and spoke to stakeholders, different people and I formed the view that the board was too arrogant. I wrote down a number of cultural shifts I wanted to effect on the board.
>
> I spend a lot of time with each of the companies, getting to know the executives.
>
> I learned as much as I could about the company both business model and key people.

As with any form of evidence-gathering, care must be taken to triangulate findings and ensure the picture of board culture is an accurate one. People will have their own views, which sometimes are coloured by emotion, personal clashes or disagreements, or fundamental lack of understanding about what the board is for. The chair will also need to draw on his or her own experience of previous boards, as noted above, have a good level of emotional intelligence and ability to empathise with other people and understand their point of view.

Create a Shared Purpose, Values and Behaviours

The purpose of assessing the culture is to understand whether and to what extent there is a clear shared purpose, values and norms of behaviour for the organisation and for the board. If these things exist, well and good; the chair's task then is to sustain that culture and make sure it continues to function. If there are misalignments and little clarity on purpose, values and behaviours, then the chair's first task is to revisit these elements, get agreement and make them clear and explicit for the board. 'The chair needs to be able to get people to agree on common cause', said one interviewee, and another added, 'the ultimate mission must be shared.'

In addition to enabling agreement around purpose and values, chairs must also find ways to embed these in practice and then reinforce them continually. One chair uses the board pack to remind every board member of purpose, values and behaviour: 'remind of purpose, values and behaviours: it's in front of every board pack.' Another chair in an NHS Trust 'starts every board meeting with a patient or carer's story. It reminds us of why we are there.'

Once again, different methods will be needed for different organisations, depending on the sector and culture. The main point to be remembered is that culture is built on those three foundation stones of purpose, values and behaviours, and must be put into practice and continually reinforced. This is one of the most important—perhaps the most important—task of the chair.

Establish Boundaries Between Executives and Non-executives

As already discussed, it is highly important to establish boundaries between the non-executive and executive roles. Generally, the rule is that independent directors and chairs do not involve themselves in operational matters and confine themselves to strategic oversight and governance issues, but exactly where that boundary lies can vary from organisation to organisation.

Failure to observe these boundaries, by either side, can be a source of tension that affects the board's operating culture. Chairs often describe managing this challenge-collaboration tension as one of the most difficult aspects of their work, and getting it wrong can have unfortunate consequences for the board and the entire organisation. One chair explained how problematic it may be for a chair to intervene when there is a dispute over boundaries:

> There was a standoff between the board and the executive, with the chief executive saying, 'that is not your responsibility, the executive has to be given the space to do this and that.' In those circumstances, I felt the role was a difficult one because I didn't want to just pile in. But the board at the time just wanted to shout at the chief executive, which is quite unproductive and also I knew that that were problems and you had to scrutinise. And it ended in grief: a payoff and a public statement where all involved can go out their heads held high. How does the chair plan and embed change, and how does he evaluate progress and do his/her strategic thinking?

Another chair commented on how establishing and maintaining boundaries was easy to say but hard to do:

> I tried to keep the line between the function of a trustee director and the executive management as clear as I possibly could. Advice, not control, and not do the management for them. And that was really, really testing.

Chairs have their own different styles and approaches to chairing, and they often have different conceptions of where the line between the non-executive and the executive should be drawn. Our research suggests that there is no hard and fast delineation; much depends on the personalities involved and the challenges facing the organisation. Some chairs view the role of the non-executive as supporting the executive without being too challenging:

> The line between non-executive and executive, or chair and CEO: the non-executive must question it occasionally but generally be supportive.

Others recognise that in some instances the chair needs to be prepared to cross the line and take action, demanding better behaviour and performance from executives:

> The chair sets the tone for the company, for the board. The chairman has to get the balance right between support, but then when the difficult decisions are required to challenge and take action if necessary.
>
> The chair needs to have a certain amount of separateness, not to become too closely associated either with the executive or with the non-executives, or the CEO in particular. He must be prepared to exercise difficult judgments and sometimes disagree with the executive and say: 'this won't do, we should be looking at changing direction, changing speed or something'.

The last respondent in particular makes the point that the chair is also a leader. That 'separateness' is one of the characteristics of leadership, and it has often been noted that leaders are both part of a team and yet at the same time separate and distinct from it.[2] It is worth remembering that the chair leads the board, but is also part of the board and needs to be guided by the wishes of its members.

Finding the right line between control and collaboration is not always easy, but it is vitally important. Getting it wrong, as we have seen, can be a source of friction and problems. Getting it right, on the other hand, powerfully reinforces the culture of engaged stewardship and enables independent directors and executives to work together in a positive and supportive manner and create impact. We have already mentioned the dual assurance model of governance at the University of Exeter, but it is worth commenting again on how carefully the lines between executive and non-executive responsibility are drawn, and how both sides work together in teams to solve problems and create value.

Promote Independent Director-Only Meetings

In Chap. 4 we also mentioned the importance and value of meetings where only independent directors are present. These meetings enable directors to speak freely, without the constraints that might exist if executives were in the room. They are also useful as bonding and team-building sessions that let directors get to know each other and learn to work together more effectively:

> The independent directors now meet three or four times a year on their own, with a dinner afterwards, and there is also an away-day with the full board to discuss strategy with a facilitator.

These meetings allow a safe place where issues can be discussed, ideas shared and alignment created around particular topics of board responsibility. They enable independent directors to develop a greater understanding of each other's areas of expertise, experience, values and preventing the emergence of pluralistic ignorance, 'a situation in which virtually all members of a group privately reject group norms, but believe that virtually all other group members accept them.'[3]

It is crucial, however, that the chair maintains transparency in this process and discusses with the CEO the outcomes of such meetings in a constructive manner. If the CEO becomes uncomfortable with these meetings and what is discussed, this will damage trust and a division between executives and independent directors may start to emerge.

> One of the fundamental things the chairman does is to create an environment where the CEO isn't fearful of what independent directors discuss behind closed doors.

In essence, the creation of strong relationships among independent directors and alignment around critical issues is important for maintaining a culture of independence:

> There is no substitute for social interaction, making sure that you are spending time to get to know people, to understand individuals and how they work together, and making sure you are extracting the best contribution possible.

Have One-to-One Meetings with the CEO

One of the ways in which the chair creates trust between the CEO and the board is to have regular one-to-ones with the CEO to discuss any sensitivities, areas of concern and potential misunderstandings. 'Frequent communication is critical', said one of our interviewees, and many others made the point that developing an effective relationship and working together is highly important. The CEO and chair need to develop a strong partnership, bringing the executive and non-executive sides of the organisation together. Each communicates their needs, concerns and problems to the other; information and knowledge are exchanged, ideas discussed and tested and calibrated, and alignment of the two sides is created.

These one-to-one meetings also give the chair a chance to check on the CEO's well-being and state of mind. Being CEO of any organisation, large or small, can be a lonely role, and CEOs often speak of how lacking people to talk to can be difficult, sometimes even harmful to mental health.[4] A good partnership with the chair means the CEO has someone to lean on, a support to help him or her get through difficult times.

The mutual support and exchange of views that comes from these meetings helps to reinforce the culture of independence. If the CEO and the chair have a good relationship, the CEO will trust not only the chair but the board more generally. That reduces—though does not entirely eliminate—the chance that the CEO will try to dominate the board, or act as gatekeeper and try to control the information the board receives.

Ensure There Is Appropriate Level and Quality of Information

Part of the chair's role is to ensure that critical information is received by directors in a form which can be easily digested and analysed. Information overload can be as damaging as receiving too little information. The chair and CEO should work together to develop effective and efficient information flows, and also enable to independent directors to come back and ask for additional evidence if anything requires further investigation.

This too is a matter of trust. Knowledge is power, and the CEO must be able to trust the chair to deal with sensitive information in an honest and ethical manner. Only if there is trust can there be full transparency. The chair in turn needs to be able to trust the CEO to provide full and correct information, and not hold back anything he or she thinks might be damaging. The

CEO should be encouraged to communicate *all* important news, both good and bad. Whether the CEO does so will depend in part on the strength of the relationship with the chair.

Lead Board Meetings Effectively

The work of the chair is most visible when chairing board meetings. As we saw in Chap. 4, effective board meetings are an important part of the culture of independence.

If the steps described above—creating shared purpose, values and behaviours, establishing clarity about the boundary between non-executive and executive members, enabling independent director-only meetings and having a strong productive relationship with the CEO—have been effectively carried out, then board meetings are likely to be placed where there is openness and robust debate about the right topics. However, chairing meetings is a skill in itself. If meetings are poorly conducted, the potential of the board will not be realised and alignment and trust might be destroyed.

Exceptional chairs are able to ensure the participation of all board members through an inclusive style of chairing, inviting views from different perspectives to be openly shared and discussed:

> The chair needs to think how he can draw out as many different scenarios and alternative options and perspectives as they can. They should actually be looking for different perspectives.
>
> Some chairs think they are there creating a consensus all the time, but actually they should be encouraging different perspectives and debate.

It is not the role of chair to attempt to create consensus at all times, or at any cost. Robust debate where alternative views are discussed and scrutinised must precede any decision, and sometimes no decision is better than a false consensus. Therefore, chairs must avoid letting overly dominant individuals take control of particular topics or set the context for decisions. Sometimes these individuals will use their status, eloquence and personality to attempt to force the board to see the world their way, with the result that alternative perspectives get pushed to one side:

> The chair should avoid letting certain individuals set the guidelines or set the context of the issue before the discussion even begun.
> The chair must avoid false consensus and have an inclusive style.

One way that chairs can instil different perspectives and create cognitive tension is by encouraging some board members to play 'devil's advocate', making the case against or in favour of a particular topic. It is important that the board is able to withstand tension, disagreement and contrary views, and fully consider all available alternatives.

> Ask particular board members to make the case 'against' a topic to get perspective and contrarian views. Empower the board to challenge.
> It's about how you respond when a contrary point of view is raised.

By encouraging robust debate in the boardroom, chairs are able to manage tensions and keep the board focused. Good chairs pull together different perspectives, summarising them and enabling the board to reach higher levels of shared understanding. Alternatively, when the debate becomes too heated and/or there is a feeling that the discussion has reached a dead end, it is important that the chair pauses the debate and allows time for reflection before raising the issue again.

> Create a climate for debate and try to summarise periodically, pause the debate and then reconvene with some chats going off-line while the debate is paused.
> It is useful to pause every now and again, to reflect and try to refine the debate and then at the end bring it together.

There will also be occasions where the board is not able to agree on important issues. In these cases, the chair may need to become more assertive and take leadership of the problem, providing clarity about whatever action that is required. Once again, a balance needs to be struck. The chair does not tell the board what to do. Instead, a good chair goes over the information and evidence, providing clarity on points where there may be confusion, and then recommending points for action which the board can discuss. It is always important that the board is clear about what needs to be done next:

> Once an issue is raised, it is the role of the chair to bring the discussion to a close with some clear steps to be taken next.
> In my board I have created an environment where nobody should feel constrained about asking or saying the silliest thing. I learned very early on that creating this environment where people aren't scared, where they trust each other's judgment, is very important.

In summary, the high-performing chair creates a culture of openness and transparency, where directors can exercise their independence and are able to express their views freely. In such a culture, tension and disagreement are seen as both 'normal' and valuable. The board, led by the chair, will handle tensions in a healthy manner, maintaining group cohesion and maximising decision quality.

> Ensure that there is a culture of totally open dialogue with complete transparency where people are able to say what they think without fear or favour; where there is a spirit of constructive cooperation, but also an ability to also be critical.
>
> Ensuring that all the members of the board have the confidence to speak up. You do no service at all by suppressing disagreement. You don't want people not speaking up for fear of the consequences.
>
> Holding the board together, making sure it is properly organised, making sure that the very diverse and dissonant board of trustees are working together cohesively. It is very important to make sure the board is working with management, and that tensions don't develop and things are dealt with.

Deal with or Remove Non-performing or Toxic Board Members

Dealing with, and ultimately removing, non-performing or toxic board members is a difficult task that requires much time and patience. Examples of poor performance might include showing up late for meetings, using the phone while in meetings, challenging a colleague inappropriately, clearly not reading the board papers before the meeting and so on. Non-performing directors are like a brake on the organisation. By failing to do their duty, or by creating tensions and disagreements within the board, they compromise the board's effectiveness. To put it bluntly, they need to be got rid of.

Once again, this is easier said than done. Chairs need to be on the lookout for signs of underperformance or toxic behaviour, and take steps early to deal with it:

> The chairman needs to lead by example, and if the behaviour in meetings isn't right, you take the individual to the side and tell him/her.

If there is a toxic member and that member holds some power in the boardroom (i.e. the charity founder, a shareholder, a source of income or someone who has an affiliation with a powerful stakeholder) removal can be extremely difficult. Sometimes it can take several years and involve legal action. Chairs often have their best chance at clearing away dead wood when they first take up their position, especially during or after a crisis where there is a clear mandate for changing the board. On the other hand, during a crisis it sometimes becomes difficult for the chair to attract the right individuals to the board:

> Change a number of independent directors and support the new CEO with transforming the organisation. It was difficult, because no one with significant standing would like to sit on that board due to how exposed it was and because of reputational issues etc.

Therefore, it is best to remove poorly performing independent directors early and decisively. Delay is in no one's best interests.

Use External Board Evaluations Effectively

Board evaluation is one area of practice where our research highlighted the need for improvement. It is vitally important that boards undergo regular evaluation in order to assess the performance of individual members and the board as a whole. Evaluations can identify areas where the board needs to improve how it works together, and can also show whether individual directors are pulling their weight. There is also a positive aspect; evaluations can help the board identify areas for innovation that would make them even more effective than they already are.

Not everyone finds evaluations comfortable, and there is always a danger that evaluations can be used punitively to single out board members who are deemed too outspoken or too ready to challenge. The chair needs to ensure that evaluations take place in an atmosphere of trust and respect:

> Trust is very important and we evaluate trust in every board evaluation. It's part of the cultural aspect, and you create trust by being transparent and honest, create an environment where all directors are happy to observe on each other and there needs to be humility to accept that you can do better. I think humility is fundamental to trust.

However, as Table 7.1 shows, many of the organisations we surveyed used external evaluations infrequently. Anecdotal evidence suggests that some had never had an external evaluation at all. This is a matter for serious concern. Boards that do not undergo evaluation cannot be certain how effective they really are, and may be missing out on areas for improvement.

Table 7.1 Frequency and type of board evaluation by sector (% of respondents)

Type of evaluation	Annually (%)	2–3 years (%)	Less often (%)	Sectors
Internal, through one-to-one discussions	87.1	9.5	3.5	Sports
External, through consultants	10.3	45.7	44.0	Sports
Internal, through one-to-one discussions	74.2	19.2	6.7	Universities
External, through consultants	5.8	59.2	35.0	Universities
Internal, through one-to-one discussions	88.6	7.4	4.0	NHS
External, through consultants	17.7	64.0	18.3	NHS
Internal, through one-to-one discussions	76.0	20.0	4.0	Charities
External, through consultants	5.3	40.0	56.5	Charities

We will discuss evaluation in more detail in Chap. 10, but the main point to be made here is that the chair has responsibility for ensuring that evaluations are carried out, and then for implementing any recommendations for improvement that come out of the process.

The Effectiveness of Chairs

That is the ideal picture of what a chair should do, but how closely does it match with the reality on the ground? Evidence from other sources confirms that chairs are not always as effective as they should be. The Kakabadse Report on civil service effectiveness, for example, found that boards in government departments are often ineffective 'because of the poor chairmanship of the Secretary of State'.[5] The Henley Business School report 'Conflict and Tension in the Boardroom' agreed with the findings of our own study that good chairing is an essential element in preventing boardroom conflict, implying that where conflict does exist, chairs may not be doing their jobs properly.

Our research looked specifically at chair effectiveness and found that while many chairs are doing a very good job, there are also gaps. Figure 7.1, for example, shows that many chairs have good experience of the role they are expected to play. Analysing in more detail, we found that chairs have values that are strongly aligned with the organisation they lead, but they are weak in several key dimensions, including practical areas such as strategic thinking, developing an evidence-based approach and building effective relationships. The latter in particular, as we saw above, is vital.

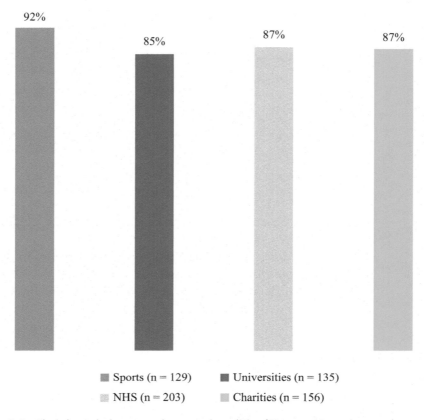

Fig. 7.1 Chair knowledge, experience and qualities (% agree/strongly agree)

Figure 7.2 reinforces this impression of lack of effective chairing in some organisations. When we looked at the responses in more detail we found significant weaknesses here in terms of taking responsibility for board composition—to be fair, our research also showed that most chairs are effective at removing non-performing or toxic directors—and in instilling confidence in key stakeholders that the organisation is well managed and well governed. There are also doubts about whether many chairs are effective in a time of crisis.

The answers to the question of how to improve chair effectiveness, and independent director performance more generally, lies in recruitment, selection, training and evaluation. We will come to those subjects in Part III of this book. For the moment, let us reiterate the statement made at the start of this chapter; the chair is at the heart of the culture of engaged stewardship. The chair creates and sustains that culture, and makes it possible for other

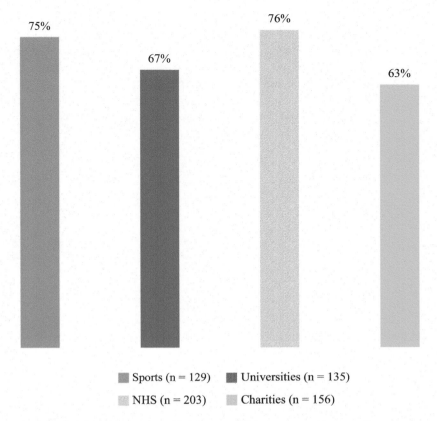

75%

67%

76%

63%

■ Sports (n = 129)   ■ Universities (n = 135)

▨ NHS (n = 203)   ▨ Charities (n = 156)

Fig. 7.2 Chair role and practice effectiveness (% agree/strongly agree)

directors to be truly independent. Without that culture, and without independence, there is little chance that the board will be able to make positive impact. But for a truly independent board with a strong culture, the sky is the limit.

Notes

1. Our thanks to Nada Kakabadse for contributing this study of the transformation of England Hockey.
2. For example, in Richard Bolden, Beverley Hawkins, Jonathan Gosling and Scott Taylor, *Exploring Leadership: Individual, Organizational and Societal Perspectives*, Oxford: Oxford University Press, 2011.

3. Dale Miller, Benoit Monin and Deborah Prentice, 'Pluralistic Ignorance and Inconsistency Between Private Attitudes and Public Behaviours', in Deborah Terry and Michael Hogg (eds), *Attitudes, Behaviour and Social Context: The Role of Norms and Group Membership*. New York: Lawrence Erlbaum (2000: 103), *cited in* Westphal and Bedner (2005: 264).
4. Ron Ashkenas 'How to Overcome Executive Isolation', *Harvard Business Review*, https:/bbt.org/2017/02/how-to-overcome-executive-isolation.
5. Kakabadse Report, p. 3.

8

Making Impact

So, what exactly is impact? There is no single definition; the nature of impact differs from organisation to organisation, from sector to sector. Broadly speaking, it means two things: first, improving the ability of the organisation to deliver, and second, a consequent improvement in people's lives and in society as a whole. Impact can take many forms: improved quality and customer satisfaction, more innovative services that give people goods and services they need, better working conditions and more meaningful work for employees, returns on investment to shareholders, improvements in health, education and community life, and many others. Importantly, impact does *not* just mean increasing shareholder value, or spending taxpayers' money wisely. The onus is on organisations in every sector to deliver positive impact for the whole community, not just a favoured few. One of the tasks of the independent director is to ensure that this is done.

We can think about impact in two ways. First, there is the impact on the organisation itself. At the University of Exeter, good governance has had an impact on the university by enabling better decision-making and stronger relationships between executives and independent directors. This has been achieved through the dual assurance model of governance, and we can take this as an example of how governance has real impact on organisations and on society.

© The Author(s) 2020
G. Brown et al., *The Independent Director in Society*,
https://doi.org/10.1007/978-3-030-51303-0_8

Dual Assurance at the University of Exeter

How can boards make a positive impact on the organisations they serve? What does this impact look like? To answer these questions, let us look at the dual assurance model of governance employed at the University of Exeter. Dual assurance is an excellent example of how good governance really can make a difference.

When Sir Steve Smith arrived at the University of Exeter in October 2002, the university viewed itself as extraordinarily strong. However, the evidence did not match the university's self- image. Since university league tables began in 1992 Exeter had never risen above the thirtieth position in the UK. Student numbers and entry grades were modest and research earnings were in the region of £10 million per annum.

An ambitious transformation plan was needed, but the governance of the university was not able to bring about the kind of value and stewardship that was required to support such a plan. The University Council was very large with about thirty-two members, and met as little as four times per year for an average of three hours each time. Council members would receive board packs with up to 600 pages of material, with an implicit presumption that lay members—as they were then called—were there to agree with management. The role of 'lay members' was therefore not well understood and valued and there was a sense of lack of independence. The council was indeed seen as a 'rubber stamping' institution. There was a strong belief that changes to governance were required to ensure long-term, sustainable success.

Introducing Dual Assurance Governance

With the departure of the incumbent secretary and registrar, the university sought another experienced individual who could assist in creating the right governance for the university and its new ambitions. David Allen, who had held similar positions at the universities of Birmingham and Nottingham, was appointed in 2003 and brought about significant changes by introducing the Dual Assurance model of governance. According to one of our interviewees, 'Dual Assurance has altered fundamentally the way we undertake governance at Exeter and it has massive pluses.'

The DA model requires the appointment of independent council members to be the dual assurance lead in particular areas such as infrastructure, fundraising, education, research and so on. The council will therefore, in each area, be assured not just by the executive responsible for that area but also by an independent director (known at Exeter as independent council members). The first step in implementing the model is to identify which areas are to be dual assured. Independent directors are nominated as 'assurance leads' due to their particular expertise and experience in that area. Indeed, directors are recruited with an eye to any gaps in the skill set needed for dual assurance. Independent directors will receive the same information and meet monthly with the executive who leads the area as well as comment and speak at the council after any area-specific presentation. In this way, dual assurance enables independent director to triangulate information and provide an independent view.

This model both requires and encourages a much greater involvement and engagement by the independent members. At Exeter, the council today meets six times a year for up to one and a half days, and the independent leads meet the executive counterpart at least three times a year. There is also a strategy away day, but there are comparatively fewer committees and particularly no finance committee. There is, however, an audit committee that carries out part of the finance committee functions, but other financial matters are fully discussed at council, and are for the council as a whole to decide. There is also a remuneration committee and a nominations committee. Dual assurance, it is not primarily about making decisions, it is about effective checks and balances leading to effective council decisions:

> Dual assurance doesn't make any decisions. Investment doesn't happen as a result of a dual assurance meeting. The dual assurance member will consider proposals to go to the council and will give advice as to the sort of things the council might wish to consider. But ultimately, it is the full council that makes the requisite evaluation.

Handling the Tensions of Dual Assurance

Dual assurance is not without tensions. Those at the University of Exeter who have worked with the model have found that three fundamental tensions exist.

Stepping over the executive line and losing independence. Sometimes independent members become too close to the organisation and start to feel responsible for the particular agenda that they assure. This can mean that the independent member is tempted to go over the executive line or to become too close to the executive. In turn, this means they are unable to challenge executives and hold them to account.

Particular agendas becoming dominant vis-à-vis the more fundamental collective purpose. Where independent members and executives work close together, particular 'assurance agendas' might come to dominate. While these agendas might be individually important, it is easy to pay too much attention to them and neglect the wider purpose. Mechanisms need to be put in place to maintain a collective, unified purpose and keep focused on the longer- term goals.

A tendency to judge every proposal against the same yardstick. Many independent members come from a business background, meaning they tend to measure the value of particular initiatives against economic criteria. Management leads sometimes have to explain to the independent directors that the KPIs (key performance indicators) of a university are not simply the bottom line. Given that every investment proposal of £1 million or more requires full council approval, tensions between management and more finance-oriented independent directors can sometimes arise.

It is up to the chair to ensure that these tensions inherent in the model are constructive and do not make the council dysfunctional. At Exeter the current chair, Sarah Turvill, conducts regular one-to-one meetings with the executives, encourages independent directors to visit operations and meet and debate among themselves, and ensures that all stakeholders are taken into consideration during decision-making. While everyone is required to play their part, it is generally accepted that the Dual Assurance model requires a chair that understands these points of tension and works continually to realign behaviour and agendas, reminding everyone of the higher purpose the university seeks and serves:

> I think it is probably a team effort [to reach decisions beyond particular agendas], but obviously the biggest weight is on the chair.

Improved Council Composition, Dynamics and Decision-making

The use of the Dual Assurance model has created an attractive governance culture which makes the role of independent member of council much more enjoyable and effective. Highly accomplished, experienced and skilled people are usually unwilling to join a council where the dynamics do not allow a real contribution. Under the Dual Assurance model, people value the role far more because they are fully involved in a meaningful way:

If you understand the underpinning and you can engage with stuff intellectually, then actually they enjoy it far more. I find people are hungry for more information and more engagement rather than less.

At Exeter, this has actually made it easier for the council to attract people. Today, the university has a group of independent directors who are very much in touch with the university, both with regard to their specific areas of dual assurance and with the institution as a whole. Independent directors are truly committed to the university and are provided with the means to challenge constructively executive proposals, thus ensuring better, more effective decision-making.

One of the greatest issues confronting university councils is the danger of having all information that reaches directors channelled through the vice-chancellor/CEO. This presents a real barrier to effective independent scrutiny. The DA model gets around this barrier by helping independent directors gather information through other channels. The model requires them to visit different parts of the university, talk to people and hear their views and concerns, and of course also to meet with the executive lead. By getting out into the organisation and seeing and hearing for themselves, independent directors can triangulate information and have fully informed debates with the executive lead and with the full council.

In turn, because everybody feels more informed and confident to speak up, there is robust challenge and discussion at various levels, including during council meetings. People feel that the process works. Proposals put before the council receive a level of scrutiny that would not be possible under a more classical model of governance.

As noted earlier, one of the strengths of dual assurance is that it allows all stakeholders to have a voice. At universities, this is particularly true where students are concerned. Over recent years, particularly since the introduction of tuition fees, the student voice has become more important than ever. At Exeter the presidents of both student unions, the Students Guild and the FXU, are permanent council members. The Students' Guild CEO also has the right to sit at council to support the two presidents. There is a general feeling that students' concerns really are taken into account, and the student voice is genuinely heard and influences decision-making:

We have a really constructive relationship—as critical friends—between the Student Union and the University here, and that is something that we work hard to maintain and really cherish.

For example, a group of students called Ethical Exeter campaigned for all university investments to be as ethical as possible. As a response, the Exeter Council embedded an ethical approach in its investment policy. Students were represented in the panel that chose which investment companies were commissioned. On another occasion, students opposed a council recommendation to extend the teaching day by an hour to cope with constraints in physical space due to growth, arguing it would harm the student experience. The objections were taken on board by council and a different solution was reached.

Ultimately, it is felt that dual assurance not only allows for better decisions to be made, but it also enables better, constructive relationships between the council and the senior executive team:

> I think it makes better decisions because the other council members can question the dual assurance person about why, rather than having to go to the executive who may be rather defensive or whatever about it.

A Virtuous Cycle of Sustainable Success

What difference had dual assurance made? What impact has it had? At the University of Exeter, leadership, governance and performance have changed beyond recognition. Exeter is today amongst the leading group of UK Universities known as the Russell Group. It has increased the number of students whilst maintaining high quality average entry grades (AAA, AAB). It was able to build from the ground up prominence in STEM (Science, Technology, Engineering and Mathematics) subjects both in terms of teaching and research. It is consistently ranked as a top ten UK university in all the major rankings, and also amongst the top 12–15th universities in research earnings, averaging £100 million per year. Today, the university and its council are well-positioned to face a very challenging higher education sector with confidence, and to build on past achievements after Sir Steve Smith steps down from his post in 2020. All of these things mean the university is carrying out its mission more effectively than before (Fig. 8.1).

STEP 1: Ensure vice-chancellor and the chair are well-aligned and buy-in to DA

STEP 2: Identify the areas to be dual-assured

STEP 3: Assess via a skills matrix whether council is appropriately skilled and experience in all areas

STEP 4: Set the expectations for the level of engagement required from independent members

STEP 5: Change the title from lay members to independent members

STEP 6: Educate everyone about dual assurance

STEP 7: Ensure that the right information and KPIs are in place and available

STEP 8: Put in place formal and informal mechanisms to handle tensions inherent in the model

STEP 9: Make financial decisions a full-council matter

STEP 10: Review how everything is working through robust governance evaluations

Fig. 8.1 10 key steps to implement dual assurance

Making Impact, Reaching Goals

The Exeter story is just one example of how good governance can make a real, positive and measurable impact on organisations. Good governance has led to expansion and growth, higher rankings and more investment in the form of research funding. However, none of this would have mattered if it had not enabled the university to do the things it is supposed to do: to provide high-quality education and to generate new knowledge through research. These are its goals; these are why any university exists in the first place.

In other examples, Ardwick Green was in a precarious position, to say the least; good governance turned it around and enabled it to become financially sustainable, meaning it could carry on delivering its vitally necessary services. By bringing in support from 4global, Carmarthenshire County Council and the ECB have invested heavily in the provision of new services which will have a real impact on communities. England Hockey rose from the ashes of a dysfunctional organisation and began to really shine. More people are now playing hockey and the national teams are now higher in the championship rankings and winning more medals, including Olympic gold. London Ambulance Service went from being in special needs to an organisation rated from good to outstanding, and has made a real impact on the lives of the people of London.

Ultimately, the task of the independent director is to make sure the organisation achieves its goals and to help it do so. That is the end game. The independent director is the servant of the organisation, but the organisation in turn is the servant of society. Some of those social goals represent formidable challenges. But if directors can meet them—if they can have genuine impact—then the rewards for all of us are potentially enormous.

Business

Much has already been written about the problems of the business world and the need for corporations to be governed more responsibly, in the interests of all their stakeholders and not just a few favoured ones (like shareholders). In his book *Confronting Capitalism*, for example, economist and marketing thought-leader Philip Kotler argues that companies that pay low wages are effectively cutting their own throats. If employees were paid better, they would have more disposable income, would purchase more goods and services and contribute to economic growth. Ironically, by keeping wages down, companies are helping to depress the economy and stifle growth.[1]

Good governance in business focuses not solely on making profits, but on rendering a service to society (which, as Kotler points out, is how profits are made). Healthy flourishing businesses provide employment, which allows people to live comfortably, educate their children well and be happy. They also pay taxes, rather than requiring taxpayer money to bail them out when they fail, and make a net positive contribution to the public purse. And, of course, they return money to shareholders, some of whom then use that money to pay our pensions when we finally retire from work.

A large part of good governance in business concerns protecting the reputation of the company itself. Reputation feeds into many other aspects including brand value, the willingness of customers, employees and suppliers to trust the company and engage with it, and the ability to negotiate with governments. A wealth of research over the past hundred years shows that how customers perceive a brand depends in large part on whether they trust the company behind it. Companies that are not trusted by employees will struggle to recruit high-calibre staff, and this again impacts on how well they can deliver value to customers. Losing reputation becomes a vicious circle, in which trust erodes everywhere and the company goes into a downward spiral.

As well as trust in individual businesses, there is also a larger issue of trust in business generally. Waves of bankruptcies and collapses, like Royal Bank of Scotland and more recently Carillion, along with scandals involving fraud and corruption—Satyam, Wells Fargo, Enron, Parmalat, Global Crossing and many others are names that continue to echo around the world—erode popular trust in business. So do accounting irregularities like those that brought down Royal Ahold and badly damaged Tesco, and cases of tax avoidance like the accusations that have dogged Amazon in Europe. The phone hacking scandal that embroiled the British press a few years ago killed one newspaper and caused a massive loss of confidence in the press more generally. Facebook is still struggling with the fallout of the Cambridge Analytica scandal, but trust in all social media platforms has suffered as a result.

Good governance could and should have meant that these issues never arose in the first place. Boards are the ultimate guardians of the company's reputation, and it is up to them to ensure that the company has a strong culture based on ethical principles where abuses do not occur. Any scandal damages not just the company affected, but the entire business world.

How then do we define impact in business? At heart, it means ensuring the company is run as it should be run, honestly and in the interest of all its stakeholders. Impact can then be seen in the form of jobs created, satisfied customers, a thriving economy and a happy society. It goes without saying that if the company is having this kind of impact, then provided it is run efficiently, it will also make a profit.

Charities

As of September 2018 there were 168,000 registered charities in the UK with an annual income of 77.4 billion. The vast majority of these were small; 85% had an income of less than £500,000.[2] The public function of some is also less than straightforward—for example, political think-tanks and public schools—and governance is not always as transparent as it might be.

Yet the work these institutions do is vital. Charities provide an immense range of services, ranging from medical research (e.g. Cancer Research UK), social deprivation (Shelter), the arts (Welsh National Opera), children (NSPCC), the elderly (Help the Aged), overseas aid (Red Cross, Oxfam) and many others.

In effect, charities plug the gap between private sector and public sector provision of services. That which business deems it unprofitable to do, and government deems it uneconomical to do, falls to charities. Without them, our society would probably fall apart.

Earlier we described the example of Ardwick Green, a small charity providing grief counselling services to children following cases of bereavement, suicide, exploitation or domestic abuse. We know how scarring these experiences can be, and how often they lead to mental illness and other problems later in life. What could be more important than providing children with support during these terrible experiences to enable them recover and go on to live full and rewarding lives? Yet Ardwick Green nearly collapsed thanks to the weakness of its board, and that essential service nearly came to an end.

For independent directors of charities, then, impact consists in making sure that the charity can continue to function and deliver its service, and then to improve that service and make certain it reaches more people who need it and meets their needs more fully. Improving efficiency is one obvious area. Of the £77 billion raised, £46 billion is spent directly on delivering services. This is a formidable total, but it could be larger; the residue is spent on areas such as fundraising and administration. Reducing overhead costs and directing more money towards services and their end users is a clear strategic imperative for many charities. Here is the challenge for directors of charity boards: how can they get those costs down? Because if they can spend more money on services, there will be a direct impact on society.

As well as cutting costs, charities need to increase their income. Most charity funding takes the form of donations and bequests, sponsorship, contract income derived from other sources (usually government) or some combination of the three. There are plenty of areas here where independent directors can have impact; chairing and sitting on fundraising committees, using networks to make contacts with potential donors and sponsors, supporting and advising contract negotiations and joining discussions with commissioners, helping the organisation set realistic income targets and so on. Again, the principle is clear; the more money the charity brings in and is able to spend efficiently, the more people will benefit from its service and the greater the social impact will be.

Independent directors are the custodians of the charity's reputation, and that reputation in turn determines how easily the charity can attract funding. As stewards of the organisation, they must ensure that the charity lives up to the highest possible standards and always acts in the best interests of its beneficiaries. Doing so increases its reputation and, in turn, the strength and sustainability of the organisation. Scandals, on the other hand, like Oxfam and Kid's Company damage not only those individual charities but the entire principle of 'charity' itself. In November 2019 the Charities Commission took the unusual step of writing to every charity in the UK to remind them of its rule on political campaigning, pointing out that endorsing political causes or parties can damage public trust in charities. For independent directors, impact means protecting and guarding that reputation and preserving that trust.

Reputation is also very important in terms of attracting staff and volunteers. Wages in the charity sector tend to be lower than elsewhere, and staff choose to work in this sector because they are looking for job satisfaction and the desire to make a difference rather than remuneration (which is not to say that pay is unimportant). Volunteers are also looking for a chance to make an impact and be involved with a cause they care about. Another form of impact, then, lies in attracting the best and most committed people. This means service quality will be high and this in turn means an increase in impact on the community.

Enthusiastic and eager though charity staff and volunteers may be, our research uncovered a worrying lack of professionalism in this sector. Independent directors can help close the gap and bring greater professionalism, either though acting as mentors and coaches to senior staff, or helping to establish and expand training programmes, bringing in outside providers of training, and even sharing their own experiences and wisdom with staff through formal (training programmes) and informal (away days, social events) interaction. Greater professionalism should lead to more efficient use of resources, better service quality and, once again, greater social impact.

Health

According to the King's Fund, the 2019/20 NHS budget stands at £139.3 billion, and will rise to £143.4 billion the following year.[3] For the directors of NHS Trusts, the challenge is to ensure that vast budget is spent wisely. Just as with charities, the more money that can be directed at front-line services, the greater the social impact will be in terms of improved health and wellbeing and greater longevity.

As the old saying goes, 'When you have your health, you have everything.' Health care services keep us alive and healthy, but the ultimate impact is much more than that. Health care enables all of us, including those affected by disabilities, to stay fit, to work, and to participate fully in society. That means we are more productive and have more to give back to the rest of our community, but it also means we are able to live our own dreams and be what we want to be. Physical and mental health are a pre-requisite for happiness.

One way in which independent directors can have impact is by helping boards to step back and take a more strategic picture. Such are the pressures on the NHS that, as our interviewees told us, many boards spend much of their time firefighting, trying to cope with day-to-day events. Again, they are being too reactive and not looking at bigger issues which have real potential to create efficiencies. One of these is supply chain management. As we saw earlier, better IT management and improvements in technology should enable to NHS to make efficiency savings in its supply chain of 10–20%, equivalent to over £1 billion. If that £1 billion could be re-directed to front-line services, that would make a tremendous difference and increase social impact.

More generally, the NHS needs to invest more in innovation. Partnership with technology companies could lead to improvements in diagnostic technology and also health education. Encouraging people to measure their own heart rate, blood pressure and so on has the potential to lead to both earlier diagnosis of medical conditions and the adoption of more healthy lifestyles. Here is a case where bringing in more independent directors from outside the health service could pay dividends. Directors with backgrounds in medical technology and/or contacts with technology companies could have impact by helping build those links and spreading better health.

The nature of demand for health care is changing over time. An ageing population means that complex illnesses such as dementia are on the increase, while poor diet and a more sedentary lifestyle have led to rises in obesity and Type 2 diabetes. Another role concerns preventive health; is the organisation working with other institutions to change lifestyles and make the population more healthy, thus reducing demand? Are issues like health education and diet being addressed? Has the organisation considered services such as MOTs (Ministry of Transport) for people over fifty, to spot signs of long-term illness early? Directors coming in from outside the health care system can use their personal networks to build links to other providers of services, for example in social prescribing. More generally, this is another example where directors can take a strategic approach and urge their organisations to become more proactive and put more resources into prevention which, as many studies have shown, is less costly and more effective than treating people once they are already ill.

Health care delivery is not solely the responsibility of the NHS, and many services are provided and/or funded in part by other agencies including local government. Care homes are a particularly complex example, with care home provision often contracted out to private providers, much of whom are badly funded and struggling to remain afloat financially. While executives have front-line responsibility for managing this system, independent directors can play an important supporting role in building and maintaining networks with other institutions and ensuring efficient and effective delivery of care.

Other issues need addressing too. There is at the moment a crisis in GP recruitment and also in recruitment of nurses, with numbers falling below the levels needed to provide an efficient service. Government initiatives in both areas have so far failed to make impact. Trust and CCG boards need to address this squarely and start taking measures of their own to improve recruitment. Trusts also need to become more commercial. With the NHS budget still falling short of what is needed to provide an efficient service, other sources of income need to be considered, such as philanthropic income (donations or bequests), or working with pharmaceutical companies to raise income by selling anonymised patient data for clinical trials. The last is bound to be controversial, but directors need to think about patients and communities and what they need.

Sport

Sport is entertainment, but it is much more than that. Some sporting events, like the 2012 Olympics or the big international football championships, can draw us together nationally, even if only for a brief space of time. The cricket World Cup held in Britain in 2019 got people who are not normally cricket fans suddenly talking about cricket. Sport even affects business; there is evidence that when national sporting teams win, stock markets experience a positive boost, while defeats will pull stock indices down.[4] At the same time, sport and exercise also help keep us fit and contribute powerfully to both physical and mental health. Without them, we would struggle to be healthy and happy.

But is sport having the impact that it could? A report in 2016 found UK sports fans spend over £20 billion a year on tickets, travel, merchandise, satellite broadcasting packages, live streaming and so on.[5] Yet only 15% of the population regularly take exercise, and obesity is on the rise, including among young people. The increase in people taking up sport that was predicted after the 2012 Olympics has largely failed to materialise. One way in which directors of sports organisation can have greater social impact is to increase participation. The headline news about England Hockey is the improved performance of the national teams, but the organisation has arguably had greater impact by encouraging more people—including more women—to take up the sport at an amateur level.

Widening the appeal of sport to attract more women, both as players and as fans, is another target independent directors can set for themselves. Thanks in part to increased funding, the success of the Lionesses and the Red Roses, England women's football and rugby teams respectively, is an example of how this can be done. During the last women's football world cup, England matches were pulling in more television viewers than matches featuring England's men's team (the former were on Freeview, the latter were on pay television) and both women's football and women's rugby have now established solid fan bases. Crucially, this is also leading to more women taking up both sports. Similarly, getting more disabled people into sport should be a major target. With role models like Tanni Grey-Thompson, Hannah Cockcroft, Kadeena Cox and Ellie Simmonds available, boards have plenty to work with. This is an area where massive impact could be generated in a comparatively short space of time.

Of course, one of the things that puts people off sports is corruption, be it the financial corruption that has dogged FIFA, doping in sports like cycling and athletics, or bullying, racism and sexual abuse such as has been revealed in the academies of professional football clubs. Many recent scandals were covered up for years because no one held the organisation to account. Financial problems like those at Bury Football Club also went undetected because no one at the top was aware of the problem until it was too late. By being alert for signs of malfeasance, independent directors can protect their organisation from scandal and loss of reputation. And, in terms of social impact, they can help protect those who play and officiate sports from harm.

And finally, of course, sport faces a real challenge in rebuilding after the pandemic. Loss of revenue from gate receipts, broadcast rights and sponsorships has driven even some large and powerful sporting organisations to the brink. Even more importantly, people's inability to watch or participate in sports during the lockdown may well have a detrimental impact on physical and mental health. Sport faces a social challenge as well as a financial one, and needs to get the nation—quite literally—back on its feet again.

Universities

The problems facing UK universities do not always make the headlines, but they are deep and real. There are 162 higher education institutions in the UK, with a turnover in 2016/17 of £33 billion, £14.4 billion of which was spent on teaching and research. These universities hosted 2.3 million students, including 1.7 million undergraduates.[6] What is less widely known is that the Office for Students, the government body that oversees universities has reported a weakening of financial performance across the sector, and around 20% of universities are now estimated to be in financial difficulties.

As a society we sometimes undervalue higher education, and successive governments had treated universities as little more than places where young people learn the skills they need to make them productive members of society; at best, they have been seen as incubators for a future generation of leaders. The directors and executives we spoke to in the universities sector argue that university is about much more than training. It expands horizons and broadens minds, gives people the chance to travel and interact with people from other cultures; and of course, universities are also vital sources of research and innovation, leading to ground-breaking new technologies like grapheme and new advances in AI. Universities impact on society in many ways, often without society being aware of it.

One of the biggest problems is the pension deficit, now estimated to be £6 billion. Attempts by universities to engage with this problem have been sporadic, half-hearted and—most importantly—too late. Independent directors at universities need to tackle this challenge head on. If not, the negative impact will be that some universities will have to downsize, merge or even fail. As noted in Chap. 2, some universities have also merged; more mergers or closures could be on the way.

More generally, a positive impact for universities would be to improve their financial performance all around. Generating more research income, bringing in more philanthropic donations, attracting more high-paying international students are all ways of improving university finances and tackling growing costs (and attracting international students is going to be particularly challenging in the next few years, with Brexit reducing numbers from Europe and post-pandemic travel restrictions likely to cut into numbers coming from Asia). Currently, most research does not recover more than 75% of costs on average, and this figure needs to improve. As with the NHS, bringing in directors from outside the sector with financial experience could allow boards to have much more impact. So too would more widespread use of the dual assurance model, which has been showing to improve governance and generate real impact.

The same is true of the digital revolution, which universities have so far failed to get to grips with. Boards need to recruit more directors with digital experience to enable them to have more impact. Finally, too, the introduction of tuition fees means there is a need to help students receive greater value for money. Digital has a role to play here, too, broadening the channels through which education is delivered and giving students a better, stronger experience. And, of course, after graduation those students will go out into society and make their own impact.

The problem, as we discussed in detail in part I, is that too many organisations are failing to meet their social goals. Failures and collapses make headlines, but just because an organisation has *not* failed or collapsed does not mean we should assume all is well. Many other organisations are struggling or underperforming, and all too often this happens because of poor governance. The independent directors, whatever their qualities as individuals, are not able to have impact.

Where does impact come from? Ultimately, as we saw in Chap. 3, it comes from independence. Directors with a truly independent mindset have the confidence to engage with their organisations and align their values with the culture of the organisation and the board. Once that engagement and alignment are achieved, directors can then start adding value. And once the entire board is working together harmoniously, directed and facilitated by the chair, that value adds up to impact.

In Chap. 4, we discussed the three roles of the independent director, monitoring, stewardship and resource provision. How well directors are able to carry out these roles determines how much impact they have. Can the independent directors scrutinise and challenge the actions of executives? Can they support the executives and help them do their job more effectively? Can they debate and discuss freely the directions in which the organisation should go, and what it needs to do to fulfil its mission? If the honest answer to all three questions is 'yes', then there is a good chance that there will be impact. If the answer to any of these questions is 'no' or 'maybe', then somewhere within the organisation there are barriers.

We have already discussed some of these barriers, including lack of knowledge and evidence, lack of confidence in the role, poor communication and interaction with other board members and the executive, and so on. One of the most important barriers, however, is lack of time spent on the job. Put bluntly, it is difficult for independent directors to have impact and help the organisation meet those social goals if they do not put in the hours.

Constraints on Independent Director Engagement

One important feature of the University of Exeter example is the greater frequency of full board meetings. Previously the board met four times annually, meaning directors spent a total of about twelve hours a year with each other. Common sense would suggest that it is quite difficult to make much impact on a large and complex organisation in twelve hours. The dual assurance model sees more frequent and much longer board meetings, as well as direct contact between independent directors and executives. The amount of contact time has increased by an order of magnitude.

Many independent directors spend relatively little time dealing with the issues their organisations face. However, we should not judge them too harshly. While corporate independent directors are usually well remunerated, this is not always the case elsewhere. Many charities do not pay directors at all, not even expenses. For those who are paid, the fees are often very modest. In effect, these independent directors are volunteers, giving up their own time to serve. That explains why many directors are older, and retired or semi-retired; they have more free time to devote to their duties. Younger people still in full-time work, without understanding employers who are willing to grant them flexibility, often struggle to find time to commit.

For whatever reason, many independent directors do not devote enough time to their job, and of course this constrains their ability to have impact. Board meetings are often infrequent and of short duration (again constrained by the time directors are available to attend meetings). Figure 8.2 shows the average frequency of board meetings across the four sectors we studied, and Fig. 8.3 shows the average duration of those meetings.

On average, then, charity boards and university councils are spending eighteen hours a year in board meetings; the figure for sports boards is eighteen and a half hours. Once again, it seems unlikely that real impact can be had in eighteen hours of meetings. The NHS has more and longer meetings, with boards meeting for an average of forty-six hours a year, but given what we have already seen about the overwhelming complexity of the task NHS boards and directors face, this is not surprising.

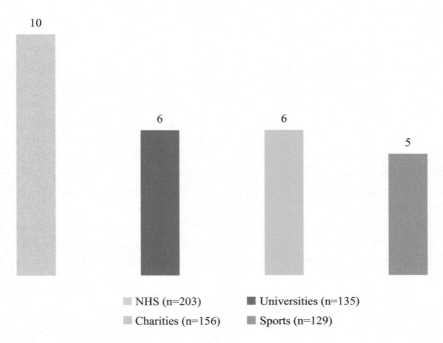

Fig. 8.2 Average number of board meetings per year

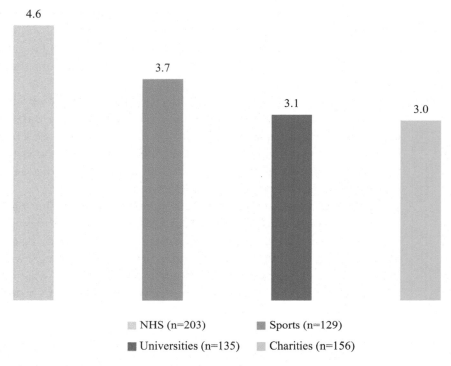

Fig. 8.3 Average duration of board meetings in hours

Of course these figures are averages, and the data shows considerable variations in practice. Some university councils and charity boards have ten or twelve meetings a year, and sometimes those meetings last for six hours or even more. There is, however, a long tail of organisations where meetings are fewer and shorter. More than 50% of sports organisations and more than 40% of charities meet four times a year or fewer, and more than 40% of charity board meetings last for two hours or less. So, depressingly, do more than 15% of university council meetings. It is pretty much impossible for boards to be effective in such a short space of time.

Equally important is the amount of time spent preparing for board meetings and, more generally, understanding the challenges that organisations face. It is not enough to simply show up at meetings; board papers must be read, questions asked, additional data gathered. Given that NHS Trusts tend to have more frequent board meetings, it is unsurprising that NHS directors spent more time preparing for meetings, but only 35% spent more than one day per month. Only 16% of directors of sports organisation and charities spent an equivalent amount of time; for universities, the figure drops to 13%.

With so little time spent on preparation, we must question how effective these board meetings are. We have already made the point that an independent mindset depends in part on knowing and understanding the issues. Do directors who spend only a few hours each month on preparing for meetings really understand what is going on at those meetings?

And even when we factor in other activities such as travel, meetings with executives or fellow directors outside of board meetings, site visits and so on, the amount of time many independent directors spend on their role is often quite low. Figure 8.4 shows the average number of days directors devote to their work in the four sectors we surveyed, but once again the figures mask a high proportion of people who spend very little time. In sports organisations, for example, 36% of directors spent less than half a day per month preparing for board meetings; when we asked how much time they spent understanding the challenges their organisations face, that figure jumped to 42%. Universities and charities were not far behind.

Again, we are not intending to criticise those directors who also have full-time jobs and parental responsibilities. Sandwiching director duties between

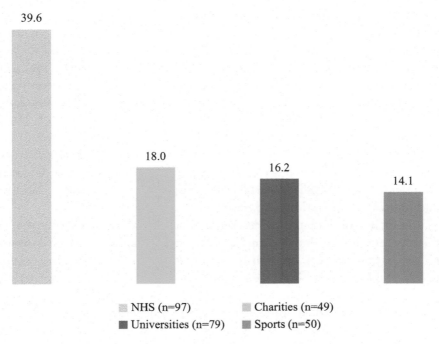

Fig. 8.4 Average number of days per year devoted by independent directors to the role

other commitments can be difficult. However, the truth needs to be faced; directors who do not devote enough time to their role will face difficulties in making an impact. International research confirms that lack of time spent on the role of independent director correlates with lack of effectiveness.[7] In far too many organisations, board meetings are infrequent and short. Too many directors do not spend enough time getting to grips with their duties and the needs of their organisations. This in turn means their impact is limited, which means poor governance, less effective decision-making and, potentially, management drift, higher levels of risk, loss of impact for stakeholders and, in some cases, failure and collapse.

Compliance and Stewardship

The twin duties of the independent director, compliance and stewardship, are demanding and require a commitment of time. Both are very necessary roles, and both require engagement with the organisation in order to control and guide it.

First and foremost, of course, independent directors have an impact in terms of how well the organisation is governed at a very basic level. Is it operating in a manner which is compliant with the law? Are staff following correct procedures, or are they doing things which could put the organisation or its stakeholders at risk? If so, then directors must take action. We saw in the example of Wells Fargo how directors received evidence of non-compliance and outright fraud but failed to take action, not just for a few months but for many years.

However, good governance is about more than just the prevention of wrongdoing. It also encourages best practice and ensures that executives and independent directors work together to see that the organisation is not just compliant but, if possible, ahead of the curve and seeking ways to innovate and improve its operations and service.

The dual assurance model described at the start of this chapter is a very good example of how compliance and stewardship blend together. Collaboration between executives and independent directors drives innovation and quality; working together, they become a kind of 'brains trust' or think-tank, generating ideas, testing them and working out how to take the organisation forward. At the same time, the independent directors are constantly scrutinising what the executives are doing and holding the latter to account. Rather than opposites, compliance and stewardship are simply two halves of the same coin.

The balance between them, between refereeing and coaching, will always be different depending on the organisation and the circumstances in which it finds itself. How compliance and engagement are exercised will change too, and may look very different at different times. During a crisis, tight control may be needed in order to ensure the organisation conforms to legal requirements and sticks to financial plans, while engagement might mean supporting the executive team with advice and encouragement. In periods of growth, engagement might mean helping to define the vision and lay out a strategy, while control could include scrutinising budgets and plans prepared by executives to ensure they are realistic and will meet agreed goals.

To have impact on the organisation, the independent director needs knowledge, evidence, the courage and confidence to speak and act, and an understanding of (a) what impact means at that time and place, and (b) how to make it. There is no recipe for impact, because impact itself varies with time and place. Making impact relies on a mindset, a way of thinking rooted in experience and, above all, a spirit of independence.

Directors need constantly to examine and re-examine themselves and their own role. The first question they need to ask themselves is, how and where can we add value? And once that is answered, the next question is, how can we ensure our ideas are accepted and implemented?

How Can the Independent Director Add Value?

Answering this question requires an ability to read the context and see what is required. What does the organisation need at this particular moment? Where is it underperforming or falling short of its goals? Are there opportunities it is failing to take advantage of? If so, how can one's knowledge and experience help them do so? Knowing how to add value is a matter of matching what one knows and can do with what the organisation needs. Ideally, a director should know at least part of the answer to this question before putting themselves forward for independent director posts in the first place. The rest will come with time and experience.

This is important, because if one cannot add value or make an impact, then one is not fulfilling our role as directors and probably should not be on the board in the first place. This is one of the questions chairs need to ask when evaluating directors, but in fact directors should also be asking this question about themselves as part of their own constant self-evaluation. The role is all about service, and if they are unable to serve effectively then they need to step aside and make way for someone else who can.

Where Should the Independent Director Add Value?

Experienced and knowledgeable directors will probably find it fairly easy to find ways of adding value. The question then becomes one of where and when to intervene. New directors will quickly learn that it is not possible to do everything, and certainly not everything at once. Not only are many organisations strapped for resources, they also lack the management capacity to take on projects that are not absolutely essential. Executives are pressed for time and have many priorities as they battle with the complexities of their own organisation and the external environment, and they will not thank directors who constantly bombard them with their own pet projects.

Independent directors need to learn what is possible and what is not, and also what is necessary and what is not, for the health of the organisation. They must pick the battles they think they can win. Priority projects, the ones like to get done, are ones that are (a) clearly of overwhelming importance in terms of the organisation's goals, including survival, (b) ones that will be relatively easy to implement or (c) ones that are cheap. Especially in the public sector and third sector, where finances have often been cut to the bone, frugal innovation is the order of the day. The trick is to find fixes that won't break the bank.

How Do Directors Get Their Ideas onto the Agenda? How Do They Influence and Engage Other Directors?

Having identified what needs to be done and where value can be added, the next task is to persuade other people to share the director's point of view. There may well be resistance to ideas; other directors will have projects of their own they want to see through, the executives may have other priorities and so on.

Directors need to be absolutely certain that they can convince other people of the importance of their project. It needs to be more than just a nice idea; they have to be able to demonstrate clearly the value it will create, for the organisation and for its stakeholders. They need to define the impact as clearly as possible so that other people can see it, hear it, imagine it. They also need to talk to the other people involved; the chair, the executives, other directors, other staff. Is what they are proposing important and worth doing? Is it a priority? Should it be?

The aim here is to build a coalition of support for ideas. If that support is strong enough, and if both the board and the executives can see a clear rationale, then the project can be put on the agenda and discussed.

How Do Directors Influence the Board and the Executive to Make Changes and Follow Them Through?

Even once the board approves our ideas, the task is still not done. Good ideas often fall by the wayside, and directors need to continue to champion their idea, monitor its progress and be sure it is carried out.

Here again we come back to the twin tracks of control and engagement. Rather than turning their backs and assuming the executives will get on with it, they need to continue to engage with them, working with them to give support and help overcome any problems that might arise while at the same time holding the executives to account and making sure the job gets done. Once again, the example of dual assurance shows us how this can work. Independent directors and executive leads collaborate to ensure that projects are carried through and that impact can be demonstrated and measured.

Conclusion

Boards do not exist simply to perpetuate the organisation, or themselves. Impact is their *raison d'etre*. Boards exist to ensure the organisation is well run and delivers the goods and services that stakeholders need. If the board does not do so, then it is failing in its purpose.

To deliver impact, directors need to carry out those twin duties of compliance and stewardship, control and engagement. Once again, these are the two faces of the same coin. Control ensures that organisations are run responsibly; engagement ensures that they are run well. Together, they drive the organisation forward so that it meets the needs of the people.

Notes

1. Philip Kotler, *Confronting Capitalism: Real Solutions for a Troubled Economic System*, New York: AMACOM, 2015.
2. https://www.gov.uk/government/publications/charity-register-statistics/recent-charity-register-statistics-charity-commission

3. https://www.kingsfund.org.uk/projects/nhs-in-a-nutshell/nhs-budget
4. Alex, Edmans, Diego Garcia and Oyvind Norli, (2007), Sports Sentiment and Stock Returns. *Journal of Finance 62*(4). Edmans et al. studied results across 39 countries, and found that defeats of international football teams led to an average share price fall of 0.5%. Lower but still substantial drops were found when studying rugby, cricket and basketball.
5. http://www.mynewsdesk.com/uk/post-office/pressreleases/uk-sports-fans-spent-over-ps20-billion-last-year-1438275
6. https://www.universitiesuk.ac.uk/facts-and-stats/data-and-analysis/Documents/patterns-and-trends-in-uk-higher-education-2018.pdf
7. For example, Vann Ees, H., Laan, G.V.D., and Postma, T.J.B.M., (2008). Effective Board Behavior in the Netherlands. *European Management Review*, 26: 84–93; Zona, F., and Zattoni, A. (2007). Beyond the black-box of demography: Board processes and task effectiveness in Italian firms. *Corporate Governance International Review*, 15(5):852–864; Wan, D., and Ong, C.H. (2005). Board structure, process and performance: evidence from publicly listed companies in Singapore, *Corporate Governance International Review*, 13(2): 277–290.

Part III

Making Boards More Effective

9

Selection, Training and Evaluation

We come now to the final section of the book, where we discuss the improvements and changes that need to be made in order to ensure that boards have better and stronger positive impact. Some of these recommendations concern boards themselves, specifically:

- Improved board composition and diversity
- Improved certification and training
- Improved board evaluation and performance appraisal

These are things that directors and boards need to consider, in our view as a matter of urgency. We make separate recommendations for policy makers in the following chapter.

The three recommendations given above are closely linked and can be seen as part of a greater question: how do we populate our boards with people who can make impact, and how do we build that culture of engaged stewardship? Part of the answer lies in the people who join boards and whether they are fit for the task, and that means who we recruit and how we recruit them are both issues that need attention. Then, once we have found the right people, we also need to pay more attention to training and development in order to promote independence and strengthen the culture. Finally, evaluation also plays an important role, enabling boards to see where and how they are making impact and what more needs to be done.

Boards need people who are intelligent and experienced, confident and strong-minded, who are good analysts and good relationship builders, and who have integrity and a strong moral compass and are not afraid to do what

© The Author(s) 2020
G. Brown et al., *The Independent Director in Society*,
https://doi.org/10.1007/978-3-030-51303-0_9

is right. They also need a good mix of people from diverse backgrounds. The question is, are they finding them?

The evidence suggests not. The Harvey Nash/London Business School board report for 2018/19 found that 29% of respondents were dissatisfied with the pool of talent they were offered for independent director appointments, most because of a lack of diversity.[1] Our research at Henley suggests that when searching for that talent, many organisations do not cast the net widely enough.

There is still a significant emphasis on personal networks such as those of the chairman and CEO as a source of potential candidates. About 43% of charities directors, 34% of directors of sports organisations, 33% of universities directors and 16.6% of NHS directors were recruited in this way. The recommended form of recruitment, a formal search and interview process guided by a nomination committee, is mostly used in universities (54.4%). The use of external recruitment or executive search agencies is most common in the NHS (48.5%) and sports (32%).

Compounding this, selection processes are often less than rigorous. In our research, 43% of charity directors, 17% of university directors and 14% of sports directors considered the selection processes in their organisations was 'not at all' intensive, and only 20% of university directors and 10% of charity directors consider the process 'very' intensive, contrasting with 40% for NHS and 32% for sports. ('Intensive' in this context means how thorough the selection process was, whether more than one interview was involved, how many other types of assessments were used and so on.)

The people we interviewed for the project confirmed that this attitude to recruitment tended to produce people who came from very similar backgrounds. Some believed this was a deliberate choice:

> I think there needs to be greater independence in the process. You may have a group of independent people who apply, but if it's the current board or the executives staff that are running the recruitment process, they'll end up selecting people who they think will give them a less challenging time.
> The chair and the executive staff treat [appointments to] the board as a reward. I call it 'disguised compliance'. It's basically ticking a box.

Another respondent commented on a lack of professionalism in the recruitment process and suggested that many boards and chairs are not sufficiently experienced at assessing CVs and conducting interviews.

A lot of interviewers aren't very good at interviewing, and a lot of interviewees actually aren't very good at being interviewed. Often the interviewee looks better if he or she has got a portfolio or whatever, and some people's CVs look more impressive than they really are because their company did well when they were there. And sometimes you can have somebody who it looks as if they were a bit of a disaster when they were in charge, but actually it could have been even worse had they not been there. Then it's important to say, well actually, that person is a stronger candidate because they know what it's like to be in tough times. Actually they have done better than the other person who simply got lucky. But so often it is the blind leading the blind; you have the chairman not used to interviewing and the candidate not used to being interviewed, and they miss things out.

As a result, we found that independent directors come from a very narrow range of profiles. Figure 9.1 shows that progress is being made towards a better balance of male and female independent directors, particularly in charities where parity has almost been achieved. However, the picture in Figs. 9.2 and 9.3 show that the overwhelming majority of directors are middle-aged white people, and Fig. 9.4 confirms that representation of people with disabilities on boards in charities and sports organisations remains very poor.

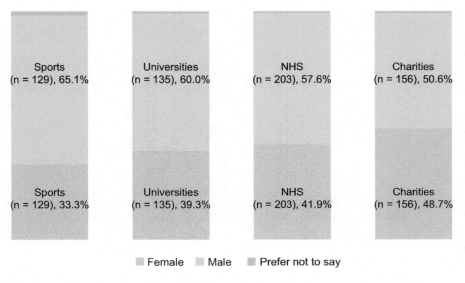

Sports (n = 129), 65.1%   Universities (n = 135), 60.0%   NHS (n = 203), 57.6%   Charities (n = 156), 50.6%

Sports (n = 129), 33.3%   Universities (n = 135), 39.3%   NHS (n = 203), 41.9%   Charities (n = 156), 48.7%

Female   Male   Prefer not to say

Fig. 9.1 Gender balance (as a percentage of respondents)

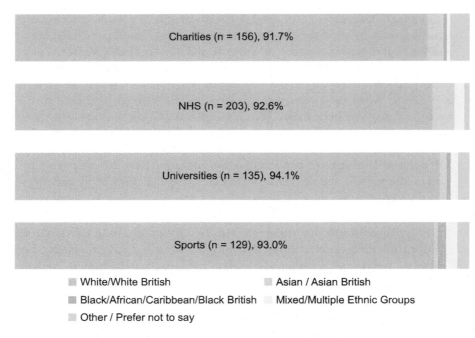

Fig. 9.2 Ethnic background (as a percentage of respondents)

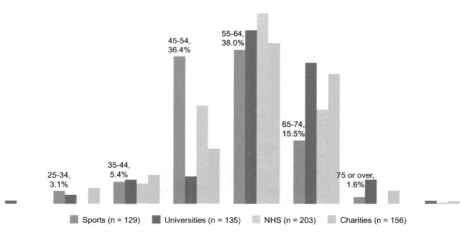

Fig. 9.3 Age range (as a percentage of respondents)

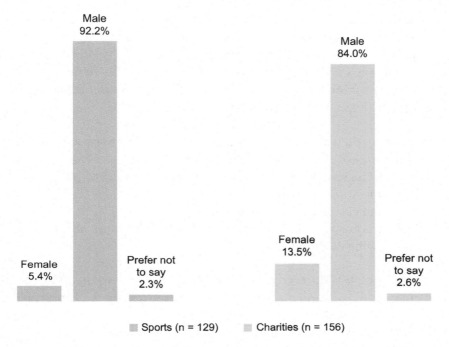

Fig. 9.4 Directors with a disability (as a percentage of respondents; charities and sports organisations only)

Diversity and Independence

Diversity and independence tend to go hand in hand. If directors look alike, act alike and think alike, then all we see is a row of nodding dogs around the boardroom table. Diversity means different mindsets, different worldviews and different ways of thinking, and out of these come challenge and stretch; the hallmarks of an independent director.

Diversity has its challenges, of course. There is another paradox here, in that we are expecting a group of people from different cultures and backgrounds to come together and work as one. That is not always easy. People from different milieus may have trouble understanding how and why other people think as they do. Chairing a diverse board requires patience and diplomacy. The results, however, are worth the effort.

There is much talk about diversity, but too often this is only lip service. We still don't fully understand what diversity is or why it is needed. The Harvey Nash/LBS report argues that 'diversity is a way of thinking, not a box-ticking exercise', and found increasing awareness of diversity as an issue on boards, but also suggests that companies are still failing to recruit a truly diverse range of independent directors. More than half of directors surveyed expressed concern about lack of diversity in the boardroom.[2]

There is a wealth of research on the subject of diversity, and a strong correlation between diversity and effectiveness. Most of this research comes to the same conclusions. An article in *Forbes* back in 2013 summed up the main reasons why diversity is important:

- The real world is diverse, something companies need to be sensitive to
- Healthy debate can lead to better decisions
- Diverse backgrounds mean diverse approaches to problem-solving
- Great ideas come from the disruption of the status quo
- Clients and customers are also diverse
- A variety of backgrounds can make the company more adaptable in an ever-changing environment[3]

Another article in the Harvard Law School Forum on Corporate Governance and Financial Regulation made the point that diversity sends a strong message to the outside world about the organisation's commitment and values, especially around issues like fairness, justice and commitment to equal opportunity: 'a diverse board signals that women's and minorities' perspectives are important to the organization, and that the organization is committed to inclusion not only in principle but also in practice.' The same article also made the point that 'corporations with a commitment to diversity have access to a wider pool of talent and a broader mix of leadership skills than corporations that lack such a commitment.'[4]

However, more recent research published in *Harvard Business Review* warned that board diversity can easily become a box-ticking exercise and that there is still not sufficient 'diversity of thought' on boards. In some cases this is because boards recruit from their own networks, or from restricted groups such as former CEOs and CFOs. The article quoted one director as saying: 'The problem is how boards get formed and how you fill vacancies. It might be unconscious bias. Sometimes, it's laziness. "Oh, we have an opening, who do we know?"' This was an American example, but our own research for this book found the same views being expressed in the UK.[5]

The answer, according to the article, is for boards to recruit on the basis of what they need rather than who they know. Boards should undertake an audit of gaps in their knowledge and recruit independent directors who can fill those gaps. The management search firm Russell Reynolds Associates conducted its own research on diversity and came up with a three-part model showing how the perspective of individual directors is shaped:

- Experiential attributes, such as functional experience, industry experience, accomplishments and education
- Demographic attributes, including gender, race, region and generational cohort
- Personal attributes, including personality, interests and values[6]

We all have these things in some combination, but that combination is different in every person, as their experience, origin and outlook on the world will differ to some degree. Like the *Harvard Business Review* authors, Russell Reynolds recommends mapping the perspectives of individuals, looking for areas of overlap and then also looking for gaps where certain perspectives may be lacking. Recruitment of new directors should then aim to fill those gaps.

To sum up, then, as well as ethnicity, gender, disability, age experience and cultural diversity we also need to consider 'diversity of thinking'. This depends in part but not entirely on background. We need boards who are collections of diverse individuals working together, debating, discussing, challenging and finally reaching consensus in the best interests of the organisation and society. These directors are truly independent, and by working in this way they are creating a real, vibrant and effective culture of engaged stewardship. The ultimate aim of recruitment, then, should be the creation of diverse boards that work together.

Individual organisations need to try harder to attract a diverse pool of potential recruits, but this issue needs broader attention too. Better public awareness of what boards and independent directors do would certainly encourage more people from different backgrounds to come forward. The media has a role to play here, as do industry associations and similar bodies in the public and third sectors. Remuneration for independent directors is also an option that should be considered, and we will come back to this in the next chapter.

Principles for Recruitment

All of the regulatory codes lay out principles for board composition and recruitment. The UK Corporate Governance Code, for example, lays down the following principles:

J. Appointments to the board should be subject to a formal, rigorous and transparent procedure, and an effective succession plan should be maintained for board and senior management. Both appointments and succession plans should be based on merit and objective criteria and, within this context, should promote diversity of gender, social and ethnic backgrounds, cognitive and personal strengths.

K. The board and its committees should have a combination of skills, experience and knowledge. Consideration should be given to the length of service of the board as a whole and membership regularly refreshed.[7]

Putting these principles into practice involves the following:

Appointments should be subject to a formal, rigorous and transparent process. This means moving away from personal networks and a box-ticking approach to appointments towards a more formal approach. Rigour in this context means casting the net widely and scrutinising candidates thoroughly. Transparency means making the process and selection criteria clear and ensuring a level playing field for all candidates, and also recording and documenting the process. The latter is particularly important in case an unsuccessful candidate should feel discriminated against and challenge the process.

All appointments should be based on merit and objective criteria. As noted the process needs to make the selection criteria clear. These will vary from organisation to organisation, and even from appointment to appointment; for example, if a charity is seeking to recruit a finance trustee it may be looking for a higher level of financial expertise than would be needed by an ordinary independent director. At the end of the process it should also be clear and demonstrable that the best candidate has been chosen. Anyone involved in the selection process who has a personal link to any candidate is obliged to declare a conflict of interest.

All appointments should promote diversity of gender, social and ethnic backgrounds, cognitive and personal strengths. Many countries have legal requirements in this respect; for example, the Equalities Act in the UK forbids discrimination on the basis of a number of protected characteristics. More generally, as noted above, boards should try to ensure that they have directors from diverse backgrounds who can give different points of view and draw on different skills and experience. The board and its committees should have the right combination of skills, experience and knowledge.

The board should appoint a nomination committee to lead the process. The nomination committee does not need to be a permanent standing committee, but can be assembled on an ad hoc basis when an appointment is needed. Executives and other directors can serve on nominations committees, but a majority of its members should be independent directors. An important point, reiterated in the Corporate Governance Code, is that the chair of the board should not chair the nominations committee when it is engaging in finding the chair's successor. This is to prevent bias, conscious or unconscious, on the behalf of the outgoing chair, which could lead them to seek a like-for-like successor, when in fact the organisation might need a new chair with a very different background and/or style of chairing.

All appointments should be subject to annual review/election. At the very least, independent directors should be evaluated on an annual basis (see Chap. 10), but the Corporate Governance Code recommends annual re-appointment or election. This gives chairs and boards an opportunity to review the appointment and determine whether any directors need to be replaced, for whatever reason. This process, however, needs to be handled with care. If directors feel they are likely to be replaced after just a year, they may feel uncertain about their futures and become demotivated. Care must also be taken not to dismiss long-serving directors simply because it is their turn to go, and they should rotate out. These long-serving directors are custodians of a great deal of organisational knowledge and memory, and removing them from post risks losing access to that memory.

Open advertising and/or external search consultants should be used. Again, the point here is to move away from networks towards a more wide-ranging and transparent process. Open advertising can be done through professional or industry sector trade journals, and on the internet; there are plenty of specialist websites where jobs can be advertised. Clear job descriptions should be provided, giving candidates an idea of what to expect. External search consultants can also be used to ensure a high quality of candidates is available. Search consultants can, in theory at least, sift out the least desirable candidates and send only the best forward for long-listing and short-listing. They can also design interviews and recommend best practices for assessment and selection.

If external search firms are used, this should be disclosed in the annual report and any relationships with board members disclosed. This again is in the interests of transparency so that everyone, including the unsuccessful candidates, can be satisfied that the process was a fair one and no undue influenced was exercised.

The annual report should include a report from the nominations committee which should explain the process used for appointments. The report can be used to communicate important information such as progress on board diversity.

Criteria for Selection

The purpose of the selection process is to find directors who will be truly independent, and who will fit into the existing culture of independence. The three critical areas to consider are personal qualities, sector expertise and diversity.

Personal qualities. These include independence of thought and action, personal integrity, knowledge about strategy, technical expertise and, if a chair is being appointed, experience of chairing. Intelligence, analytical ability and financial literacy are also important, as are communications and interpersonal skills, emotional intelligence, cultural flexibility, judgement and empathy. Professional and managerial competence and entrepreneurial skills round out the picture.

Sector expertise. It is important that the board has a requisite level of sector expertise and that the board as a whole is familiar with the sector. That said, as we have pointed out before, there is real value in having a few independent directors coming from outside the sector. However, these directors must be capable of getting to grips with the sector quickly and understand the challenges the organisation faces.

Building the board. That leads us once again to diversity, and the need for different perspectives and different points of view. It cannot be stressed too often that a good board is a diverse board. This means that selection criteria must be tailored to the needs of the board and any gaps in experience or skills or perspectives that need to be filled. This does not mean tokenism or box-ticking. Appointing diverse directors simply because they are diverse is bad practice. Appointing them because their diversity adds an extra dimension to the board should be the goal.

Training

Thus far we have talked a great deal about experience, but while experience is a necessary quality for independent directors, it is not always sufficient. It used to be said—inaccurately—that leaders are born and not made. We suggest turning that sentence on its head. Independent directors are made, not born. Very few people can step into the role of independent director without prior training or experience. Training can play a vital role in helping people to understand not just the role of a director, but also the true nature of independence and how to become part of a culture of engaged stewardship.

That last point is important, because training, like selection, can sometimes be a tick-box exercise; we have completed a training programme, therefore we are trained. The reality is quite different, and far too many training programmes are focused on getting people through to the end rather than imparting real knowledge or wisdom. The purpose any training programme should be to help the director become more independent and more engaged with the organisation and its culture. If it does not do these things, then the value of training will be limited, to say the least.

Experience has to start somewhere; for every independent director, there is a first-time appointment. Training can play an important role in helping the would-be director to prepare for that first appointment (and also, the presence of formal training programmes on a CV will reassure boards that they are appointing someone who takes the role seriously and has prepared for it).

But training is a journey, not a destination, and ongoing training is required if independent directors are to keep pace with change. When starting any new role, even if in a familiar sector and environment, an induction programme is essential to introduce the new director to their organisation, its structure and its culture. Ongoing training and refresher courses are important aids in keeping up to date on issues such as new legislation or new technology. And finally, personal development is an area that no independent director should neglect. Coaches, mentors and critical friends can help directors improve their soft skills and become more effective.

Appendix 1 gives a list of current formal training programmes for independent directors. While all these programmes have worthy objectives and deliver valuable training, they do not even begin to provide full coverage. Tens of thousands of independent directors across the country and hundreds of thousands more around the world have little or no access to training. Part of this is for reasons of cost. The programmes above are, rightly, expensive; they represent a gold standard in terms of service delivery. But few unpaid independent directors of charities or sports organisation or universities can afford to dip into their own pocket and pay these fees, and their cash-strapped organisations cannot afford the cost either.

In addition to cost, there is also time. These are residential programmes, and it is often difficult for directors to give up their own time to travel and attend lectures and workshops. We have already seen how many directors struggle to find time to prepare for and attend board meetings. Asking them to give up still more time is unlikely to work. Locally, smaller organisations such as specialist trainers and consultancy firms will offer training for directors on specific issues such as digital skills or GDPR, but the quality of these is variable, and they too are often costly and are usually delivered on the provider's premises, necessitating travel and an expenditure of time.

We need to think more creatively about how training is delivered. Training *in situ*, on the premises of the organisation, perhaps even in conjunction with board meetings, would be more convenient and less expensive. Online delivery of some kinds of training is also possible; all that is needed is content development—case studies, exercises and so on—and a delivery channel. Like any service, training needs to be delivered at a time and place that suits the customer, and at a cost they can afford. At the moment, high-quality training for independent directors is only available to those whose organisations have deep pockets.

Finally, we need also to develop more training programmes for full boards, not just independent directors. Boards need to learn from best practice in areas such as teamworking, communication, managing meetings and so on, and full board programmes would enable people to work together, develop skills and build stronger relationships. Again, full board training requires a commitment of time and money, but the rewards in terms of increased board cohesiveness should be worth the price.

Induction

Our research shows that most organisations provide board induction programmes, although there are significant gaps in the charities sector. Figure 9.5 shows the percentage of respondents who reported that their organisation has an induction programme.

However, there are induction programmes, and then there are induction programmes. Anecdotal evidence suggests the quality of these programmes is patchy. Some throw so much information at the new director that it is impossible to digest everything in a short period of time or ask informed questions. Others cover up weaknesses in the organisation and try to create a favourable impression in the mind of the new director; a favourable impression that may mask a rather less favourable reality. Even with the best of intentions, induction programmes don't always give a full picture of what the organisation does or how it functions, and it can take a long time—months, sometimes even years—for an independent director to completely get their feet under the table.

It is important that induction programmes present a realistic and comprehensive picture of the full organisation. This will give incoming directors a chance to hit the ground running and begin making impact as soon as possible. A good induction programme should include the following:

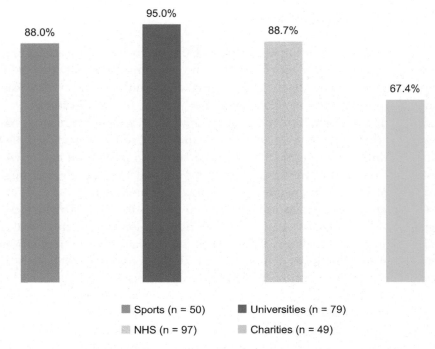

Fig. 9.5 Presence of induction programmes (as a percentage of respondents)

- An organogram or organisational flowchart that clearly explains how the organisation is structured and the flow of communications and identifies who has responsibility for key aspects of operations.
- A copy of the current business strategy, followed by a full strategic briefing by the CEO and/or the chair—preferably both, separately—to identify key business risks and opportunities.
- A full set of accounts, followed by a detailed briefing from the finance director to highlight any current or expected issues and problems, along with an assessment of whether current financial control systems are sufficiently robust.
- A meeting with the operations director or equivalent for briefing about how the organisation produces and delivers products/services, in order to get a full and complete understanding of the value chain
- Meetings with staff at various levels, unsupervised by other directors or CEO, to gauge organisational culture and get a look at any human problems
- A physical tour, not just of the offices but also field visits, with further chances to speak to staff and also to customers/clients/service users to gain an impression of how they perceive the organisation. The new director should be allowed to pick who they interview, to avoid the possibility of Potemkin villages.

Ongoing Sector Training

Refresher training is an important part of the independent director's career, keeping them up to date with changes in the environment. Ideally this should be provided or arranged by the organisation, and again, training in many cases should be provided to the whole board, not just one or two directors.

Sometimes, though, if resources or capacity are lacking, directors may have to arrange their own training. In this case they need to familiarise themselves with the kind of training they might need, and who provides it and at what cost. Here are some of the kinds of training that independent director might need to consider on an ongoing basis, annually or bi-annually.

Compliance training, ensuring the director is up to date with changes in legislation and regulations. Laws and regulations are constantly being tweaked, and procedures are updated. Compliance is important from a reputational perspective, and failures of compliance can also lead to the possibility of penalties, fines or even prosecution. GDPR is a good example of an area where directors needed—and in many organisations, still need—to make themselves familiar with changes in law.

Safeguarding training, designed to ensure that vulnerable people in the organisation's care are protected. Sports organisations, charities, universities and health care organisations all look after young people and/or people with special needs. It is important to update safeguard procedures, partly for compliance and partly to ensure best practice is followed. Under this heading we would also include training for Prevent, the government's programme for tackling radicalisation among young people.

Health and safety training, designed to protect employees and clients/customers while they are on the organisation's premises. As well as training in safety procedures, the current emphasis in health and safety training focuses on cultural change, for example the 'zero harm' programmes being introduced in heavy industries and construction.

Digital economy training, to bring directors up to date on new technologies and new skills in areas ranging from web design, data management, artificial intelligence and nanotechnology. The digital world is changing rapidly, so rapidly that many organisations have trouble keeping pace. Independent directors don't have to become digital experts—though it would help if the board has one or two directors who are—but they do need to be aware of what the technological trends are and where the threats and opportunities lie.

Mentoring and Coaching

As we said above, it is important that independent directors continue to stretch and challenge themselves, to make them more effective in their roles. Mentors, coaches and critical friends can all play an important role here. This is particularly true of the chair. As we noted in Chap. 7, chairs serve as useful sounding boards and critical friends for the CEO, but chairs also need someone to play that role for themselves. In business boards, the senior independent director (SID) often plays this role. SIDs are less common on public sector and third sector boards but sometimes another board member such as the vice-chair also serves as the chair's critical friend, formally or informally.

Mentoring and coaching by experienced senior professionals can be one of the most effective forms of personal development. It is important that the mentor or coach is someone who also has a strongly independent mindset and has experience of working a strong culture of engaged stewardship. That personal experience will provide many learning points, including how to deal with particularly challenging issues. In the course of their work, directors will have to deal with some hard issues: budget cuts and financial pressures, misbehaviour or malfeasance by members of staff, difficult relationships with other stakeholders or within the board itself and many others. All of these things can be sources of stress. The mentor or coach can also keep an eye on the directors they are working with and ensure that their own stress levels are being managed and their mental health is not suffering.

On a more positive note, mentors and coaches can provide a personal example for the independent director to follow. Hard though the job sometimes is, mentors and coaches show it can be done. By developing the mindset of independence and closer engagement with the organisation, mentors and coaches are strengthening independent directors and making them more perceptive and more resilient. This improvement in personal strength and mental toughness is an asset beyond price, to boards and to directors themselves.

As well as using personal contacts, there are also organisations that facilitate mentoring. European Women on Boards provides mentoring services for women executives and independent directors across Europe, and there are other similar organisations in America and India, helping women break through the glass ceiling.

Evaluation

Board evaluation is the means by which boards check on themselves and see how effective they are at doing their job of governance. As a recent article in *Harvard Business Review* put it, 'The purpose of the exercise is to ensure that boards are staffed and led appropriately, that board members are effective in fulfilling their obligations, and that reliable processes are in place to satisfy important oversight requirements.'[8] In other words, are the right people on the board, and are they doing the right things?

Board evaluation should be carried out annually. The New York Stock Exchange requires annual board evaluations for all member companies, and the UK Corporate Governance Code recommends annual evaluation as well. Most of the time, self-evaluation—board members look at themselves and each other and evaluate their own performance—is sufficient, but it is also recommended that every so often boards should also have an independent evaluation carried out by an external agency.

A number of consultancy firms offer board evaluation services, although there will be a fee for the service, and this could deter some smaller organisations and not-for-profits. In the UK, the National Audit Office offers free sample board evaluation questionnaires for public sector organisations, and also holds workshops on how to conduct evaluations.[9] ICSA, the Chartered Governance Institute, offers free advice to charities on how to design and carry out evaluations.[10]

Despite these resources, the evidence suggests that far too many companies are managing the evaluation process poorly, or simply not conducting evaluations at all. The Harvey Nash/London Business School 2018–2019 Alumni Report found that 46% of corporate boards had not completed an external evaluation in more than three years, and 31% had never conducted an external evaluation at all.[11] As a result, these boards are reliant almost entirely on their own opinion of themselves, and this is dangerous. If carried out honestly and truthfully, self-evaluation can be a very powerful tool for understanding board strengths and diagnosing weaknesses. Too often, board delude themselves into thinking that all is well when in fact it is not, and the self-evaluation exercise degenerates into a combination of self-congratulation and navel-gazing.

Certainly the authors of the *Harvard Business Review* article, 'How Boards Should Evaluate Their Own Performance', found this to be the case. Their study of American companies found that only 55% of companies that conduct board evaluations actually evaluate the performance of individual directors (which begs the question: what exactly *are* they evaluating?), and only 36% of respondents to their survey believe that their company does a good job of assessing the performance of directors.

The impact of this failure on board performance is considerable. According to the authors, 'Only around two-thirds (64%) strongly believe their board is open to new points of view, only half strongly believe their board leverages the skills of all board members, and less than half (46%) strongly believe their board tolerates dissent.' Nearly half believe that a cabal of board members dominates the agenda and has excessive influence over the chairman and CEO, and many believe that at least one fellow board member is not competent and should be removed.[12]

Other research comes to the same conclusions. According to the consultancy Spencer Stuart, 46% of directors believe that one of their fellow directors should be replaced; 20% believe that two or more should be replaced. They agree that board evaluation should be used to identify these underperforming or non-performing directors and ease them out, replacing them with people who can contribute more effectively.[13]

Our own research suggested that most organisations do carry out evaluations of some type, with the exception of charities. As Fig. 9.6 shows, fewer than half of charities carry out regular board evaluations.

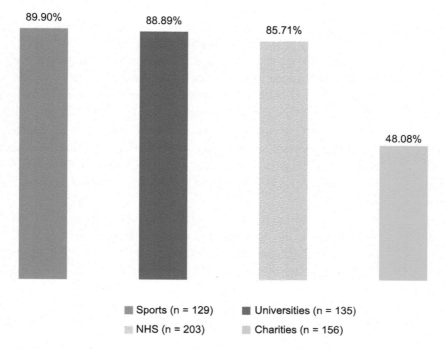

Fig. 9.6 Board carries out a regular formal performance evaluation (as a percentage of respondents)

Table 9.1   Frequency and type of board evaluation by sector

Type of evaluation	Annually (%)	2–3 years (%)	Less often (%)	Sectors (%)
Internal, through one-to-one discussions	87.1	9.5	3.5	Sports
External, through consultants	10.3	45.7	44.0	Sports
Internal, through one-to-one discussions	74.2	19.2	6.7	Universities
External, through consultants	5.8	59.2	35.0	Universities
Internal, through one-to-one discussions	88.6	7.4	4.0	NHS
External, through consultants	17.7	64.0	18.3	NHS
Internal, through one-to-one discussions	76.0	20.0	4.0	Charities
External, through consultants	5.3	40.0	56.5	Charities

Digging into the matter further, we find that some form of board evaluation does happen, but it seems that sometimes this is quite informal, a matter of one-to-one discussions (perhaps between the chair and individual directors), and that this usually does take place annually. External evaluations are less common; the NHS is most rigorous about carrying these out, but 44% of sports organisation, 35% of universities and 56% of charities have not carried out an external evaluation in more than three years. As we discussed in Chap. 7, there are discrepancies between sectors as well; as a reminder, Table 9.1 shows the responses from each sector we surveyed and how some are clearly more rigorous in their approach to evaluation than others.

Our research also looked at what issues are covered during board evaluations, We found that leadership dynamics of the board, quality of dialogue and debate, culture and climate in the boardroom, organisation of the board (i.e. agendas, length and frequency of meetings, etc.) and board composition tended to receive most attention across sectors. Issues such as degree of involvement and engagement, the role of committees and development needs of board members tend to receive less attention, and communication with key stakeholders and performance of individual board members receive least attention of all.

As Figure 9.6 shows, there are also variations across sector. Each sector clearly prioritise some issues over others, and it is interesting to see which issues receive *less* attention and to consider the implications. For example, NHS boards pay least attention to board composition, communication with key stakeholders, succession planning and individual members' performance feedback. Universities pay relatively less attention during board evaluations to communication with key stakeholders, succession planning and individual members' performance feedback. This suggests that these boards may be taking a task-oriented view and are more concerned with effectiveness in the short term. There is an obvious risk that board composition and the effectiveness of individual members may not be getting enough attention, which questions whether the board is functioning as well as it could. Does the board have the right people? Do they contribute as well as they should?

Sports organisations tend to downplay the role of committees, communication with key stakeholders and individual members' performance feedback, and charities pay relatively less attention to quality of dialogue and debate, communication with key stakeholders and individual members' performance feedback. A couple of points need to be made here. First, failure to prioritise communication with key stakeholders means that boards are running the risk of becoming isolated, and not really understanding how their stakeholders think and feel about them. If this is so, then how can the board know whether it is truly effective? Board evaluation deteriorates into an assessment of how well the board *thinks* it is doing, rather than the impact it is really having on stakeholders. We are back once again to navel-gazing.

Second, failure to appraise the performance of individual directors is a mistake. As the *Harvard Business Review* pointed out, without such an assessment, the board cannot know what its strengths and weaknesses are. It cannot tell with any certainty whether it is leveraging the skills of its directors—largely because it doesn't even know what those skills are—and on the opposite side of the coin, it cannot tell with any certainty which directors are underperforming and may need to be replaced.

Self-evaluation

The Chartered Governance Institute in the UK states that a board evaluation should:

- assess the balance of skills within the board
- identify attributes required for new appointments
- review practices and procedures to improve efficiency and effectiveness
- review practices and procedures of the board's decision-making processes
- recognise the board's outputs and achievements.

The consultants at Spencer Stuart argue that board evaluations should concentrate on improving board effectiveness in several key areas including leadership, continuous improvement, board culture and personal dynamics. They suggest six key questions that need to be addressed:

1. How effectively does the board engage with management on the company's strategy?
2. How healthy is the relationship between CEO and board?
3. What is the board succession plan?
4. What is the mechanism for providing individual director feedback?
5. What is the board culture and how well does it align with the strategy?
6. What processes are in place for engaging with shareholders/other stakeholders?

An evaluation checklist should include the following in some form:

- Overall impression of the board
- Organisation
- Committee organisation
- Board composition
- Board involvement and engagement
- Communication with stakeholders
- Looking forward
- Overall board effectiveness
- Effectiveness of the chair

As an example, the council of the University of Exeter's self-evaluation form is divided into six sections: role and performance of the council; development, selection, recruitment and induction; operating processes; culture of the board; council contribution to strategy and relationship with management; and the performance of the chair. Each section offers a number of statements, which respondents score on a scale from 1 to 7 with 1 meaning 'strongly disagree' and 7 meaning 'strongly agree'. Under 'role and performance of the council', the statements are as follows:

- Council has the required experience and expertise to support the university in achieving its strategy.
- Matters reserved for Council are appropriate and adequate
- Financial performance is reviewed incisively
- Quality of debate is high: facts are surfaced and confronted, executive team proposals are considered critically
- There is clarity over the role of the Senate within the university and its relationship with the Council

- Independent members understand the nature of the role well, including duties, obligations and responsibilities
- Council is always well prepared and has read the material provided ahead of Council meetings
- There is sufficient contribution from all members

In terms of self-evaluation, then, boards can either draw on existing templates or design their evaluation forms, perhaps by adapting another template. What is most important is that they carry out the exercise on a regular basis. It is all too easy for boards to believe that their members are independent, and that a culture of engaged stewardship exists. Evaluation, whether self-evaluation or carried out by an external agency, will show whether independence has been compromised and the culture has begun to erode.

Notes

1. 'The Uncomfortable Boardroom: The New Normal?' Harvey Nash/Alumni Board Report 2018/19.
2. Ibid.
3. https://www.forbes.com/sites/mikemyatt/2013/11/18/top-10-reasons-diversity-is-good-for-the-boardroom/#48daa00f1b90
4. https://corpgov.law.harvard.edu/2015/01/05/diversity-on-corporate-boards-how-much-difference-does-difference-make/
5. Stephanie J. Creary, Mary-Hunter Mcdonnell, Sakshi Ghai and Jared Scruggs, 'When and Why Diversity Improves Your Board's Performance', *Harvard Business Review*, 27 March 2019.
6. https://www.russellreynolds.com/insights/thought-leadership/different-is-better-why-diversity-matters-in-the-boardroom
7. UK Corporate Governance Code 2018.
8. David Larcker, Taylor Griffin, Brian Tayan and Stephen Miles, 'How Boards Should Evaluate Their Own Performance', *Harvard Business Review*, 1 March 2017, https://hbr.org/2017/03/how-boards-should-evaluate-their-own-performance
9. https://www.nao.org.uk/report/board-evaluation-questionnaire-4/
10. https://www.icsa.org.uk/knowledge/resources/board-evaluation-charity-sector
11. Harvey Nash 2018/19 Alumni Report.
12. Larcker et al. (2017).
13. Spencer Stuart, 'Beyond "Check the Box": Getting Real Value From Board Assessments', January 2018, https://www.spencerstuart.com/research-and-insight/beyond-check-the-box

10

Recommendations for Policy Makers

We come now to recommendations for policy makers. Too often, independent directors and boards face an uphill struggle in their quest to be more effective and make real impact. We have seen how in the NHS, in particular, governments have sometimes actively interfered with boards and made their work more difficult, compromising their independence. In many other cases boards of vitally important organisations have been left to sink or swim at times when government intervention might have been timely and helpful. If we are to resolve the crisis of governance and end the damaging stream of collapses and scandals, then boards and directors need more support from government and regulators if they are to fulfil their remit and make the kind of social impact we described in Chap. 8.

In particular, we believe that several actions need to be taken urgently. The first is to ensure that all independent directors are paid for their work. This may be controversial, but we argue that remunerating directors will solve several existing problems as well as providing fair compensation for the time they spend, or should spend, on their duties.

Our second recommendation is a thorough overhaul of governance structures across the board, in the private, public and third sectors. A culture of stewardship needs to be embedded in all of our institutions to ensure that they are run in the best interests of all their stakeholders. Additionally, it is high time that regulators were given more powers to act and intervene, to support boards that are struggling and to take corrective action in case where boards are actively failing.

In the specific case of the NHS, we argue that the organisation's broad mandate is putting too much stress on trusts and making their job very

© The Author(s) 2020
G. Brown et al., *The Independent Director in Society*,
https://doi.org/10.1007/978-3-030-51303-0_10

difficult, if not impossible to do. This issue needs further investigation, yet so far no government or political party seems prepared to confront it. Action is needed now.

And finally, we have alluded earlier in the book to the need for an inquiry into the coronavirus outbreak. We believe this inquiry should look into the lack of national preparedness for the coronavirus outbreak, not just in the health care sector but across business, government and the whole of society. It is too soon to say exactly how this inquiry should be formulated and what its detailed remit should be, but one thing is clear; we need to learn lessons so we can be better prepared for future pandemics, because this is very unlikely to be the last such event we see. This time, we were caught with our defences down. That must never happen again.

Payment for Directors

Some independent directors are paid, some are not. In the private sector virtually all board members are paid, and in large corporations they are often paid quite well. Elsewhere the picture is mixed. NHS Foundation Trusts pay their chairs and independent directors, fees ranging from £200 to £300 per day. Some universities pay chairs and directors, some pay only their chair, some do not offer payment at all. A recent report found that sixteen of the largest hundred charities paid their chairs and some of their independent directors, but the rest did not. Among smaller charities, payment is very rare indeed.[1]

The author of this report, Alison Wheaton, an experienced independent director and former member of the Higher Education Funding Council, suggests that universities have been reluctant to pay independent directors for several reasons:

- Universities are charities
- Governance is based on volunteerism
- It is an honour to act as a member of the council
- There is little difficulty in recruiting new members

The same of course applies to charities themselves and to sports bodies (many of which also have charitable status). Particularly in the UK there is a culture among charitable organisations which sees governance as a form of service, a higher level of volunteering. By agreeing to serve as an independent director, one is 'putting something back', using one's own experience and accumulated wisdom to serve the community in a selfless way. That is laudable, and those sentiments are to be encouraged. It *is* an honour to act as an independent director, and we really do need people who are willing to give time and share their skills and experience.

But there are downsides to the culture of volunteerism. In the first place, people must have spare time in which to volunteer. People who already work full-time jobs, parents of small children, carers and others will have only limited time to spare, and often are not free during the working day when most meetings are held. Some employers are willing to be flexible and give employees paid time off to attend meetings, but many insist that employees will either have to forfeit holiday time, or take unpaid leave. Parents and carers have to pay childminders or other carers to cover for them.

This has two consequences. First, many people who might be interested in serving on boards are deterred because of the cost. It is one thing to volunteer one's time, but quite another to dip into one's own pocket to subsidise that time. Not everyone can afford to do so. Second, this narrows the pool of potential recruits to those who *can* afford the time. Not just our research but study after study of the profiles of independent directors show they are overwhelmingly in their late fifties or older, retired people with comfortable incomes who have time to spare to devote to volunteer work.

We have already commented, several times, on the lack of diversity on boards. On too many boards, the independent directors all look like each other. There has been progress on greater representation by women on boards, but in other aspects of diversity—age, ethnicity, disability—progress has been glacially slow. Worse still, some boards become private clubs, where the member are all friends of each other or have some personal connection with the chair. These closed shops rarely make for good governance.

Alison Wheaton argues that remunerating directors will aid recruitment, increase board diversity and improve board effectiveness. We agree. Payment will broaden the talent pool by encouraging those who want to serve but, as things stand at present, cannot afford to do so. It will encourage people of more diverse backgrounds—young people, the disabled, those from socially disadvantaged backgrounds—to come forward. As well as improving the quality of decision-making by bringing more and different points of view, this measure will also mean that boards become more representative of the people they serve and not, as they are at the moment, overwhelmingly white and middle class.

Remuneration would need to be carefully handled. The fees paid need to be set at a level to recompense people appropriately for their time, but not so much as to risk compromising their independence, or encouraging people to apply for director posts simply for the money. Directors must not feel that being paid for their time constrains their independence or their ability to challenge and disagree with the executives.

We are aware that paying directors would of course increase administration costs. However, we believe that organisations would also benefit from having access to more high-quality directors, which would include governance and add value in many of the ways we have described in this book. The cost of paying directors would be a good investment. Some directors will not wish to be paid (indeed, our own study shows that many independent directors of charities see no reason to be paid). That is absolutely fine, and directors should be free to hand back their fees (as some in charities and universities already do). Care needs to be taken, however, that a rift does not develop within the board between directors who are paid and those who have refused their fees.

To sum up, remunerating independent directors would increase the number of potential candidates and encourage those who are not currently able to serve as directors to put their names forward. This would lead to greater diversity, better representation and better decision-making, and these things put together, we argue, would lead to greater impact. Loss of independence is a concern, but it can be addressed. We believe that government should look urgently at establishing a system of payment for all independent directors.

Overhaul of Governance Structures

Our second recommendation is that our current system of governance be reviewed in order to ensure that a culture of stewardship is thoroughly embedded in our private and public institutions, and that regulators be given the powers to challenge organisations where stewardship is perceived to be failing.

As we have already argued, stewardship means that directors and boards are acting as stewards of the organisation, taking account of the long-term best interests of stakeholders and not just the organisation itself. Pressure for the development of a culture of stewardship has been growing for some time, driven in part by social change and the growing environmental crisis. Companies, public bodies and charities are all under pressure to behave more responsibly. As a result, codes of stewardship have begun to proliferate and more than twenty countries have issued codes of stewardship, mostly for the private sector, over the past decade.

In order to be sure that they are living up to their responsibilities, stewards need to be accountable to someone. Most stewards leave this up to investors; as owners of share capital, they are given responsibility for 'guarding the guardians'. The problem with these codes, according to one report, is that they 'become a compliance document, where investors tick the boxes, rather than an exercise in real engagement between investors and the companies in which they invest'.[2] Other observers have cast doubt on whether investors have the ability, the knowledge or the time to provide the level of oversight and scrutiny that is required.

The same is true in the other sectors as well. Government is arguably the primary 'investor' in universities and the health service, but in practice its interventions tend to range from toxic interference to not-so-benign neglect. The Charities Commission exercise oversight of charities, but there is little in its activities that could be described as stewardship. Donors to charity, who might also be considered investors, will sometimes ask for reports to confirm that charitable objectives are being met, but many do not even take this step.

All this leads to a vacuum of oversight, where failing organisations and failing boards slide towards the edge of the precipice with no one there to stop their fall. The Financial Conduct Authority (FCA), which regulates the banking industry, does not intervene to prevent banks from failing (the decision to bail out several banks in 2008 was made by the government, not the FCA; instead, it picks up the pieces afterwards. The FCA has the power to discipline the directors of failed banks, but this is a case of closing the stable door after the horse has bolted. Similarly the Charities Commission will intervene to close down failed charities, but rarely if ever does it practice early intervention to help keep struggling charities afloat. The Office for Students, the government body that oversees universities, has no powers to intervene and support failing universities.

There are examples to the contrary. In education, Ofsted conducts frequent inspections of schools, usually unannounced, and has draconian powers to force improvements if they are seen to be needed, but its powers do not extend to higher or further education. In health care, the Care Quality Commission conducts regular inspections of health care facilities including GP practices and also social care organisations. It has the power to put failing organisations into special measures, or even close them down, and it has done so. However, on several occasions including at Basildon and Thurrock Hospital in 2009, Winterbourne View Hospital in 2011 and Furness General Hospital in 2012, the CQC was accused of failing to notice deficiencies and/or ignoring the views of whistle-blowers. It would seem that here again, someone needs to watch over the regulator.

In general, though, despite the scandals that have arisen and continue to arise, the position adopted by government and regulators is either (a) further regulation and compliance procedures or (b) a renewed focus on the role of the director with codes of conduct spelling out in every more exhaustive detail what director should do. Investigation has clearly shown that neither of these is effective at promoting good governance. Board failure comes from a lack of oversight and stewardship and a reluctance to exercise personal responsibility on the part of the independent directors and the board as a whole.

This is the issue that policy makers and regulators need to confront. Why is stewardship not promoted or highlighted as a fundamental part of what boards do? Why is it not seen as a critical part of the director development? Certainly stewardship cannot be legislated for, but the vital nature of its role needs to be emphasised. The board is responsible for compliance, but stewardship is about much, much more. Thus far, discussions of stewardship have been mostly just words. But telling directors they should be stewards and enshrining this in a code of conduct is far different from actually explaining what stewardship is and embedding it in board and corporate culture. That is what needs to be done now.

To date, enabling and enforcing a culture of stewardship has been left to investors, in whatever form they come. This is not working. Investors are clearly failing to engage with the organisations they invest in and scrutinise their activities. Far from ensuring that the boards these organisations are acting as good stewards, they are failing to behave like stewards themselves. This is not entirely the fault of investors themselves; they cannot be everywhere at once, paying attention to everything. This is an area where government needs to intervene, on several levels.

First, as we have already argued, more and better training needs to be provided for independent directors, and the concepts of stewardship and engagement need to be embedded in that training. A thorough review of training provision for independent directors in all types of organisations needs to be carried out as a matter of urgency, and support for new training programmes is required. These training programmes must have the concept of stewardship at their heart, and aim to embed this in boards and directors across every sector. We recommend that as a first step, the Department of Trade and Industry should convene a working group including the CBI and the Institute of Directors to consider a professional qualification for independent directors.

Second, regulators need to be given more powers to inspect and intervene across a much wider range of organisations. The vacuum of oversight needs to be filled. It is painful to contemplate putting a university, a charity or a bank into special measures, but how much damage is caused when they fail? Far more than money is involved here. Jobs are lost, careers are cut short or wrecked, lives are blighted, the economy suffers, society as a whole feels the impact. In some cases, where ill or vulnerable people are involved, the end result can be harm or even death.

For this reason, we need regulators—who are themselves fully aware of their own responsibilities and capable of acting as good stewards—who can intervene when needed and get organisations back on track before they fail. There will be cost, to government, to society, to all of us, but the cost of failure is far greater. We need to turn the culture of governance around, and we need to do it now, before any more damage is done. Independent directors are one of society's greatest assets. They need protection, encouragement and support. If they receive it, then we will all feel the impact, and our lives will be better for it. If we let them fail, then at the end of the day it is us that foot the bill.

We also recommend that NHS mandate needs to re-examined and over-hauled. Nowhere is the crisis of governance more strongly apparent than here. The first mandate between the government and the NHS was issued in 2012, and every year since it has failed to be met. Our own research showed that 20% of NHS directors now do not believe it *can* be met. Unfortunately, no government or political party has been prepared to deal with this steadily worsening problem. Given the complexity of the issue, which involves not just government and the NHS but also local councils, the private sector, the voluntary sector, staff, carers and patients themselves, we believe a Royal Commission should be established to look into this as a matter of urgency.

Independent directors are society's unsung heroes. They have no public image or face, and there is widespread ignorance about what they actually do. They rarely receive credit when things go well, although society is all too happy to blame them—often with good reason—when they do not. Many are underpaid, or receive no pay at all for the service they give. Yet without them, the vitally important institutions that serve society and bring benefit to us all would collapse. We need to recognise the role that they play, and we need to give them the support and assistance they deserve so they can carry out their role more fully. Investing in support for independent directors will be repaid many times over, in the forms of more efficient and effective institutions, contributions to tax income, a prospering economy and a healthy, happy society. The time to begin reforms and end the crisis of governance is now.

Notes

1. Alison Wheaton, 'Payment for University Governors? A Discussion Paper', Higher Education Policy Institute report 118, 2019, https://www.hepi.ac.uk/wp-content/uploads/2019/07/HEPI-Payment-for-university-governors-A-discussion-paper-Report-118-11_07_19.pdf.
2. Didier Cossin, Boon Hwee Ong and Sophie Coughlin, 'Stewardship: Fostering Responsible Long-Term Wealth Creation', IMD, 2015.

Appendices

A1: Board and director demographics
A2: Board operation and director time
A3: Director recruitment, selection, induction, remuneration and evaluation
A4: Board challenges
A5: Board and director behaviour
A6: List of interviewees
A7: Desk review references by sector
A8: List of case studies and contributors
A9: Training courses for independent directors

Methodological Note

This book is the result of a two-year research programme conducted by a team of researchers at Henley Business School.

The team has conducted in-depth qualitative interviews with fifty key opinion leaders (e.g. chairs, vice-chancellors, CEOs, independent directors) across the NHS, charity, sports and university sectors. The interviews explored board governance across these sectors and focused independence and the independent director role. It asked one key question: how can independence be gained, sustained and lost? The ensuing report identified a number of themes and insights that subsequently formed the base for the survey design. The survey was tested with directors both face to face and online to eliminate ambiguities, duplications and clarify questions.

© The Author(s) 2020
G. Brown et al., *The Independent Director in Society*,
https://doi.org/10.1007/978-3-030-51303-0

After this process the length of the survey was substantially reduced. The final version of the survey was also discussed with key stakeholders in each sector who have made some final suggestions. These include:

- Health sector: NHS Providers, NHS Confederation and NHS Improvements;
- University sector: Committee of University Chairs (CUC) and Association of Heads of University Administration (AHUA).
- Charity sector: The Association of Chairs (AoC) and the NCVO (National Council of Voluntary Organisations).
- Sports sector: Sport England (SE)

With the support of these organisations, the survey was sent to be completed by directors in each of these sectors. The survey returned 623 completed responses from across the 4 sectors including: NHS ($n = 203$), university ($n = 135$), sports ($n = 129$) and charities ($n = 156$). In addition, the research team has undertaken a desk review of latest literature on each of the sectors, as well as conducting case studies in each of the four sectors under scrutiny.

There follows a Table of Correspondence which shows where the issues relating to each figure or table are discussed in the text of the book.

Table of Correspondence

Table number	Table name	Corresponding chapters
Table 1	Respondents by organisation size	Chapter 1, Chapter 9
Table 2	Respondents by role/sector	Chapter 1
Figure 1	Gender balance	Chapter 1, Chapter 9
Figure 2	Ethnic background	Chapter 1, Chapter 9
Figure 3	Directors with a disability	Chapter 1, Chapter 9
Figure 4	Directors age range	Chapter 1, Chapter 9
Figure 5	Board size	Chapter 1, Chapter 4
Figure 6	Number of independent directors on the board	Chapter 1, Chapter 4
Figure 7	Non-executive director tenure	Chapter 4, Chapter 9
Figure 8	Number of board meetings per year	Chapter 8
Figure 9	Average duration of board meetings	Chapter 8
Figure 10	Strategy-only board meetings	Chapter 8
Figure 11	Number of additional directorships of directors	Chapter 1, Chapter 4
Figure 12	Average number of days/year directors devote to role	Chapter 4, Chapter 5, Chapter 8
Figure 13	Average time/month spent on strategic direction	Chapter 4, Chapter 5, Chapter 8

(continued)

(continued)

Table number	Table name	Corresponding chapters
Figure 14	Average time/month spent on monitoring performance	Chapter 4, Chapter 5, Chapter 8
Figure 15	Average time/month spent on succession planning	Chapter 4, Chapter 5, Chapter 8
Figure 16	Average time/month spent on communicating with key stakeholders	Chapter 4, Chapter 5, Chapter 8
Figure 17	Average time/month spent on risk management	Chapter 4, Chapter 5, Chapter 8
Figure 18	Average time/month spent on auditing	Chapter 4, Chapter 5, Chapter 8
Figure 19	Average time/month spent on governance and compliance	Chapter 4, Chapter 5, Chapter 8
Figure 20	Average time/month spent on preparing for board meetings	Chapter 4, Chapter 5, Chapter 8
Figure 21	Average time/month spent on preparing for committee meetings	Chapter 4, Chapter 5, Chapter 8
Figure 22	Average time/month spent on understanding challenges faced	Chapter 4, Chapter 5, Chapter 8
Table 3	Director use of data and evidence	Chapter 5, Chapter 6
Figure 23	Directors recruitment sources	Chapter 9
Figure 24	Directors process selection intensity	Chapter 9
Figure 25	Directors induction	Chapter 9
Figure 26	Should directors be appropriately remunerated for the role they play	Chapter 10
Figure 27	Board undergoes a regular performance evaluation	Chapter 9
Table 4	Frequency and type of board evaluation by sector	Chapter 9
Table 5	Items covered by board evaluation per sector	Chapter 9
Figure 28	Board competency to handle challenges faced	Chapter 5, Chapter 6, Chapter 8
Figure 29	Ability of directors to articulate a different perspective	Chapter 4, Chapter 8
Figure 30	Ability of directors to contribute to a shared purpose at the board	Chapter 4, Chapter 8
Figure 31a	A culture of independence	Chapter 4
Figure 31b	A culture of independence (constraints)	Chapter 4
Figure 32a	Monitoring role effectiveness	Chapter 4
Figure 32b	Stewardship and resource provisioning role effectiveness	Chapter 4
Table 6	Chair qualities	Chapter 7
Table 7	Chair role and practice	Chapter 7
Table 8	Non-executive director qualities	Chapter 4, Chapter 5
Table 9	Board qualities	Chapter 8
Figure 33	Ability of board to handle awkward/sensitive discussions	Chapter 7, Chapter 8
Table 10	Consequences if awkward/sensitive discussions effectively handled	Chapter 7, Chapter 8

Appendix A (A1): Organisation, Board and Director Demographics

Table 1 Respondents by organisation size/sector (in %)

Organisation Size	Sports (*n* = 129)	Universities (*n* = 135)	NHS (*n* = 203)	Charities (*n* = 156)
Up to 499 staff	98	17	1	92
500–999 staff	2	14	3	2
1000–2499 staff	0	21	18	2
2500–4999 staff	0	35	43	4
5000–9999 staff	0	7	31	0
10,000 staff or more	0	6	4	0

Table 2 Respondents by role/sector (in %)

Roles	Sports (*n* = 129)	Universities (*n* = 135)	NHS (*n* = 203)	Charities (*n* = 156)
Chairman/Chairwoman	43.2	26	28.1	57
Non-executive Director/ Trustee /Lay Member	39	58	48	25.3
Chief executive	2.3	0	3.5	6.4
Other executives	5.4	4	13	1.3
Others	10.1	12	7.4	10

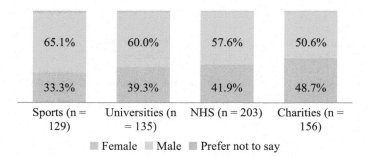

Fig. 1 Gender balance (as a percentage of respondents)

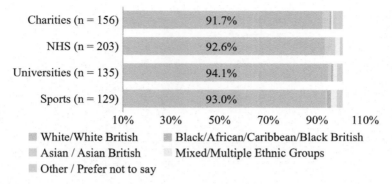

Fig. 2 Ethnic background (as a percentage of respondents)

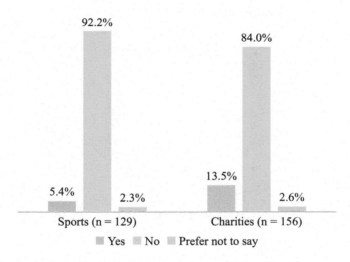

Fig. 3 Directors with a disability (as a percentage of respondents)

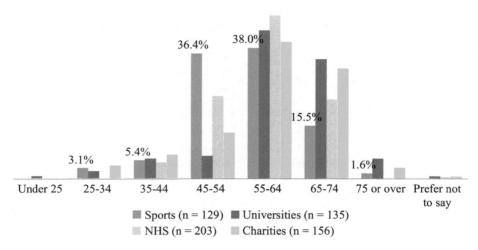

Fig. 4 Directors age range (as a percentage of respondents)

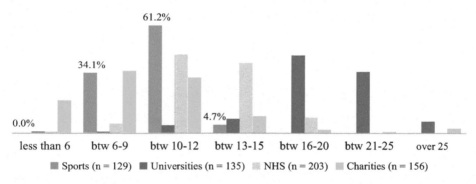

Fig. 5 Board size (as a percentage of respondents)

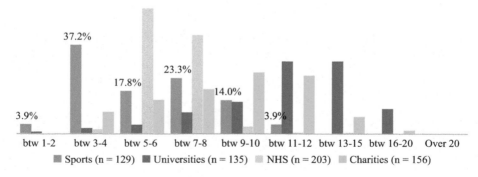

Fig. 6 No. of Independent Directors on the board (as a percentage of respondents)

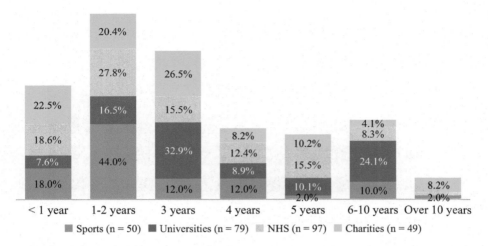

Fig. 7 Non-executive director tenure (as a percentage of respondents)

Appendix B (A2): Board Operation and Non-Executive Director Time

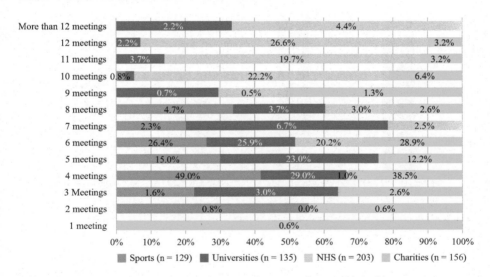

Fig. 8 No. of board meetings/year (as a percentage of respondents)

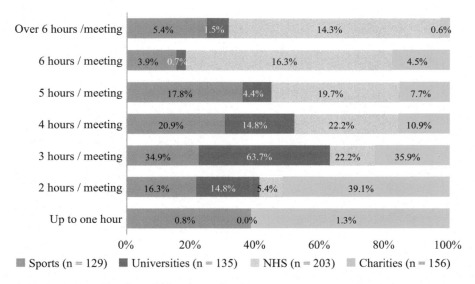

Fig. 9 Average duration of board meetings

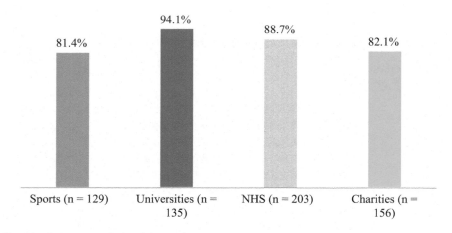

Fig. 10 Strategy-only board meetings

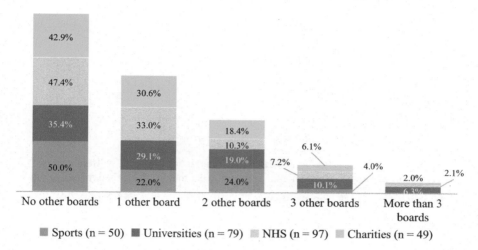

Fig. 11   No. of additional directorships of NEDs

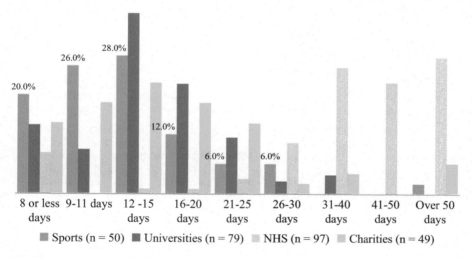

Fig. 12   Average no. of days/year NEDs devote to the role

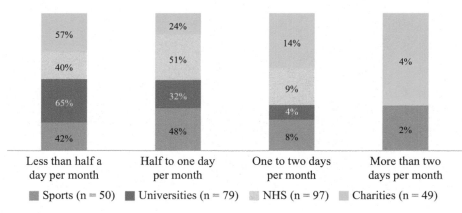

Fig. 13 Average time/month spent on **Strategic Direction**

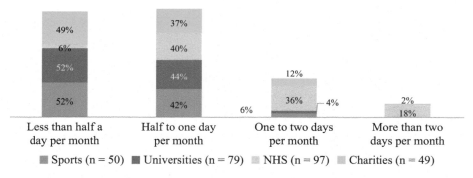

Fig. 14 Average time/month spent on **Monitoring Performance**

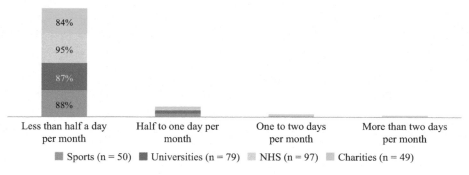

Fig. 15 Average time/month spent on **Succession Planning**

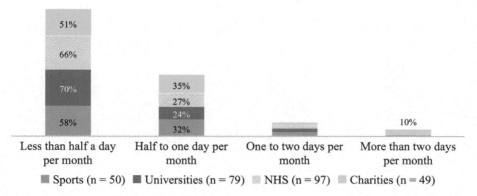

Fig. 16   Average time/month spent on **Communicating with Key Stakeholders**

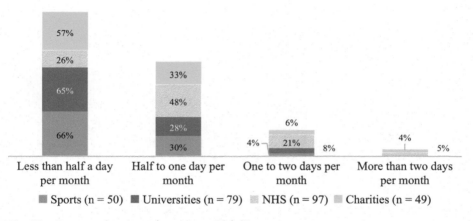

Fig. 17   Average time/month spent on **Risk Management**

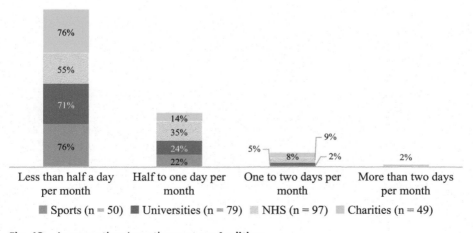

Fig. 18   Average time/month spent on **Auditing**

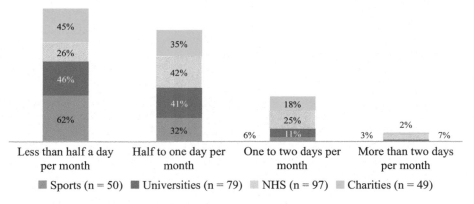

Fig. 19   Average time/month spent on **Governance Compliance**

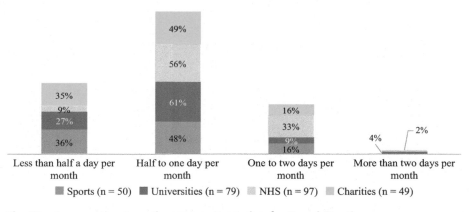

Fig. 20   Average time/month spent on **Preparing for Board Meetings**

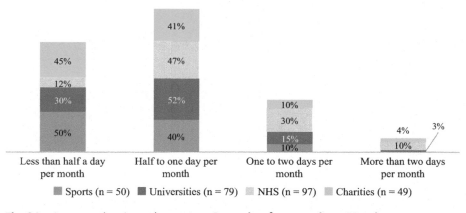

Fig. 21   Average time/month spent on **Preparing for committee Meetings**

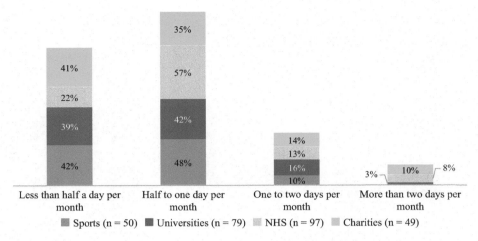

41%
22%
39%
42%

35%
57%
42%
48%

14%
13%
16%
10%

3% — 10% — 8%

Less than half a day per month   Half to one day per month   One to two days per month   More than two days per month

■ Sports (n = 50)   ■ Universities (n = 79)   ▨ NHS (n = 97)   ▨ Charities (n = 49)

Fig. 22 Average time/month spent on **Understanding the Challenges Faced**

Table 3 NED use of data and evidence (% agree/strongly agree)

Use of data/evidence	Sports (n = 50)	Universities (n = 79)	NHS (n = 97)	Charities (n = 49)
To familiarise myself with the charity I often visit operations and talk to other layers of management	56	58	78	76
To ensure the quality of information is credible, other directors/managers or an external expert/advisor is often brought in to present to the Board	78	71	78	69
I have an effective dialogue with the other directors, to cross-check information and ensure that the data/evidence is robust	90	87	95	92
I work with the other directors to ensure that appropriate action is taken at Board level based on available data/evidence	92	85	94	83
I believe I am given all the data/ information necessary for the Board agenda to play an effective role during meetings	86	75	84	78
The chief executive is open and transparent in ensuring that all relevant information is shared/made readily available	90	87	93	78
I can effectively analyse data/ information by focusing on the key messages	92	82	86	86

Appendix C (A3): Director Recruitment, Selection, Induction, Remuneration and Evaluation

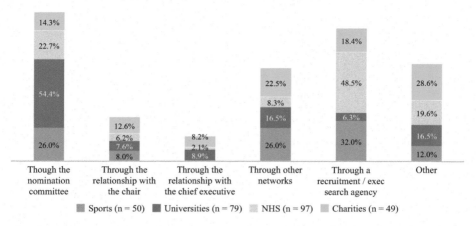

Fig. 23   NEDs/trustees recruitment sources

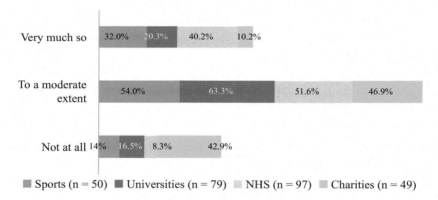

Fig. 24   NEDs/trustees selection process intensity

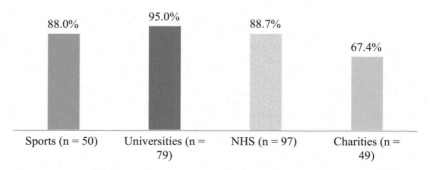

Fig. 25   NEDs/trustees induction (% of respondents with induction process)

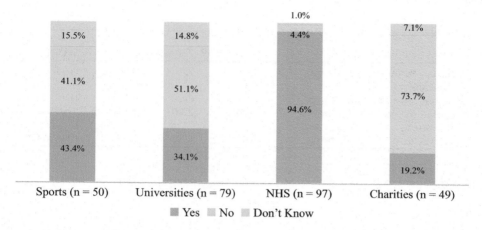

Fig. 26 Should NEDs be appropriately remunerated for the role they play?

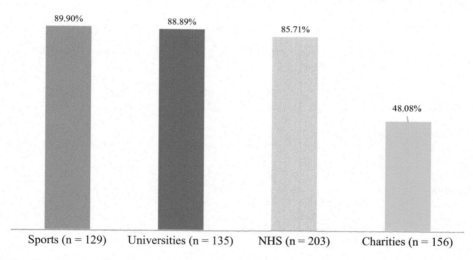

Fig. 27 Board undergoes a regular formal performance evaluation (% of respondents)

Table 4 Frequency and type of board evaluation by sector (% of respondents)

Type of evaluation	Annually	2–3 years	Less often	Sectors
Internal, through one-to-one discussions	87.1	9.5	3.5	Sports
External, through consultants	10.3	45.7	44.0	Sports
Internal, through one-to-one discussions	74.2	19.2	6.7	Universities
External, through consultants	5.8	59.2	35.0	Universities

(*continued*)

Table 4   (continued)

Type of evaluation	Annually	2–3 years	Less often	Sectors
Internal, through one-to-one discussions	88.6	7.4	4.0	NHS
External, through consultants	17.7	64.0	18.3	NHS
Internal, through one-to-one discussions	76.0	20.0	4.0	Charities
External, through consultants	5.3	40.0	56.5	Charities

Table 5 Items covered during board evaluations per sector (% of respondents)

Topics	Sports (n = 116)	Universities (n = 120)	NHS (n = 174)	Charities (n = 75)
Leadership dynamics of the board	86.10	86.44	89.08	80.82
Quality of dialogue/debate	80	82	75	68
Culture and climate in the Boardroom	75.65	79.66	78.74	78.08
Organisation of the Board (e.g. agendas, length and frequency of meetings)	84.35	91.53	86.78	84.93
The role of committees	66.96	80.51	83.91	73.97
Board composition (e.g. size, balance, degree of independence)	80	82	68	77
Degree of Board involvement and engagement	70.43	69.49	68.97	80.82
Communication with key stakeholders	60	42	49	41
Succession planning (executive and independent directors)	68.70	62.71	54.60	82.19
Development needs of board members	66.10	72.88	75.86	79.45
Performance of its individual members (e.g. 360 feedback)	55.65	44.07	58.62	61.64

Appendix D (A4): Board Challenges

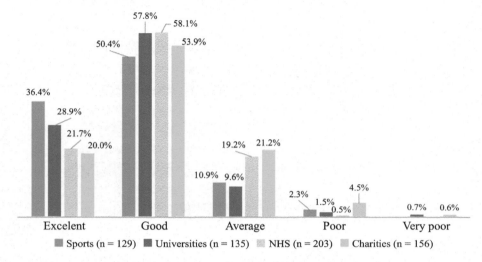

Fig. 28 Board competency to handle challenges faced (% of respondents)

Appendix E (A5): Board and Director Qualities and Behaviour

Independence and Culture of Independence

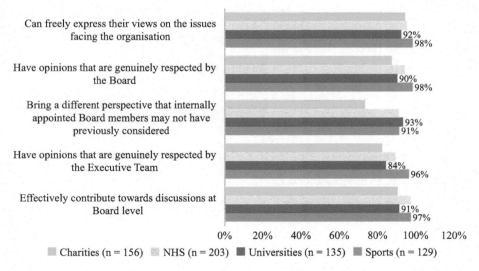

Fig. 29 Ability of INED to articulate a different perspective (% agree/strongly agree)

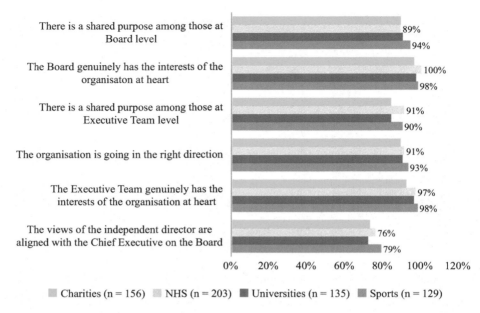

Fig. 30 Ability of INED to contribute to a shared purpose at the board (% agree/strongly agree)

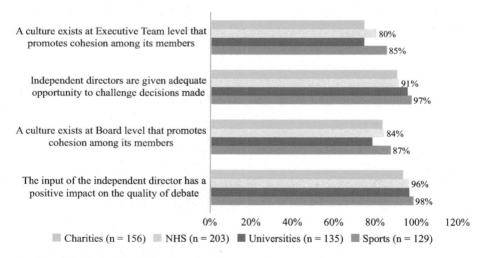

Fig. 31a Culture of independence

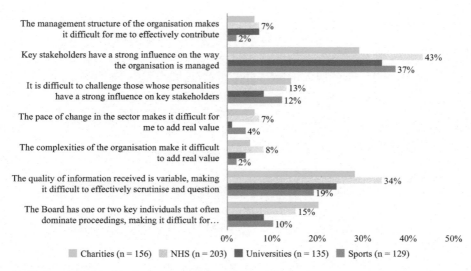

Fig. 31b   Culture of independence (constraints to)

Non-Executive Director Role Effectiveness

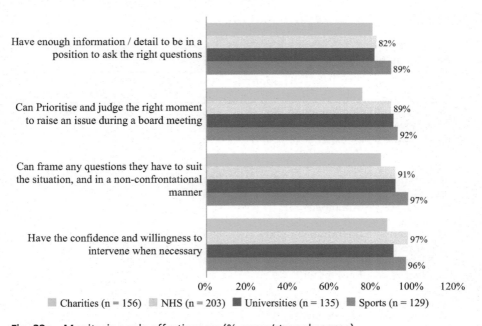

Fig. 32a   Monitoring role effectiveness (% agree/strongly agree)

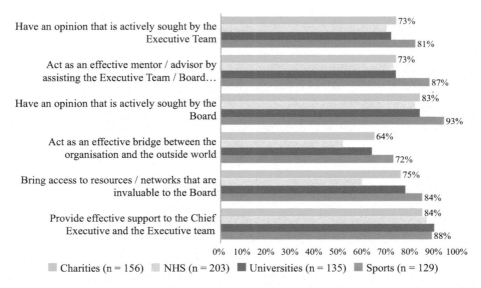

Fig. 32b Stewardship and resource provision role effectiveness (% agree/ strongly agree)

Chairperson Qualities, Role and Practice

Table 6 Chair qualities (% agree/strongly agree)

Chair qualities	Sports (n = 129)	Universities (n = 135)	NHS (n = 203)	Charities (n = 156)
Is skilful at facilitating debate at Board level	93	85	88	88
Effectively uses their experience from a similar role in another charity	86	90	82	65
Is a strategic thinker	95	84	84	86
Takes a long-term view of what it takes to be a sustainable organisation	95	88	86	90
Has experience in operating in a similar role in another sector	80	73	74	69
Leads by example	94	84	90	91
Has effective relationships with others	92	89	91	94
Demonstrates high moral values	98	90	96	95
Has values that are aligned with those of the organisation	97	89	96	98
Uses an evidence-based approach	92	84	84	83

(continued)

Table 6   (continued)

Chair qualities	Sports (*n* = 129)	Universities (*n* = 135)	NHS (*n* = 203)	Charities (*n* = 156)
Has an in-depth understanding of the organisation	91	84	86	92
Is effective in their role	94	84	89	88
Total average	**92**	**85**	**87**	**87**

Table 7   Chair role and practice (% agree/strongly agree)

Chair role and practice	Sports (*n* = 129)	Universities (*n* = 135)	NHS (*n* = 203)	Charities (*n* = 156)
Creates a shared purpose, values and norms of behaviours that guides the future of the Board/organisation	92	80	90	90
Establishes the boundaries between independent directors and executive and is prepared to cross them if necessary	79	62	74	70
Promotes independent directors-only meetings to discuss issues, share ideas and thinking, and gain greater alignment	41	45	79	62
Ensures there is an appropriate level and quality of information for debate	91	80	85	85
Effectively deals with/removes non-performing and/or disruptive Board members	55	44	55	47
Takes responsibility for Board composition	88	84	88	75
Conducts a thorough appraisal of the Chief Executive	80	76	82	62
Effectively takes responsibility for the composition of committees and how they operate	77	78	80	60
Ensures that the board is independently evaluated on a regular basis	77	77	73	39
Has effective relations with external stakeholders	85	63	87	65
Instil confidence in key stakeholders in the way the organisation is run	81	70	83	70
Is effective in times of crisis	72	62	71	67
Has positive relations with the media	42	42	47	33

(*continued*)

Table 7 (continued)

Chair role and practice	Sports (n = 129)	Universities (n = 135)	NHS (n = 203)	Charities (n = 156)
Effectively maps board skills against the challenges the organisation/board faces	86	74	76	62
Average	**75**	**67**	**76**	**63**

Non-Executive Director Qualities

Table 8 Non-executive director qualities (% agree/strongly agree)

Director qualities	Sports (n = 129)	Universities (n = 135)	NHS (n = 202)	Charities (n = 156)
Have a sense of duty to see things are done both ethically and morally	97	98	98	97
Are experienced enough and comfortable with organisational complexity	95	92	92	78
Are aware of the challenges facing the charity	98	95	94	88
Clearly understand what is required of them in the role	94	85	88	80
Have the capacity to be effective in the role	93	90	90	81
Are effective in building relationships	91	88	88	79
Have a diverse range of skills that adds value	95	95	95	87
Are effective in putting forward a well-articulated case for debate	95	88	90	81
Are adaptable/flexible to changing needs/priorities	89	86	88	73
Can easily adapt to working with people from different cultures/backgrounds	88	84	85	74
Effectively use their experience and expertise from working in other sectors	95	91	92	88
Have the necessary commercial acumen	81	84	82	63
Communicate effectively	94	91	94	84
Are truly independent	96	93	94	83
Total	**93**	**90**	**91**	**81**

Board Qualities

Table 9 Board qualities (% agree/strongly agree)

Board qualities	Sports (n = 129)	Universities (n = 135)	NHS (n = 203)	Charities (n = 156)
Uses the codes, guidance and regulations that exist for the sector to positively influence behaviours on the Board	86	87	85	79
Ensures that the role that the Trustees play is clearly understood by other Board members	89	85	86	84
Has a long-term strategy that is taking the charity in the right direction	86	88	84	79
Would be able to proactively deal with/handle a potential crisis	89	88	87	86
Is responsive in taking ownership of problems/issues	88	85	89	84
Understands the financial implications of the decisions it makes	88	89	90	85
Has a diverse range of backgrounds, experience and opinions that contribute towards the Board's effectiveness	87	87	85	80
Has a vision that is clearly understood by its members	81	85	84	80
Has a shared understanding of the strategy among its members	83	84	83	78
Comprises the best quality people	83	80	80	77
Is decisive	83	81	81	79
Effectively monitors performance of its members (e.g. through KPIs)	76	77	84	67
Has clear criteria for Board member replacement	86	82	80	76
Effectively balances short-term pressures vs long-term objectives	81	81	76	76
Is risk averse	47	36	30	34
Is innovative	64	56	56	59
Creates value	82	80	79	81
Is effective in the role it plays	85	84	83	81
Average	**81**	**80**	**79**	**76**

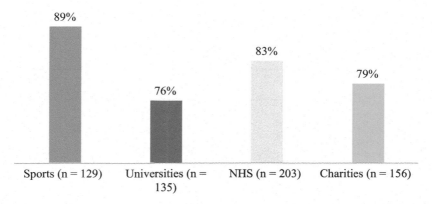

Fig. 33   Ability of Board to handle awkward/sensitive discussions (% excellent/good)

Table 10 Consequences if sensitive/awkward discussions effectively handled (% agree/ strongly agree)

Impact	Sports (n = 129)	Universities (n = 135)	NHS (n = 203)	Charities (n = 156)
Better quality debate	92	99	91	87
Better decision-making capability	91	97	92	88
Better solutions for challenges faced	91	97	92	90
Improved ability to cope with change	89	96	92	91
Better quality of relationships	88	96	90	87
More forward thinking	90	98	92	88
Improved performance of one or more members of the Board	89	93	90	88
Improved performance of one or more members of the Executive Team	90	94	91	93

Table 11 Consequences of board ineffectiveness

Consequences of an ineffective board	NHS	Universities	Charities	Sports	Overall
Lack of resources to cope with day-to-day pressures	89.1%	76.5%	89.7%	87.6%	86.2%
Inability to cope with future challenges	89.0%	72.6%	80.0%	82.9%	82.0%
Lost opportunities to develop the organisation	82.1%	73.3%	75.6%	86.8%	79.6%
Long-term damage to reputation/image	82.6%	78.8%	65.2%	68.2%	74.3%
Inefficient use of resources	70.7%	40.8%	54.9%	51.6%	56.3%

Appendix F (A6): Interviewee List

Name	Organisation	Role
1. Sir Steve Smith	University of Exeter	Vice-Chancellor
2. Sir Andrew Likierman	London Business School	Former Dean
3. David Bernstein	Football Association	Former Chairman
	British Red Cross	Executive Chairman
4. Peter Waine	Hanson Green	Founder and CEO
5. Stephen Ross	The Education and Training Trust of the Chartered Insurance Institute	Independent Trustee
6. Roger Barker	Institute of Directors	Director of Governance
7. David Gregson	LTA—Tennis for Britain	Chairman
8. Leigh Pomlett	Walsal Football Club	NED
9. Stephen Gamble	Walsal Football Club	CEO
10. Sir Laurie Magnus	Historic England	Chairman
11. Professor Nick Pearce	Bath University	Director of the Institute for Policy Research (IPR), Professor of Public Policy
12. John Carrier	North Middlesex University Hospital NHS Trust	Chairman
13. Sir William Wakeham	University of Southampton	Former Vice-Chancellor
14. Sir David Bell	University of Reading	Former Vice-Chancellor
15. David Allen OBE	University of Exeter	Former Deputy Vice-Chancellor and Registrar
16. Chris Collins	British Horseracing Authority	Former Chairman
	Forth Ports plc	Former Chairman
17. Professor Dorothy Griffiths, OBE	Central Northwest London NHS Foundation Trust	Chairwoman
18. Sir David Eastwood	University of Birmingham	Vice-Chancellor
19. Lord Nigel Crisp	NHS/Department of Health	Former Chief Executive and Permanent Secretary
20. Professor Brian Quinn, CBE	Celtic PLC	Chairman
21. Professor Steven Hodgkinson	British & Foreign School Society	Chairman
22. Sir Michael Barber	Office for Students	Chairman
23. Penny Egan, CBE	US-UK Fulbright Commission	Executive Director
	University of Reading	Lay Member of the Council

(continued)

(continued)

Name	Organisation	Role
24. Anne Marie Phelps, CBE	British Rowing	Chairwoman
25. Dr Ann Limb, CBE	London Stansted Cambridge Consortium	Chairwoman
	South East Midlands Local Enterprise Partnership	Former Chairwoman
		Former Chairwoman
	Scout Association	
26. Peter Wanless, CB	NSPCC	CEO
27. Prof. John Caldwell	Mid-Staffordshire NHS Foundation Trust	Former Chairman
	Health Education Thames Valley	Chairman
28. Chris Hopson	NHS Providers	CEO
29. John Lauwreys	University of Southampton, Royal Holloway	Former Secretary and Registrar
30. Matthew Blagg	Critical Eye	Founder & CEO
31. Ed Warner	UK Athletics	Former Chairman
32. Dame Angela Pedder	Royal Devon and Exeter Foundation Trust	Former CEO
33. Sir Peter Thompson	NFC, plc	Former Chairman
	Community Hospitals PLC	Former Chairman
34. Dr Dipti Amin	Johns Hopkins All Children's Hospital	Chief Medical Informatics Officer
	Buckinghamshire Healthcare NHS Trust	Non-Executive Director
35. James Brent	Plymouth Argyle	Chairman
36. Elizabeth Drew	Helen & Douglas House	Chairwoman
37. Professor Roger Brown	Southampton Solent University	Former Vice-Chancellor
38. Steve Edge	Slaughter & May	Principal Partner
39. Susie Rodgers, MBE	British Athletes Commission	Non-Executive Director
40. Baroness Grey-Thompson	UK Active	Chairwoman
	Sports Aid	Board Trustee
41. David Pitt-Watson	KPMG	INED,
	Sarasin & Partners	Chairman
	Aviva	Advisor
42. Ralph Krueger	Southampton FC	Chairman
43. Richard Sargeant	University of Exeter	Independent Board Member a
	ASI Data Science	CCO

Appendix G (A7): Desk Review References by Sector

A desk review of most recent and relevant policy, practitioner and academic literature was undertaken. The references of the documents reviewed per sector are as follows:

Charity Sector References

CASS Business School (2017). Taken on Trust: The awareness and effectiveness of charity trustees in England and Wales. Available at https://assets.publishing.service.gov.uk/government/uploads/system/uploads/attachment_data/file/658766/20171113_Taken_on_Trust_awareness_and_effectiveness_of_charity_trustees.pdf, accessed 13 December 2018.

Charity Commission (2018a). Whistleblowing disclosures made to the Charity Commission for England and Wales 2017–2018, available at https://www.gov.uk/government/publications/whistleblowing-disclosures-made-to-the-charity-commission-for-england-and-wales-2017-2018/whistleblowing-disclosures-made-to-the-charity-commission-for-england-and-wales-2017-2018.

Charity Commission (2018b). Accounts Monitoring Review: concerns highlighted by auditors in their audit reports. Available at https://www.gov.uk/government/publications/accounts-monitoring-concerns-highlighted-by-auditors-in-their-audit-reports-2017, accessed 06 January 2019.

Charity Commission (2018c). Accounts Monitoring Review: telling the story well: public benefit reporting by charities. Available at https://assets.publishing.service.gov.uk/government/uploads/system/uploads/attachment_data/file/609953/AMR_Telling_your_story_well_public_benefit_reporting_by_charities.pdf, accessed 10 January 2019.

Charity Governance Code Steering Group (2017a). Charity Governance Code for Smaller Charities. Available at https://www.charitygovernance-code.org/en/pdf, accessed 10 February 2019.

Charity Governance Code Steering Group (2017b). Charity Governance Code for Larger Charities. Available at https://www.charitygovernance-code.org/en/pdf, accessed 10 February 2019.

Charity Today (2017). The charity sector's place in the national fabric and daily life and recent and future challenges faced by charities. Available at file:///C:/Users/mi907468/Downloads/%E2%80%98Charity%20Today%20%E2%80%93%202017%E2%80%99%20

%E2%80%93%20Briefing%20and%20Stats%20FINAL%20(1).pdf, accessed 13 December 2018.

Civil Society Futures (2018). The Independent Inquiry. Interim Report: End of Year 1, April 2018. Available at https://cdn.baringfoundation.org.uk/ wp-content/uploads/CSF_1Year_ResearchReport.pdf, accessed 6 January 2019.

Cornforth, C. (2001). What makes boards effective? An examination of the relationships between board inputs, structures, processes and effectiveness in non-profit organisations. *Corporate Governance: an International Review*, 9(3):217–227.

Cornforth, C. (2011). Nonprofit governance research: Limitations of the focus on Boards and suggestions for new directions. *Nonprofit and Voluntary Sector Quarterly*, 41(6): 116–1135.

Cornforth, C., and Simpson, C. (2002). Change and continuity in the governance of non-profit organizations in the United Kingdom: The impact of organizational size. *Non-profit Management and Leadership*, 12(4): 451–470.

Fundraising Regulator (2018). Annual Review 2017/2018. Available at https://www.fundraisingregulator.org.uk/sites/default/files/2018-07/ Annual-review-2017-18.pdf, accessed 14 January 2019.

Grant Thornton (2016). Charity Governance Review: Transmitting trust through good governance. Available at https://www.grantthornton.co.uk/ insights/charity-governance-review-2016/, accessed 10 December 2018.

House of Lords (2017). Stronger charities for a stronger society. Select Committee on Charities, Report of Session 2016–17, HL Paper 13. Available at https://publications.parliament.uk/pa/ld201617/ldselect/ ldchar/133/133.pdf, accessed 28 November 2018.

ICAEW and Charity Commission (2014). Findings from the ICAEW AND Charity Commission Project on Strategy Development, Implementation and Review. Available at https://www.icaew.com/-/media/corporate/files/ technical/charity-and-voluntary/volunteering/findings-from-the-icaew- and-cc-review-project.ashx?la=en, accessed 9 December 2018.

Kirchner, A. (2007). Leading leaders: a snapshot into the minds of CEOs, ACEVO, Available at https://www.cass.city.ac.uk/__data/assets/pdf_ file/0003/37290/leading_leaders.pdf, accessed 16 December 2018.

NCVO (2016). Fast facts about the charity sector. National Council for Voluntary Organisations. Available at https://www.ncvo.org.uk/images/ documents/about_us/media-centre/fast-facts-about-the-voluntary-sector. pdf, accessed 17 December 2018.

NCVO (2018a). A Review of the voluntary sector's operating environment: The Road Ahead, January, 2018. Available at http://www.ncvo.org.uk/ images/documents/policy_and_research/Road-Ahead-report-2018-summary.pdf, accessed 7 January 2019.

NCVO (2018b). Brexit and the voluntary sector: Preparing for change, October, 2018. Available at https://www.ncvo.org.uk/images/documents/ policy_and_research/europe/NCVO-Brexit-factsheet.pdf, accessed 20 December 2018.

Puyvelde, S.V., Brown, W.A., Walker, V., and Tenuta, B. (2018). Board effectiveness in Nonprofit organizations: Do interactions in the boardroom matter?, *Nonprofit and Voluntary Sector Quarterly*, 47(6): 1296–1310.

NHS Sector References

Alderweick, H., and Ham, C. (2017). Sustainability and transformation plans for the NHS in England: what do they say and what happens next? British Medical Journal, 77

British Medical Association (2017). *Funding for ill-health prevention and public health in the UK*. Available at file:///C:/Users/mi907468/Downloads/ Funding-for-ill-health-prevention-and-public-health-in-the-UK.pdf.

CQC (2018). Trust-wide well-led. Inspection Framework: NHS Trusts and Foundation Trusts. Available at https://www.cqc.org.uk/sites/default/ files/20180921_9001100_trust-wide_well-led_inspection_framework_v5.pdf.

FRC (2018). The UK Corporate Governance Code. Available at https://www. frc.org.uk/getattachment/88bd8c45-50ea-4841-95b0-d2f4f48069a2/2018-UK-Corporate-Governance-Code-FINAL.PDF.

Gainsbury, S. (2016). Feeling the crunch: NHS finances to 2020. Nuffield Trust.

Grant Thornton (2017). The Board: Creating and Protecting Value. A cross sector review of board effectiveness. Available at https://www.grantthornton.co.uk/globalassets/1.-member-firms/united-kingdom/pdf/publication/board-effectiveness-report-2017.pdf.

Grant Thornton (2015). NHS Governance Review 2015: Uncharted waters. Available at https://www.grantthornton.co.uk/globalassets/1.-member-firms/united-kingdom/pdf/publication/2015/gt.1110-nhs-governance-review-2015-final.pdf.

Jha, A.K., and Epstein, A.M. (2013). A Survey of Board Chairs of English Hospitals Shows Greater Attention to Quality of Care Than Among Their US Counterparts. *Health Affairs*, 32(4): 677–85.

Jiang, H.J., Lockee, C., Bass, K., Fraser, I., Norwood, E. (2009). Board Oversight of Quality: Any Differences in Process of Care and Mortality?, *Journal of Healthcare Management*, 54(1): 15–30.

Lee, S-Y. D., Alexander, J.A., Wang, V., Margolin, F.S., and Combes, J.R. (2008). An Empirical Taxonomy of Hospital Governing Board Roles, *Health Research and Educational Trust*, 43(4): 1223–1243.

Mannion, R., Davies, H., Freeman, T., Millar, R., Jacobs, R., and Kasteridis, P. (2015). Overseeing oversight: governance of quality and safety by hospital boards in the English NHS, *Journal of Health Services Research & Policy*, 20(1S): 9–16.

McDonagh, K.J. (2006). Hospital Governing Boards: A study of their effectiveness in relation to organisational performance, *Journal of Healthcare Management*, 51(6): 377–391.

Millar, R., Mannion, R., Freeman, T., and Davies, H.T.O. (2013). Hospital Board Oversight of Quality and Patient Safety: A Narrative Review and Synthesis of Recent Empirical Research, *The Milbank Quarterly*, 91(4): 738–770.

Monitor (2015). Well-led framework for governance reviews: guidance for NHS foundation trusts. Available at https://assets.publishing.service.gov.uk/government/uploads/system/uploads/attachment_data/file/422057/Well-led_framework_April_2015.pdf.

Monitor (2014). The NHS Foundation Trust Code of Governance, available at https://assets.publishing.service.gov.uk/government/uploads/system/uploads/attachment_data/file/327068/CodeofGovernanceJuly2014.pdf.

National Leadership Council (2013). The Healthy NHS Board Principles for Good Governance. Available at https://www.leadershipacademy.nhs.uk/wp-content/uploads/2013/06/NHSLeadership-HealthyNHSBoard-2013.pdf.

NHS (2014). *Five Years Forward View*. Available at https://www.england.nhs.uk/wp-content/uploads/2014/10/5yfv-web.pdf.

NHS Confederation (2016). Lords debate on the implications of the EU referendum result on ensuring safe staffing levels in the NHS and social care services. NHS Confederation, available at http://www.nhsconfed.org/-/media/Confederation/Files/public-access/Lords_debate_staffing_levels_NHS_post_Brexit_July_2016_Final.pdf.

NHS Confederation & Foundation Trust Governor's Association (2013). A match made in heaven? How NEDs and governors can form effective working relationships. NHS Confederation, Discussion Paper, Issue 15.

NHS Improvement (2018a). Performance of the NHS provider sector for the quarter ended 30 June 2018. Available at https://improvement.nhs.uk/documents/3209/Performance_of_the_NHS_provider_sector_for_the_month_ended_30_June_18_FINAL.pdf.

NHS Improvements (2018b). Monitor: Annual Report and Accounts 2017/18, available at https://assets.publishing.service.gov.uk/government/uploads/system/uploads/attachment_data/file/725242/Monitor_annual_report_and_accounts_201718_web.pdf.

NHS Improvements (2018c). Guidance for boards on Freedom to Speak Up in NHS trusts and NHS foundation trusts, available at https://improvement.nhs.uk/documents/2468/Freedom_to_speak_up_guidance_May2018.pdf.

NHS Improvement (2017). Single Oversight Framework. Available at https://improvement.nhs.uk/documents/400/Single_Oversight_Framework___update_Nov_2017_Oct2018.pdf.

NHS Improvement (2016). Monitor: annual report and accounts 2015/16. Available at https://assets.publishing.service.gov.uk/government/uploads/system/uploads/attachment_data/file/539624/56333_HC_401_Monitor_AR_Web_pdf__2_.pdf.

NHS Providers (2016). The state of the NHS provider sector. Available at www.nhsproviders.org/resource-library/reports/state-of-the-nhs-provider-sector-1116.

NHS Providers (2015). The Foundations of Good Governance: a compendium of good practice, 3rd Edition, available at http://nhsproviders.org/media/1738/foundations-of-good-governance-web-file.pdf.

Ellwood, S., and Garcia-Lacalle, J. (2015). The Influence of Presence and Position of Women on Boards of Directors: The Case of NHS Foundation Trusts, *Journal of Business Ethics*, 130: 69–84.

Pritchard, C., and Harding, A.J.E. (2014). An analysis of National Health Service Trust websites on the occupational backgrounds of 'Non-Executive Directors' on England Acute Trusts, *Journal of the Royal Society of Medicine Open*, 5(5): 1–5.

Prybil, L.D., Bardach, D.R., and Fardo, D.W. (2014). Board Oversight of Patient Care Quality in Large Nonprofit Health Systems, *American Journal of Medical Quality*, 29(1): 39–43.

Higher Education Sector References

Bacon, E. (2014). *Neo-collegiality: Restoring academic engagement in the managerial university. Stimulus paper.* London: Leadership Foundation for Higher Education.

Committee of University Chairs (2014). The Higher Education Code of Governance. Available at https://www.universitychairs.ac.uk/wp-content/uploads/2015/02/Code-Final.pdf.

De Boer, H., Huisman, J., and Meister-Scheytt, C. (2010). Supervision in 'modern' university governance: boards under scrutiny. *Studies in Higher Education*, 35(3): 317–333.

Deem, R, Hillyard, S, and Reid, M (2007) Knowledge, Higher Education and the New Managerialism, Oxford: OUP.

Gibbs, P. (2011). A marriage made in heaven. Clore Social Leadership. www.cloresocialleadership.org.uk/userfiles/documents/Research%20reports/2010/Research,%20Penelope%20Gibbs,%20FINAL.pdf

Greatbatch, D. (2014). *Governance in a changing environment: Literature review.* Leadership Foundation for Higher Education, London.

HEFCE (2010). Model financial memorandum between HEFCE and institutions. Available at https://www.ncl.ac.uk/executive/assets/documents/SAppendixII.pdf.

Highman, L. (2017). Brexit and the issues facing UK higher education. Policy Briefing No. 2, Centre for Global Higher Education.

Horvath, A., and Courtois, A. (2018). United Kingdom: 'The impact of Brexit on UK higher education and collaboration with Europe', in Courtois, A. (Ed.) "Higher education and Brexit: current European perspectives", pp. 159–184, Centre for Global Higher Education, Oxford.

Lambert, R. (2003). Lambert review of business-university collaboration. London: HM Treasury.

Lapworth, S. (2004). Arresting decline in shared governance: Towards a flexible model for academic participation. *Higher Education Quarterly*, 58(4): 299–314.

Larsen, I.M., Maassen, P., and Stensaker, B. (2009). Four basic dilemmas in University Governance Reform. *Higher Education Management and Policy*, 21(3): 41–58.

Leadership Foundation for Higher Education (2017). *Governors' views of their institutions, leadership and governance.* Higher Education Leadership Management Survey: London.

Leadership Foundation for Higher Education (2017). *Getting to grips with trustee responsibilities in higher education: A guide for governors.* Leadership Foundation for Higher Education: London.

Leadership Foundation for Higher Education and CUC (2011). A framework for identifying governing body effectiveness in higher education. Available at https://www.lfhe.ac.uk/en/research-resources/research-hub/2011-research/a-framework-for-identifying-governing-body-effectiveness-in-higher-education.cfm.

Lumby, J. (2018). Leadership and power in higher education. *Studies in Higher Education*, https://doi.org/10.1080/03075079.2018.1458221.

Middlehurst, R. (2013). Changing internal governance: Are leadership roles and management structures in United Kingdom universities fit for the future? *Higher Education Quarterly*, 67(3): 275–294.

PWC (2018). Managing risk in higher education: Higher education sector risk profile. Available at https://www.pwc.co.uk/government-public-sector/education/documents/higher-education-sector-risk-profile-2018.pdf.

Schofield, A. (2009). What is an effective and high performing governing body in UK higher education? London: Leadership Foundation for Higher Education and CUC.

Shattock, M. (2013). University governance, leadership and management in a decade of diversification and uncertainty, *Higher Education Quarterly*, 67(3): 217–233.

Shattock, M. (2017). University governance in flux. The impact of external and internal pressures on the distribution of authority within British universities: a synoptic view. Centre for Global Higher Education, Working Paper No. 13, pp. 1–22.

Sherer, M.J., and Zakaria, I. (2017). Mind the gap! An investigation of gender imbalances on the governing bodies of UK universities. *Studies in Higher Education*, 43(4): 719–736.

Rushforth, J. (2017). Managing the chair/vice-chancellor relationship. Leadership Foundation for Higher Education, London.

Waring, M. (2017). Management and leadership in UK universities: exploring possibilities of change. *Journal of Higher Education Policy and Management*, 39(5): 540–558.

Waugh, W. L. (1998). Conflicting values and cultures: the managerial threat to university governance. *Policy Studies Review*, 15(4): 61–73.

Sports Sector References

Birkbeck College and Moore Stephens. The state of sports governance: Are you leading or lagging?, available at http://www.sportbusinesscentre.com/wp-content/uploads/2018/03/FINAL-REPORT-the-state-of-sports-governance.pdf.

Grey-Thompson, T. (2017). Duty of Care in Sport: Independent Report to Government. April 2017, available at https://assets.publishing.service.gov.uk/government/uploads/system/uploads/attachment_data/file/610130/Duty_of_Care_Review_-_April_2017__2.pdf.

ICSA (2018). Organisational culture in sport: assessing and improving attitudes and behaviour. Available at https://www.icsa.org.uk/assets/files/policy/research/Organisational-culture-in-sport.pdf.

Nelson, P. (2017). What is the role of an independent non-executive director on the board of a national governing body of sport?, Birkbeck, University of London, Birkbeck Sport Business Centre.

Sport England and UK Sport (2018). A code for sports governance, April 2017, available at https://www.sportengland.org/media/11193/a_code_for_sports_governance.pdf.

Walters, G., Trenberth, L., and Tacon, R. (2010). Good governance in sport: A survey of UK national governing bodies of sport. Birkbeck Sport Business Centre, University of London.

Walters, G., Tacon, R., and Trenberth, L. (2011). The role of the board in UK National Governing Bodies of sport. Birkbeck Sport Business Centre, University of London.

Appendix H (A8): List of Case Studies and Contributors

1. The University of Exeter: Dual Assurance Governance and Sustainable Success

Thanks to the following individuals from the University of Exeter who gave time for individual interviews about its governance:

- Mike Shor-Nye, Head of Administration and Registrar
- Professor Janice Kay, Provost and Senior Deputy Vice-Chancellor
- Professor Ken Evans, Pro Vice-Chancellor and Executive Dean of the College of Engineering, Mathematics and Physical Science

- Professor Nina Wendell, Professor of Evolutionary Biology
- Professor Roy Sambles, Professor of Physics, Former President of the Institute of Physics
- Professor Wendy Robinson, Pro Vice-Chancellor and Executive Dean of the College of Social Sciences
- Sarah Turville, Chair of the Council
- Sir Steve Smith, Vice-Chancellor
- Tracey Costello, Chief Executive of the University of Exeter Students' Guild

2. On the Brink of Collapse: The Case of Ardwick Green

Thanks to Professor Nada Kakabadse for writing the case and to the former chairman and two other former board members for their account of the case.

3. Hockey England: From Greek Tragedy to Gold Medal

Thanks to Professor Nada Kakabadse for writing the case study on Hockey England, and the following individuals from Hockey England who gave time for individual interviews about its governance:

- Ian Wilson, Company Secretary and Finance Director
- Royston Hoggarth, Chairman
- Sally Munday, CEO

4. London Ambulance Service (LAS)

Thanks to the following individuals from LAS who gave time for individual interviews about its governance:

- Heather Lawrence (Chair of the Board)
- Garett Emmerson (CEO)
- Philippa Harding (Director Corporate Governance)

5. 4Global: How Can Boards Make the Most of Technology?

- Thanks to Chris Phillips for contributing the account of 4Global and its work.

6. University and Technology: Is an Avalanche Coming?

- Thanks to Richard Sargeant for contributing the account on University and Technology

Appendix I (A9): Training Courses for Independent Directors

Several institutions offer formal training programmes for current and prospective independent directors. A brief list of these follows below.

Institute of Directors

The Institute of Directors (IOD) holds frequent one-day programmes entitled The Role of the Non-Executive Director. Most of these are delivered in London, but programmes are sometimes delivered in other centres (in late 2019, programmes were on offer in Guildford and Nottingham). The programmes are designed and delivered by experienced independent directors and other experts in fields such as law and corporate governance. The programme is aimed at both aspiring and serving independent directors, and topics for the day include:

- Identifying the key attributes of an effective independent director
- Recognising the legal and practical responsibilities of the independent director
- Identifying how an independent director can help to create an effective board
- Appreciating how an independent director can add value in and out of the boardroom
- Applying knowledge and skills to effectively deal with a range of boardroom challenges in different types of organisations
- Building your profile through an extended peer network
- Effectively applying and preparing for an independent director position

The cost for the one-day workshop is £1090 for IOD members, and £1310 for non-members.

Henley Business School

The Board Directors Programme at Henley Business School is a two-day residential programme for both current and aspiring independent directors and executive directors; a typical programme sees representation from both groups, allowing them a chance to get to know each other and practise working together. The programme is delivered by a mixture of industry experts and Henley Business School faculty, the latter drawing on their own research with boards around the world. Topics include:

- The composition, role and dynamics of boards: the nature and complexities of board dynamics, director relationships and their effect on the functioning of the board
- Board diversity
- The contribution of sub-committees and independent directors.
- How to engage fully with all stakeholders
- When boards become dysfunctional: how to influence and effectively manage board relations
- Competitive advantage and how to maximise it
- Governance and its role in sustainable success
- The importance of corporate, social and community responsibility and reputation, including avoiding the pitfalls of international trade.

The programme runs twice a year, and the cost in 2019 was £2550 including residential costs. In the interests of transparency we should state that the director of the programme, Professor Andrew Kakabadse, is also one of the authors of this book.

Henley also offers an MSc in regulation and compliance, a three-year part-time programme which has been adapted to the requirements of the Level 6 Senior Compliance and Risk Specialist Apprenticeship standard in financial services. This programme includes modules that touch on many of the aspects of governance discussed in this book.

PWC/Cass Business School

The Professional Development Programme for Aspiring Non-Executive Directors is a one-day workshop run out of Cass Business School in London in association with PWC. The workshop is aimed at aspiring independent directors rather than currently serving directors and serves as an introduction to the role and its responsibilities. Aims include:

- Understanding the important role boards play in corporate life
- Understanding the importance of strategic direction and corporate governance
- Gaining insights into the contribution expected from NEDs as independent and external to the management of companies
- Appreciating how group dynamics can influence decision-making
- Unravelling the complexities of effective board membership
- Planning and preparing for a first move into the board arena[1]

The cost in 2018 was £995 for the full workshop.

University of Edinburgh

In 2017 the University of Edinburgh Business School in association with FWB Park Brown launched its Non-Executive Director Programme, a series of workshops on key topics of interest for independent directors. Each session is delivered by experienced chairs and directors. There are eight evening sessions, and the 2019 programme includes the following topics:

- Financing and Funding Growth Companies and Managing the Investor
- The Role of the Non-Executive Director in Growing a Company
- The Data Revolution: Understanding the Landscape
- The Data Revolution: Ethical Challenges
- Boardroom Dynamics and Crisis Situation
- The Audit Committee
- The Fusion of New Technology with Financial Services
- The Remuneration and Nominations Committees

There is no formal qualification, but the programme offers opportunities for networking and making contacts. The cost is £400 per session, with discounts for booking multiple sessions.[2]

Financial Times

The *Financial Times* offers a variety of programmes and workshops to support independent directors through its Board Director Programme.[3]

So You Want To Be A Non-Executive Director? A one-day introductory workshop offered several times a year, primarily for those interested in the role of independent director and wanting to know more about the role and its responsibilities. Participants typically have no prior independent director experience, and use the workshop as a way of learning and deciding whether the role is for them. Topics covered include the duties and liabilities of the independent director, effective boardroom behaviour and advice on how to apply for a first independent director post, along with tips on CV writing and interview techniques. The price in 2019 was £750.

The Effective Non-Executive Directors Programme. This is a two-day programme, also held several times a year in either London or Hong Kong. It is aimed principally at newly appointed independent directors, and is delivered by a mixture of experienced independent directors and consultants. The June 2019 version of the programme covered subjects including legal responsibilities, corporate governance, the role of the remuneration committee, the role of the audit committee, characteristics of effective boards, boardroom dynamics, personal behaviour in the boardroom, removing directors and characteristics of an effective independent director. Case studies and guest speakers are used to bring in real-life experience. The 2019 price for the two days is £1500.

The Non-Executive Director Diploma. This is a six-month post-graduate diploma programme, based on the UK Corporate Governance Code and covering a wide range of skills and knowledge required by non-executive directors. It is divided into five modules: the effective non-executive director, directors' duties and liabilities, board structure and performance, risk management and internal control, and audit and financial reporting. While the headings are largely the same as for the two workshops above, the diploma programme goes into much greater detail on the legal and financial issues in particular. The programme also offers a formal qualification which should boost the recipient's chances of getting top independent director posts in the corporate world in particular. The price is likely to deter directors from the public and third sectors: £5450 for the six-month programme.

Board Masterclass. The board masterclasses are half-day workshops designed to help experienced independent directors stay up to date and learn about new and emerging issues. Each workshop addresses a different topic, and the cost for the half day is £375. At time of writing, upcoming topics include reputational risk and its roots, international board dynamics, cyber security and appointing the right CEO. The FT Board Director Programme website offers an updated list of topics going forward: https://bdp.ft.com/Masterclass.

Notes

1. https://execed.economist.com/cass-business-school/professional-development-programme-aspiring-non-executive-directors-2018-10-17.
2. https://www.business-school.ed.ac.uk/event/non-executive-director-programme-2.
3. https://bdp.ft.com/.

Index[1]

---

[1] Note: Page numbers followed by 'n' refer to notes.

© The Author(s) 2020
G. Brown et al., *The Independent Director in Society*,
https://doi.org/10.1007/978-3-030-51303-0